THE

WORKS

Of the REVEREND

WILLIAM LAW, M.A.,

Sometime Fellow of *Emmanuel*
College, *Cambridge.*

———

In Nine Volumes.

———

Volume III.

A PRACTICAL TREATISE upon
Christian Perfection.

Wipf and Stock Publishers
150 West Broadway • Eugene OR 97401
2001

Volume III-A Practical Treatise upone Christian
Perfection

By Law, William

ISBN: 1-57910-617-X

Reprinted by *Wipf and Stock Publishers*
150 West Broadway • Eugene OR 97401

Previously published by G. Moreton, Setley, 1892.

Prefatory Advertisement.

A Practical Treatise
upon *Christian Perfection.*

THIS Treatise is WILLIAM LAW'S fourth Work in the Order of Publication; published in the year 1726, when he was about forty years of age.

MR. WALTON records a Tradition to the effect that shortly after the publication of the 'Christian 'Perfection,' when *William Law* was one day waiting 'in the Shop 'of his Publisher, in *London,* a person, habited as a Gentleman's 'servant, accosted him, inquiring if he were the Rev. Mr. *Law ;* 'and being answered in the affirmative, placed a letter in his 'hands and departed. Upon opening the letter, it was found to 'contain a Bank-note for £1,000 from some anonymous in-'dividual.' *Walton* suggests that 'if this anecdote be true,' it was probably with this donation that *William Law* endowed the Girls' School in his Native place of King's Cliffe: and it is equally probable that the publication of this excellent Treatise procured him the appointment of Tutor in the *Gibbon* family.

In the course of *William Law's* controversial writings his mind may have become impressed with the importance of setting forth in a practical manner the True Profession of Christianity, as the best method of further refuting erroneous doctrines and opinions; such as he had already felt called upon in the defence of True Christianity to expose—hence this Treatise.

The 'Christian Perfection' has exercised an immense influence over the lives of many of its readers; and it may indeed be regarded as a Practical Guide to Christianity. It is the first Work of *William Law's* which really, as a Beacon, directs the Wayfarer through the strait gate into that narrow way, with its pitfalls and manifold difficulties which he knew so well, and along which he himself has passed.   The popularity of this Work has however been exceeded by that of the ' Serious ' Call,' which was *William Law's* next work ; but is for the most part merely the ' Christian Perfection ' reduced into a Formula or System of Religion, with Rules for Devotion, appointed Hours for, and Subjects of, Prayer.   Hence the extreme but unmerited, popularity of the 'Serious Call' far beyond *William Law's* other writings—for ' Man is a bundle 'of Habits,' and the majority of even religious people, from want of sufficient earnestness, require to be led and instructed by ' Rules' at every step, as if they were mentally and spiritually blind.

It is in the ' Christian Perfection ' that the following sentence respecting the Light of Revelation occurs : which, in the infinite comprehensiveness of its idea, is amongst the most beautiful that *William Law* ever wrote :

' This Light (of Revelation) has dispersed all the Anxiety of ' Man's vain Conjectures.   It has brought him acquainted with ' God ; and, by adding Heaven to Earth and Eternity to Time, ' has opened such a glorious View of Things as makes Man, even ' in his present Condition, full of a Peace of God which passes all ' Understanding.'

G. B. M.

A

PRACTICAL
TREATISE

UPON

CHRISTIAN

PERFECTION.

By *WILLIAM LAW*, M. A.

Not as though I had already attained,
either were already perfect.
Phil. iii. 12.

LONDON:

Printed for WILLIAM and JOHN INNYS,
at the West-End of St. *Paul's.* 1726.

The Contents.

The Introduction.

CHAPTER VIII.

CHAPTER IX.

CHAPTER X.

CHAPTER XI.

CHAPTER XII.

CHAPTER XIII.

CHAPTER XIV.

A
Practical Treatise

UPON

Christian Perfection.

The Introduction.

C HRISTIAN Perfection will perhaps seem to the common Reader to imply some State of Life which everyone need not aspire after ; that it is made up of such Strictnesses, Retirements, and Particularities of Devotion, as are neither necessary, nor practicable by the Generality of Christians.

But I must answer for myself, that I know of only one common Christianity, which is to be the common Means of Salvation to all Men.

If the Writers upon Christian Perfection have fancied to themselves some peculiar Degrees of Piety, or extraordinary Devotions which they call by that Name, they have not done Religion much Service, by making Christian Perfection to consist in anything, but the right Performance of our necessary Duties.

This is the Perfection which this Treatise endeavours to recommend ; a Perfection that does not consist in any singular State or Condition of Life, or in any particular Set of Duties, but in the holy and religious Conduct of ourselves in every State of Life.

It calls no one to a *Cloister*, but to a right and full Performance of those Duties, which are necessary for all Christians, and common to all States of Life.

I call it *Perfection*, for two Reasons, first, because I hope it contains a full Representation of that Height of Holiness and Purity, to which Christianity calls all its Members : Secondly, that the *Title* may invite the Reader to peruse it with the more Diligence, as expecting to find not only a Discourse upon moral Virtues, but a regular Draught of those holy Tempers which are the perfect Measure and Standard of Christian Piety.

Now as Perfection is here placed in the right Performance of our necessary Duties, in the Exercise of such holy Tempers as are equally necessary and equally practicable in all States of

Life, as this is the highest Degree of Christian Perfection, so it is to be observed, that it is also the lowest Degree of Holiness which the Gospel alloweth. So that though no Order of Men can pretend to go higher, yet none of us can have any Security in resting in any State of Piety that is lower.

And I hope this will be taken as a Sign that I have hit upon the true State of Christian Perfection, if I show it to be such, as Men in *Cloisters* and religious Retirements cannot add more, and at the same time such, as Christians in all States of the World must not be content with less.

For consider, what can Christian Perfection be, but such a right Performance of all the Duties of Life, as is according to the Laws of Christ? What can it be, but a living in such holy Tempers, and acting with such Dispositions as Christianity requires? Now if this be Perfection, who can exceed it? And yet what State, or Circumstance of Life, can allow any People to fall short of it?

Let us take an Instance in some one particular Temper of Christianity. Let it be the Love of God, Christians are to love God with *all their Heart and all their Strength.* Now can any Order of Christians exceed in this Temper? Or is there any Order of Christians who may be allowed to be defective in it?

Now what is thus true of the Love of God, is equally true of all other religious Duties; and consequently all those holy Tempers of Heart which constitute the Perfection of Christian Piety, are Tempers equally necessary for all Christians.

As there is but one Faith and one Baptism, so there is but one Piety, and one Perfection, that is common to all Orders of Christians.

It will perhaps be here objected, that this supposes that all People may be equally good, which seems as impossible in the Nature of Things, as to suppose that all People may be equally wise.

To this it may be answered, that this is neither altogether true, nor altogether false.

For to instance in Charity, it is true that all People may be equally charitable; if we understand by Charity that Habit of the Mind which stands rightly disposed to all Acts of Charity; in this Sense all People may be equally charitable. But if we take Charity for Alms-giving, or a liberal Assistance of the Poor, in this Sense it is false, that all People may be equally charitable.

Now as it is the Habit of the Mind, that constitutes the Excellency of Charity, so this is the Charity to which Christians are called, and in which they may all be equally perfect.

Again, are not all People obliged to be equally honest, just, and true and faithful? In these Virtues all are to be eminent and exact in the same Degree, there are no Abatements to be made for any Rank or Order of People.

Now as to the external Exercise of these Duties, there may be great Difference. One Man may have great Business in the World, and be honest and faithful in it all; another may have small Dealings and be honest in them; but provided that there be in both of them the same Justice and Integrity of Mind, they are equally honest, though their Instances of Honesty, as to external Acts of it, are as different, as great Things are different from small.

But as it is the Habit of the Mind, which is the Justice which Religion requires, so in this Respect all People may be equally just.

Now this may serve to show us in what Respect all People may be equally virtuous, and in what Respect they cannot.

As to the external Instances or Acts of Virtue, in these they must differ according to the Difference of their Circumstances, and Condition in the World; but as Virtues are considered as Habits of the Mind, and Principles of the Heart, in this Respect they may all be equally virtuous, and are all called to the same Perfection.

A Man cannot exercise the Spirit of Martyrdom, till he is brought to the Stake; he cannot forgive his Enemies till they have done him Wrong, till he suffers from them. He cannot bear Poverty and Distress till they are brought upon him. All these Acts of Virtue depend upon outward Causes, but yet he may have a Piety and heroic Spirit equal to those who have died for their Religion. He may have that Charity of Mind which prays for its Enemies, he may have that Meekness and Resignation to the Will of God, as disposes People to bear Poverty and Distress with Patience and humble Submission to the Divine Providence.

So that they are only the external Instances and Acts of Virtue, which depend upon outward Causes and Circumstances of Life; a Man cannot give till he has something to give; but the inward Piety of the Heart and Mind which constitutes the State of Christian Perfection, depends upon no outward Circumstances. A Man need not want Charity because he has no Riches, nor be destitute of a forgiving Spirit, because he has no Persecutors to forgive.

Although therefore we neither are, nor can be all in the same Circumstances of Life, yet we are to be all in the same Spirit of Religion; though we cannot be all equal in Alms-giving, yet we are to be all alike in Charity; though we are not all in the same State of Persecution, yet we must be all in the same Spirit that forgives and prays for its Persecutors; though we are not all in Poverty and Distress, yet we must all be full of that Piety of Heart which produces Meekness, Patience, and Thankfulness, in Distress and Poverty.

From these Considerations it is easy to apprehend, how Persons may differ in Instances of Goodness, and yet be equally good; for as the Perfection of Piety is the Perfection of the Heart, so the Heart may have the same Perfection in all States and Conditions of Life. And this is that Perfection which is common to all States, and to which all Orders of Christians are equally called.

Again, There may be another Difference of Virtue founded in the different Abilities of Persons; one may have a more enlightened Mind than another, and so may see further into his Duty, and be able to practise it with greater Exactness, but then as his Goodness seems to consist in this, that he is true and faithful to what he knows to be his Duty, so if another is as true and faithful to that Measure of Light and Knowledge which God has given him, he seems to be as good a Man, as he that is true and faithful to a greater Light.

We can hardly reconcile it with the Divine Goodness to give one Man two Talents, and another five, unless we suppose that he is as high in his Master's Pleasure who makes the right use of two, as he that makes the right use of five Talents.

So that it still holds good, that it is the Perfection of the Heart, that makes the Perfection of every State of Life.

It may perhaps be further objected, that the different Degrees of Glory in another Life, supposes that good Men and such as are accepted of God, do yet differ in their Degrees of Goodness in this Life.

I grant that it does.

But then this is no Proof that all Men are not called to the same Goodness, and the same Perfection.

Perhaps it cannot be said of the best of Men that ever lived, that they performed their Duty in such Perfection in all Instances, as they might have done.

Now as it suits with the Divine Mercy to admit Men to Happiness, who have not been in every Respect so perfect as they might have been, notwithstanding that he gave them such a Rule of Perfection; so it equally suits with the Divine Mercy to admit Men to different Degrees of Happiness, on Account of their different Conduct, though he gave them all one common Rule of Perfection.

Did not God pardon Frailties and Infirmities, the best of Men could not be rewarded. But consider now, does God's pardoning of Frailties and Infirmities in the best of Men, prove that the best of Men were not called to any other Perfection, than that to which they arrived? Does this prove that God did not call them to be strictly good, because he receives them to Mercy with some Defects in Goodness? No, most surely.

Yet this is as good an Argument, as to say, that all Men are not called to the same State of Goodness, or Perfection, because they are admitted to different Rewards in the other Life.

For it is as right Reasoning, to say, God rewards frail and imperfect Men, therefore they were called to no higher Perfection; as to say that because God rewards different Degrees of Goodness, therefore Men are not called to one and the same Goodness.

For as God could reward none, unless he would reward such as had Failings, so their Difference in their Failings may make them Objects of his different Mercy and Rewards, though the Rule from which they failed, was common to them all.

It therefore plainly appears, that the different Degrees of Glory in another Life, are no more a Proof that God calls some Persons to different and lower States of Goodness, than others, than his pardoning Variety of Sinners is a Proof that he allowed of those Kinds of Sin, and did not require Men to avoid them. For it is full as good an Argument to say, God pardons some Sinners, therefore he did not require them to avoid such Sins, as to say God rewards different Degrees of Goodness, therefore he did not call People to higher Degrees of Goodness.

So that the different Degrees of Glory in the World to come are no Objection against this Doctrine, that all Christians are called to one and the same Piety and Perfection of Heart.

Lastly, it may be farther objected, that although the Law of God calls all Men to the same State of Perfection, yet if there are different Degrees of Glory given to different Degrees of Goodness, this shows that Men may be saved, and happy, without aspiring after all that Perfection to which they were called.

It may be answered, That this is a false Conclusion: For though it may be true, that People will be admitted to Happiness, and different Degrees of Happiness, though they have not *attained* to all that Perfection to which they were called; yet it does not follow that any People will be saved who did not *endeavour* after that Perfection. For surely it is a very different Case, to *fall* short of our Perfection after our best Endeavours, and to *stop* short of it, by not endeavouring to arrive at it. The one Practice may carry Men to a high Reward in Heaven, and the other cast them with the unprofitable Servant into outer Darkness.

There is therefore no Foundation for People to content themselves in any lower Degrees of Goodness, as being sufficient to carry them to Heaven, though not to the highest Happiness in Heaven.

For consider, thou hearest there are different Degrees of Glory; that they are proportioned to different States of Goodness in this Life, thou wilt therefore content thyself with a lower Degree of Goodness, being content to be of the lowest Order in Heaven. Thou wilt have only so much Piety as will save thee.

But consider how vainly thou reasonest; for though God giveth different Rewards, it is not in the Power of Man to take them of himself. It is not for anyone to say I will practise so much Goodness, and so take such a Reward. God seeth different Abilities and Frailties in Men, which may move his Goodness to be merciful to their different Improvements in Virtue: I grant thee that there may be a lower State of Piety which in some Persons may be accepted by God.

But consider, that though there is such a State of Piety that may be *accepted*, yet that it cannot be *chosen*, it ceases to be that State as soon as thou chooseth it.

God may be merciful to a low Estate of Piety, by reason of some pitiable Circumstances that may attend it; but as soon as thou choosest such an Estate of Piety, it loses those pitiable Circumstances, and instead of a low State of Piety, is changed into a high State of Impiety.

So that though there are meaner Improvements in Virtue, which may make some Persons accepted by God, yet this is no Ground for Content or Satisfaction in such a State; because it ceases to be such a State, and is quite another thing, for being chosen and satisfied with.

It appears therefore from these Considerations, that notwithstanding God may accept of different Degrees of Goodness, and reward them with different Degrees of Glory in another Life, yet that all Christians are called to one and the same Perfection, and equally obliged to labour after it.

Thus much may suffice to give the Reader a general Notion of Perfection, and the Necessity of endeavouring after it.

What it is, and what holy Tempers it requires, will, I hope, be found sufficiently explained in the following Chapters.

Chapter I.

The Nature and Design of Christianity, that its sole End is to deliver us from the Misery and Disorder of this present State, and raise us to a blissful Enjoyment of the Divine Nature.

THE Wisdom of Mankind has for several Ages of the World, been inquiring into the Nature of Man, and the Nature of the World in which he is placed.

The Wants and Miseries of human Nature, and the Vanity of worldly Enjoyments, has made it difficult for the wisest Men to tell what human Happiness was, or wherein it consisted.

It has pleased the infinite Goodness of God, to satisfy all our Wants and Inquiries by a Revelation made to the World by his Son Jesus Christ.

This Revelation has laid open the great Secrets of Providence from the Creation of the World, explained the present State of Things, and given Man all the Information that is necessary to quiet his Anxieties, content him with his Condition, and lead him safely to everlasting Rest and Happiness.

It is now only necessary, that the poor Wisdom of Man do not exalt itself against God, that we suffer our Eyes to be opened by him that made them, and our Lives to be conducted by him, in whom *we live, move, and have our Being.*

For Light is now come into the World, if Men are but willing to come out of Darkness.

As Happiness is the sole End of all our Labours, so this Divine Revelation aims at nothing else.

It gives us right and satisfactory Notions of ourselves, of our true Good and real Evil; it shows us the true State of our Condition, both our Vanity and Excellence, our Greatness and Meanness, our Felicity and Misery.

Before this, Man was a mere Riddle to himself, and his Condition full of Darkness and Perplexity. A restless Inhabitant of a miserable disordered World, *walking in a vain Shadow, and disquieting himself in vain.*

But this Light has dispersed all the Anxiety of his vain Conjectures; it has brought us acquainted with God, and by adding

Heaven to Earth, and Eternity to Time, has opened such a glorious View of Things, as makes Man even in his present Condition, full of a Peace of God which passes all Understanding.

This Revelation acquaints us, that we have a Spirit within us, that was created after the Divine Image, that this Spirit is now in a fallen corrupt Condition, that the Body in which it is placed, is its Grave, or Sepulchre, where it is enslaved to fleshly Thoughts, blinded with false Notions of Good and Evil, and dead to all Taste and Relish of its true Happiness.

It teaches us, that the World in which we live, is also in a disordered irregular State, and cursed for the Sake of Man; that it is no longer the Paradise that God made it, but the Remains of a drowned World, full of Marks of God's Displeasure, and the Sin of its Inhabitants.

That it is a mere Wilderness, a State of Darkness, a Vale of Misery, where Vice and Madness, Dreams and Shadows, variously please, agitate, and torment the short, miserable Lives of Men.

Devils also, and evil Spirits, have here their Residence, promoting the Works of Darkness, and wandering up and down seeking whom they may devour.

So that the Condition of Man in his natural State, seems to be, as if a Person sick of a Variety of Diseases, knowing neither his Distempers, nor his Cure, should be enclosed in some Place, where he could hear, or see, or feel, or taste of nothing, but what tended to inflame his Disorders.

The Excellency therefore of the Christian Religion appears in this, that it puts an End to this State of Things, blots out all the Ideas of worldly Wisdom, brings the World itself to Ashes, and creates all anew. It calls Man from an animal Life and earthly Conversation, to be born again of the Holy Ghost, and be made a Member of the Kingdom of God.

It crushes into nothing the Concerns of this Life, condemns it as a State of Vanity and Darkness, and leads Man to a Happiness with God in the Realms of Light.

It proposes the Purification of our Souls, the enlivening us with the Divine Spirit; it sets before us new Goods and Evils, and forms us to a glorious Participation of the Divine Nature.

This is the one sole End of Christianity, to lead us from all Thoughts of Rest and Repose here, to separate us from the World and worldly Tempers, to deliver us from the Folly of our Passions, the Slavery of our own Natures, the Power of evil Spirits, and unite us to God, the true Fountain of all real Good. This is the mighty Change which Christianity aims at, to put us into a new State, reform our whole Natures, purify our Souls, and make them the Inhabitants of heavenly and immortal Bodies.

It does not leave us to grovel on in the Desires of the Flesh, to cast about for worldly Happiness, and wander in Darkness and Exile from God, but prepares us for the true Enjoyment of a divine Life.

The Manner by which it changes this whole State of Things, and raises us to an Union with God, is equally great and wonderful.

I am the *Way, the Truth* and the *Life,* saith our blessed Saviour, *no Man cometh unto the Father but by me.*

As all Things were at first created by the Son of God, and without him was *not anything made that was made,* so are all Things again restored and redeemed by the same Divine Person.

As nothing could come into Being without him, so nothing can enter into a State of Happiness or Enjoyment of God, but by him.

The Price and Dignity of this Redemption at once confounds the Pride, and relieves the Misery of Man. How fallen must he be from God, how disordered and odious his Nature, that should need so great a Mediator to recommend his Repentance !——— And on the other Hand, how full of Comfort, that so high a Method, so stupendous a Means should be taken, to restore him to a State of Peace and Favour with God !

This is the true Point of View in which every Christian is to behold himself. He is to overlook the poor Projects of human Life, and consider himself as a Creature through his natural Corruption falling into a State of endless Misery, but by the Mercy of God redeemed to a Condition of everlasting Felicity.

All the Precepts and Doctrines of the Gospel are founded on these two great Truths, the deplorable Corruption of human Nature, and its new Birth in Christ Jesus.

The one includes all the Misery, the other all the Happiness of Man.

It is on these great Doctrines, that the whole Frame of Christianity is built, forbidding only such Things as fasten us to the Disorders of Sin, and commanding only those Duties which lead us into the Liberty and Freedom of the Sons of God.

The Corruption of our Nature makes Mortification, Self-denial, and the Death of our Bodies necessary. Because human Nature must be thus unmade, Flesh and Blood must be thus changed, before it can enter into the Kingdom of Heaven.

Our new Birth makes the Reception of God's Spirit, and the Participation of the holy Sacraments necessary, to form us to that Life to which the Resurrection of Jesus Christ has entitled us.

So that would we think and act and live like Christians, we must act suitably to these Terms of our Condition, fearing and avoiding all the Motions of our corrupted Nature, cherishing the secret Inspirations of the Holy Spirit, opening our Minds for the Reception of the Divine Light, and pressing after all the Graces and Perfections of our new Birth.

We must behave ourselves conformably to this double Capacity, we must fear, and watch, and pray, like Men that are always in Danger of eternal Death, and we must believe and hope, labour and aspire, like Christians, that are called to fight the good Fight of Faith, and lay hold on eternal Life.

This knowledge of ourselves, makes human Life a State of infinite Importance, placed upon so dreadful a Point betwixt two such Eternities.

Well might our blessed Saviour say to one, that begged first to go and bury his Father, *Follow me, and let the Dead bury their Dead.*

For what is all the Bustle and Hurry of the World, but dead Show, and its greatest Agents, but dead Men, when compared with the State of Greatness, that real Life, to which the Followers of Christ are redeemed?

Had we been made only for this World, worldly Wisdom had been our highest Wisdom; but seeing Christianity has redeemed us to a contrary State, since all its Goods are in Opposition to this Life, worldly Wisdom is now our greatest Foolishness.

It is now our only Wisdom to understand our new State aright, to let its Goods and Evils take Possession of our Hearts, and conduct ourselves by the Principles of our Redemption.

The Nature and Terms of our Christian Calling is of that Concern, as to deserve all our Thoughts, and is indeed only to be perceived by great Seriousness and Attention of Mind.

The Christian State is an invisible Life in the Spirit of God, supported not by sensible Goods, but the spiritual Graces of Faith and Hope; so that the natural Man, especially while busied in earthly Cares and Enjoyments, easily forgets that great and heavenly Condition in which Religion places him.

The Changes which Christianity maketh in the present State of Things, are all invisible, its Goods and Evils, its Dignities and Advantages, which are the only true Standards of all our Actions, are not subject to the Knowledge of our Senses.

In *God we live, and move, and have our Being,* but how unseen, how unfelt is all this!

Christ is the *Lamb slain from the Foundation of the World,* the true Light, that lighteth every Man that cometh into the World. He is the *Alpha* and *Omega*, the Beginning and End of all Things. The whole Creation subsists in him and by him; nothing is in any Order, nor any Person in any Favour with God, but by this great Mediator. But how invisible, how unknown to all our Senses, is this State of Things!

The Apostle tells us, that we Christians are *come unto Mount Sion, and unto the City of the Living God, to the heavenly Jerusalem, and to an innumerable Company of Angels, and to the general Assembly of the First-born, which are written in Heaven, and to God the Judge of all, and to the Spirits of just Men made perfect, and to Jesus the Mediator of the New Covenant, &c.**

But our Senses see or feel nothing of this State of Glory, they only show us a Society amongst vain and worldly Men, labouring and contending for the poor Enjoyments of a vain World.

We are Temples of the Holy Ghost, consecrated to God, Members of Christ's mystical Body, of his flesh and of his Bones, receiving Life, Spirit, and Motion from him our Head.

But our Senses see no farther than our Parents and Kindred according to the Flesh, and fix our Hearts to earthly Friendships and Relations.

Religion turns our whole Life into a Sacrifice to God, a State of Probation, from whence we must *all appear before the Judgment-Seat of Christ, that everyone may receive the Things done in his Body, &c.*†

But our Senses, the Maxims of this Life, and the Spirit of the World, teach quite another Turn of Mind; to enjoy the good Things of Life as our Portion, to seek after Riches and Honours, and to dread nothing so much as Poverty, Disgrace, and Persecution. Well may this Life be deemed a State of Darkness, since it thus clouds and covers all the true Appearances of Things, and keeps our Minds insensible, and unaffected with Matters of such infinite Moment.

We must observe, that in Scripture Christianity is constantly represented to us, as a Redemption from the Slavery and Corruption of our Nature, and a raising us to a nearer Enjoyment of the Divine Glory.

It knows of no Misery, but the Death and Misery which Sin has made, nor of any Happiness, but the Gifts and Graces of the Holy Ghost, which form us to a greater Likeness of God.

Thus saith the Apostle, *Jesus Christ gave himself for us that he might redeem us from all Iniquity.*‡

He was manifested to take away our Sins.§

---

* Heb. xii. 22.   † 2 Cor. v. 9.   ‡ Tit. ii. 13.   § 1 John iii. 5.

Who gave himself for our Sins, that he might deliver us from this evil World.

The same Scriptures teach us, that as we are redeemed from this State of Sin, so we are raised to a new Life in Christ, to a Participation of the Divine Nature, and a Fellowship with him in Glory.

Thus our blessed Saviour prayeth for all his Followers, *That they all may be one, as thou Father art in me, and I in thee; that they also may be one in us. And the Glory which thou gavest me, I have given them, that they may be one, even as we are one. I in them and thou in me, that they may be made perfect in one.**

Happy he that hath Ears to hear, and a Heart to feel the Majesty and Glory of this Description of our new Life in Christ!

For surely could we understand what our Saviour conceived, when he sent up this Prayer to God, our Hearts would be always praying, and our Souls ever aspiring after this State of Perfection, this Union with Christ in God.

To proceed, *In my Father's House*, saith Christ, *are many Mansions. I go to prepare a Place for you, that where I am, there ye may be also.*†

The Apostle tells us, that as *we have borne the Image of the Earthly, we shall also bear the Image of the Heavenly.*‡

And that *when* Christ, *who is our Life, shall appear, then shall we also appear with him in Glory.*§

Beloved, saith St. John, *now we are the Sons of God, and it doth not yet appear, what we shall be: but we know, that when he shall appear, we shall be like him; for we shall see him as he is.*‖

I cannot leave this Passage, without adding the Apostle's Conclusion to it. And *every Man that hath this Hope in him, purifieth himself, even as he is pure.*

Which teaches us this Lesson, that no Man, whatever he may think of his Christian Improvement, can be said to have this Hope in him, unless he shows it by such a Purification of himself, as may resemble the Purity of Christ.——But to return.

St. Paul thus breaks forth into the Praises of God, *Blessed be the God and Father of our Lord Jesus Christ, who hath blessed us with all spiritual Blessings in heavenly Places in Christ.*¶ And again, *God, who is rich in Mercy, for his great Love wherewith he loved us. Even when we were dead in Sins, hath quickened us together with Christ; and hath raised us up together, and made us sit together in heavenly Places in Christ Jesus.***

---

* John xvii. 21.   † John xiv. 23.   ‡ 1 Cor. xv.   § Col. iii. 4.
‖ 1 John iii. 2.   ¶ Eph. i. 3.   ** Eph. ii. 4.

These Passages teach us, that Christianity introduceth us into a new State, made up of invisible Goods, and spiritual Blessings, that it so alters our Condition, as to give us a new Rank and Degree even in this Life; which the Apostle expresses by making us *sit together in heavenly Places.*

So that though we are still in the Flesh, yet, as the Apostle saith, need we know no Man after the Flesh; though we are still Inhabitants of this Vale of Misery, yet are we ranked and placed in a certain Order amongst heavenly Beings in Christ Jesus.

Would we therefore know our true Rank and Condition, and what Place we belong to, in the Order of Beings, we must search after a *Life that is hid with Christ in God.* We must consider ourselves as Parts of Christ's mystical Body, and as Members of a Kingdom of Heaven. In vain do we consider the Beauty and Strength of our Bodies, our Alliances with Men, the Privileges of Birth, and the Distinctions of this World, for these Things no more constitute the State of human Life, than rich *Coffins,* or beautiful *Monuments,* constitute the State of the Dead.

We justly pity the last poor Efforts of human Greatness, when we see a breathless Carcass lying in *State.* It appears to us to be so far from any real Honour, that it rather looks like ridiculing the Misery of our Nature. But were Religion to form our Judgments, the *Life* of a proud, voluptuous, and sensual Man, though shining in all the Splendour of the World, would give us no higher an Idea of human Dignity, than that of a poor *Corpse* laid in State.

For a *Sinner,* when glorying in *the Lust of the Flesh, the Lust of the Eyes, and the Pride of Life,* shows us a more shocking Sight of a Misery ridiculed, than any Pageantry that can expose the Dead.

We have an Apostle's Authority to say, *that he who liveth in Pleasure is dead while he liveth.*

This shows us, that when we enquire what our Life is, or wherein it consists, we must think of something higher than the Vigour of our Blood, the Gaiety of our Spirits, or the Enjoyment of sensible Pleasures; since these, though the allowed Signs of living Men, are often undeniable Proofs of dead Christians.

When therefore we would truly know what our Life, our State, our Dignity, our Good, or our Evil is, we must look at nothing that is temporal, worldly, or sensible. We may as well dig in the Earth for Wisdom, as look at Flesh and Blood, to see what we are, or at worldly Enjoyments, to find what we want, or at temporal Evils to see what we have to fear.

Our blessed Saviour put an absolute End to all Enquiries of this kind, when he said, *Be not afraid of them that kill the Body, and after that have no more that they can do.**

Here our Bodies and all bodily Enjoyments are at one Dash struck out of the Account of Happiness, and the present State of Things made so very low, and insignificant, that he who can only deprive us of them, has not Power enough to deserve our Fear.

We must therefore, if we would conceive our true State, our real Good and Evil, look further than the Dim of Eyes of Flesh can carry our Views, we must, with the Eyes of Faith, penetrate into the invisible World, the World of Spirits, and consider our Order and Condition amongst them, a World which (as St. *John* speaks) *has no need of the Sun, neither of the Moon, to shine in it, for the Glory of God doth lighten it, and the Light of the Lamb.* For it is there, amongst external Beings, that we must take an eternal Fellowship, or fall into a Kingdom of Darkness and everlasting Misery.

Christianity is so divine in its Nature, so noble in its Ends, so extensive in its Views, that it has no lesser Subjects than these, to entertain our Thoughts.

It buries our Bodies, burns the present World, triumphs over Death by a general Resurrection, and opens all into an eternal State.

It never considers us in any other Respect, than as fallen Spirits; it disregards the Distinctions of human Society, and proposes nothing to our Fears, but eternal Misery, nor anything to our Hopes, but an endless Enjoyment of the Divine Nature.

This is the great and important Condition in which Christianity has placed us, above our Bodies, above the World, above Death, to be present at the Dissolution of all Things, to see the Earth in Flames, and the Heavens wrapt up like a Scroll, to stand at the general Resurrection, to appear at the universal Judgment, and to live for ever, when all that our Eyes have seen, is passed away and gone.

Take upon thee therefore, a Spirit and Temper suitable to this Greatness of thy Condition; remember that thou art an eternal Spirit, that thou art for a few Months and Years in a State of Flesh and Blood, only to try, whether thou shalt be for ever happy with God, or fall into everlasting Misery with the Devil.

Thou wilt often hear of other Concerns, and other Greatness in this World; thou wilt see every Order of Men, every Family, every Person pursuing some fancied Happiness of his own, as if

---

* Luke xii. 4.

the World had not only Happiness, but a particular kind of Happiness for all its Inhabitants.

But when thou seest this State of human Life, fancy that thou sawest all the World asleep, the Prince no longer a Prince, the Beggar no longer begging, but every Man sleeping out of his proper State, some happy, others tormented, and all changing their Condition as fast as one foolish Dream could succeed another.

When thou hast seen this, thou hast seen all that the World awake can do for thee ; if thou wilt, thou mayst go to *sleep* for awhile, thou mayst lie down and *dream ;* for, be as happy as the World can make thee, all is but sleeping and dreaming, and what is still worse, it is like sleeping in a Ship when thou should be pumping out the Water ; or dreaming thou art a Prince, when thou shouldst be redeeming thyself from Slavery.

Now this is no imaginary Flight of a melancholy Fancy, that too much exceeds the Nature of Things, but a sober Reflection justly suited to the Vanity of worldly Enjoyments.

For if the Doctrines of Christianity are true, if thou art that Creature, that fallen Spirit, that immortal Nature which Religion teaches us, if thou art to meet Death, Resurrection, and Judgment, as the Forerunners of an eternal State, what are all the little Flashes of Pleasure, the changing Appearances of worldly Felicities, but so many Sorts of Dreams ?

How canst thou talk of the Happiness of Riches, the Advantages of Fortune, the Pleasures of Apparel, of State, and Equipage, without being in a Dream ?

Is the *Beggar* asleep, when he fancies he is building himself fine Houses ? Is the *Prisoner* in a Dream, when he imagines himself in open Fields, and fine Groves ? And canst thou think that thy immortal Spirit is awake, whilst it is delighting itself in the Shadows and Bubbles of worldly Happiness ?

For if it be true, that Man is upon his Trial, if the Trial is for Eternity, if Life is but a Vapour, what is there that deserves a serious Thought, but how to get well out of the World, and make it a right Passage to our eternal State ?

How can we prove that we are awake, that our Eyes are open, but by seeing, and feeling, and living according to these important Circumstances of our Life ?

If a Man should endeavour to please thee, with fine Descriptions of the Riches, and Pleasures, and Dignities, of the World in the *Moon*, adding that its Air is always serene, and its Seasons always pleasant, would'st thou not think it a sufficient Answer, to say, *I am not to live there ?*

When thy own false Heart is endeavouring to please itself

2—2

with worldly Expectations, the Joy of this or that way of Life, is it not as good a Reproof, to say to thyself, *I am not to stay here ?*

For where is the Difference betwixt an earthly Happiness, from which thou art to be separated for ever, and a Happiness in the Moon, to which thou art never to go ? Thou art to be for ever separated from the Earth, thou art to be eternal, when the Earth itself is lost, is it not therefore the same Vanity to project for Happiness on Earth, as to propose a Happiness in the Moon? For as thou art *never* to go to the one, so thou art to be *eternally* separated from the other.

Indeed the Littleness and Insignificancy of the boasted Honours of human Life, appears sufficiently from the Things themselves, without comparing them to the Subjects of Religion.

For see what they are in themselves.

Ahasuerus, that great Prince of the eastern World, puts a Question to *Haman*, his chief Minister of State, he asks him, *what shall be done unto the Man, whom the King delighteth to honour ?**

Haman imagining that he was the Person whom the King had in his Thoughts, answered in these Words,

Let the royal Apparel be brought which the King useth to wear, and the Horse that the King rideth upon, and the Crown Royal which is set upon his Head ; and let this Apparel and Horse be delivered to the Hand of one of the King's most noble Princes, that they may array the Man withal, whom the King delighteth to honour, and bring him on horseback through the Street of the City, and proclaim before him, thus shall it be done to the Man whom the King delighteth to honour.

Here you see the Sum total of worldly Honours.

An ambitious *Haman* cannot think of anything greater to ask ; *Ahasuerus*, the greatest Monarch in the World, has nothing greater to give to his greatest Favourite ; powerful as he is, he can only give such Honours as these.

Yet it is to be observed, that if a poor *Nurse* was to please her *Child*, she must talk to it in the same Language, she must please it with the same fine Things, and gratify its Pride with Honours of the same kind.

Yet these are the mighty Things, for which Men forget God, forget their Immortality, forget the Difference betwixt an Eternity in Heaven, and an Eternity in Hell.

There needs no great Understanding, no mighty Depth of Thought, to see through the Vanity of all worldly Enjoyments ;

---

* Esther vi. 6.

do but talk of them, and you will be forced to talk of Gewgaws, of Ribbons, and Feathers.

Every man sees the Littleness of all Sorts of Honours, but those which he is looking after himself.

A private English Gentleman, that is half distracted till he has got some little Distinction, does at the same time despise the highest Honours of other Countries, and would not leave his own Condition, to possess the ridiculous Greatness of an *Indian King.* He sees the Vanity and Falseness of their Honours, but forgets that all Honour placed in external Things, is equally vain and false.

He does not consider that the Difference of Greatness, is only the Difference of Flowers and Feathers ; and that they who are dressing themselves with *Beads,* have as just a Taste of what adorns their Persons, as they who place the same Pride in *Diamonds.*

When we read of an eastern Prince, that is too great to feed himself, and thinks it a Piece of Grandeur to have other People put his Meat into his Mouth, we despise the Folly of his Pride.

But might we not as well despise the Folly of their Pride, who are ashamed to use their Legs, and think it adds to their State, to be removed from one Place to another by other People.

For he that thinks it stately to be carried, and mean to walk on Foot, has as true Notions of Greatness, as he who is too haughty to put his Meat in his own Mouth.

Again, It is the Manner of some Countries in the Burial of their Dead, to put a Staff, and Shoes, and Money, in the Sepulchre along with the Corpse.

We justly censure the Folly and Ignorance of such a poor Contrivance to assist the Dead ; but if we did but as truly understand what Life is, we should see as much to ridicule in the poor Contrivances to assist the Living.

For how many Things in Life do People labour after, break their Rest and Peace to get, which yet when gotten, are of as much real Use to them, as a Staff and Shoes to a *Corpse* under Ground ? They are always adding something to their Life, which is only like adding another Pair of Shoes to a Body in the Grave.

Thou mayst hire more Servants, new paint thy Rooms, make more fine Beds, eat out of *Plate,* and put on richer Apparel, and these will help thee to be happy, as *golden* Staves, or *painted* Shoes, will help a dead Man to walk.

See here therefore the true Nature of all worldly *Show* and *Figure,* it will make us as great as those are, who are dreaming that they are Kings, as rich as those who fancy that they have

Estates in the Moon, and as happy as those, who are buried with
Staves in their Hands.

Now this is not carrying Matters too high, or imposing upon
ourselves with any Subtleties of Reasoning, or Sound of Words;
for the Value of worldly Riches and Honours can no more be
too much lessened, than the Riches and Greatness of the other
Life can be too much exalted.   We don't cheat ourselves out
of any real Happiness, by looking upon all worldly Honours
as Bubbles, any more than we cheat ourselves by securing
Honours that are solid and eternal.

There is no more Happiness lost by not being *great* and *rich*,
as those are amongst whom we live, than by not being *dressed*
and *adorned* as they are, who live in *China* or *Japan*.

Thou art no happier for having painted Ceilings, and marble
Walls in thy House, than if the same Finery was in thy *Stables;*
if thou eatest upon Plate, it maketh thee just as happy, as if thy
Horses wore silver Shoes.

To disregard Gold, Jewels, and Equipage, is no more running
away from any real Good, than if we only despised a Feather or
a Garland of Flowers.

So that he who condemns *all* the external Show and State of
Life as equally vain, is no more deceived, or carried to too high
a Contempt for the Things of this Life, than he that only condemns the Vanity of the vainest Things.

You don't think yourself imposed upon, or talked out of any
real Happiness, when you are persuaded not to be as vain and
ambitious as *Alexander.*

And can you think that you are imposed upon, or drawn from
any real Good, by being persuaded to be as meek and lowly as
the holy Jesus ?

There is as much sober Judgment, as sound Sense in conforming to the Fulness of Christ's Humility, as in avoiding the
Height and Extravagance of *Alexander's* Vanity.

Don't therefore think to compound Matters, or that it is
enough to avoid the Vanity of the vainest Men.   There is as
much Folly in seeking little as great Honours ; as great a
Mistake in needless Expense upon thyself, as upon anything
else.   Thou must not only be less vain and ambitious than an
Alexander, but practise the Humility of the blessed *Jesus.*

If thou rememberest that the whole Race of Mankind are a
Race of fallen Spirits, that pass through this World as an Arrow
passes through the Air, thou wilt soon perceive, that all Things
here are equally great and equally little, and that there is no
Wisdom or Happiness, but in getting away to the best
Advantage.

If thou rememberest that this Life is but a Vapour, that thou art in the Body, only to be holy, humble, and heavenly-minded, that thou standest upon the Brinks of Death, Resurrection, and Judgment, and that these great Things will suddenly come upon thee, like a Thief in the Night, thou wilt see a Vanity in all the Gifts of Fortune, greater than any Words can express.

Do but therefore know thyself, as Religion has made thee known, do but see thyself in the Light, which Christ has brought into the World, and then thou wilt see that nothing concerns thee, but what concerns an everlasting Spirit that is going to God ; and that there are no Enjoyments here that are worth a Thought, but such as may make thee more perfect in those holy Tempers which will carry thee to Heaven.

Chapter II.

Christianity requires a Change of Nature : a new Life perfectly devoted to God.

CHRISTIANITY is not a *School*, for the teaching of moral Virtue, the polishing our Manners, or forming us to live a Life of this World with Decency and Gentility.

It is deeper and more divine in its Designs, and has much nobler Ends than these, it implies an *entire Change* of Life, a Dedication of ourselves, our Souls and Bodies unto God, in the strictest and highest Sense of the Words.

Our blessed Saviour came into the World not to make any Composition with it, or to divide Things between Heaven and Earth, but to make War with every State of Life, to put an End to the Designs of Flesh and Blood, and to show us, that we must either leave this World, to become Sons of God, or by enjoying it, take our Portion amongst Devils and damned Spirits.

Death is not more certainly a Separation of our Souls from our Bodies, than the Christian Life is a Separation of our Souls from worldly Tempers, vain Indulgences, and unnecessary Cares.

No sooner are we baptized, but we are to consider ourselves as new and holy Persons, that are entered upon a new State of Things, that are devoted to God, and have renounced all, to be Fellow-heirs with Christ, and Members of his Kingdom:

There is no Alteration of Life, no Change of Condition, that implies half so much, as that Alteration which Christianity introduceth.

It is a Kingdom of Heaven begun upon Earth, and by being made Members of it, we are entered into a new State of Goods and Evils.

Eternity altereth the Face and Nature of everything in this World, Life is only a Trial, Prosperity becometh Adversity, Pleasure a Mischief, and nothing a Good, but as it increaseth our Hope, purifieth our Natures, and prepareth us to receive higher Degrees of Happiness.

Let us now see what it is, to enter into this State of Redemption.

Our own Church in Conformity with Scripture, and the Practice of the purest Ages, makes it necessary for us to renounce the *Pomps and Vanities of the World,* before we can be received as Members of Christian Communion.

Did we enough consider this, we should find, that whenever we yield ourselves up to the Pleasures, Profits, and Honours of this Life, that we turn *Apostates,* break our Covenant with God, and go back from the express Conditions, on which we were admitted into the Communion of Christ's Church.

If we consult either the Life or Doctrines of our Saviour, we shall find that Christianity is a Covenant, that contains only the Terms of changing and resigning this World, for another, that is to come.

It is a State of Things that wholly regards Eternity, and knows of no other Goods, and Evils, but such as relate to another Life.

It is a Kingdom of Heaven, that has no other Interests in this World, than as it takes its Members out of it, and when the Number of the Elect is complete, this World will be consumed with Fire, as having no other Reason of its Existence than the furnishing Members for that blessed Society which is to last for ever.

I cannot here omit observing the Folly and Vanity of human Wisdom, which full of imaginary Projects, pleases itself with its mighty Prosperities, its lasting Establishments in a World doomed to Destruction, and which is to last no longer, than till a sufficient Number are redeemed out of it.

Did we see a Number of Animals hastening to take up their Apartments, and contending for the best Places, in a Building that was to be beat down, as soon as its old Inhabitants were got safe out, we should see a Contention full as wise, as the Wisdom of worldly Ambition.

To return. Christianity is therefore a Course of holy Discipline, solely fitted to the Cure and Recovery of fallen Spirits, and intends such a Change in our Nature, as may raise us to a nearer Union with God, and qualify us for such high Degrees of Happiness.

It is no Wonder therefore, if it makes no Provision for the Flesh, if it condemns the Maxims of human Wisdom, and indulges us in no worldly Projects, since its very End, is, to redeem us from all the Vanity, Vexation, and Misery, of this State of Things, and to place us in a Condition, where we shall be Fellow-heirs with Christ, and as the Angels of God.

That Christianity requires a Change of Nature, a new Life perfectly devoted to God, is plain from the Spirit and Tenor of the Gospel.

The Saviour of the World saith, *that except a Man be born again, of the Water and the Spirit, he cannot enter into the Kingdom of God.** We are told, that *to as many as received him, to them he gave Power, to become the Sons of God, which were born, not of Blood, nor of the Will of the Flesh, nor of the Will of Man, but of God.*†

These Words plainly teach us, that Christianity implies some great Change of Nature, that as our Birth was to us the Beginning of a new Life, and brought us into a Society of earthly Enjoyments, so Christianity, is another Birth, that brings us into a Condition altogether as new, as when we first saw the Light.

We begin again to be, we enter upon fresh Terms of Life, have new Relations, new Hopes and Fears, and an entire Change of everything that can be called good or evil.

This new Birth, this Principle of a new Life, is the very Essence and Soul of Christianity, it is the Seal of the Promises, the Mark of our Sonship, the Earnest of the Inheritance, the Security of our Hope, and the Foundation of all our Acceptance with God.

He that is in Christ, saith the Apostle, *is a new Creature, and if any Man hath not the Spirit of Christ, he is none of his.*‡

And again, *He who is joined to the Lord, is one Spirit.*§

It is not therefore any Number of moral Virtues, no partial Obedience, no Modes of Worship, no external Acts of Adoration, no Articles of Faith, but a new Principle of Life, an entire Change of Temper, that makes us true Christians.

If the *Spirit of him who raised up Jesus from the Dead dwell in you, he that raised up Christ from the Dead, shall also quicken*

---

* John iii. 5. † John i. 12. ‡ Rom. viii. 9. § 1 Cor. vi. 17.

*your mortal Bodies by his Spirit that dwelleth in you.** For as *many as are led by the Spirit of God, they are the Sons of God.*

Since therefore the Scriptures thus absolutely require a Life suitable to the Spirit and Temper of Jesus Christ, since they allow us not the Privilege of the Sons of God, unless we live and act according to the Spirit of God ; it is past Doubt, that Christianity requires an entire Change of Nature and Temper, a Life devoted perfectly to God.

For what can imply a greater Change, than from a carnal to a spiritual Mind ? What can be more contrary, than the Works of the Flesh are to the Works of the Spirit ? It is the Difference of Heaven and Hell.

Light and Darkness are but faint Resemblances of that great Contrariety, that is betwixt the Spirit of God, and the Spirit of the World.

Its Wisdom is Foolishness, its Friendship is Enmity with God.

All that is in the World, the Lust of the Flesh, the Lust of the Eyes, and the Pride of Life, is not of the Father.†

Worldly Opinions, proud Reasonings, fleshly Cares, and earthly Projects, are all so many false Judgments, mere Lies, and we know who is the Father of Lies.

For this Reason, the Scripture makes the Devil the God and Prince of this World, because the Spirit and Temper which reigns there, is entirely from him ; and so far as we are governed by the Wisdom and Temper of the World, so far are we governed by that evil Power of Darkness.

If we would see more of this Contrariety, and what a Change our new Life in Christ implies, let us consider what it is to be *born of God.*

St. John tells us one sure Mark of our new Birth, in the following Words, *He that is born of God, overcometh the World.*‡

So that the *new Birth,* or the Christian Life, is considered with Opposition to the *World,* and all that is in it, its vain Cares, its false Glories, proud Designs, and sensual Pleasures, if we have overcome these, so as to be governed by other Cares, other Glories, other Designs, and other Pleasures, then are we born of God. Then is the Wisdom of this World, and the Friendship of this World, turned into the Wisdom and Friendship of God, which will for ever keep us *Heirs of God, and Joint-heirs with Christ.*

Again, the same Apostle helps us to another Sign of our new Life in God. *Whosoever,* saith he, *is born of God, doth not*

---

* Rom. viii. 11.   † 1 John ii. 16.   ‡ 1 Ep. v. 4.

*commit Sin, for his Seed remaineth in him, and he cannot sin, because he is born of God.**

This is not to be understood, as if he that was born of God, was therefore in an absolute State of Perfection, and incapable afterwards of falling into anything that was sinful.

It only means, that he that is born of God, is possessed of a Temper and Principle, that makes him utterly hate and labour to avoid all Sin ; he is therefore said *not to commit Sin*, in such a Sense as a Man may be said not to do that, which it is his constant Care and Principle to prevent being done.

He cannot sin, as it may be said of a Man that has no Principle but Covetousness, that he cannot do Things that are expensive, because it is his constant Care and Labour to be sparing, and if Expense happen, it is contrary to his Intention ; it is his Pain and Trouble, and he returns to saving with a double Diligence.

Thus is he that is born of God, Purity and Holiness is his only Aim, and he is more incapable of having any sinful Intentions, than the *Miser* is incapable of generous Expense, and if he finds himself in any Sin, it is his greatest Pain and Trouble, and he labours after Holiness with a double Zeal.

This it is to be born of God, when we have a Temper and Mind so entirely devoted to Purity and Holiness, that it may be said of us in a just Sense, that we cannot commit Sin. When Holiness is such a Habit in our Minds, so directs and forms our Designs, as Covetousness and Ambition directs and governs the Actions of such Men, as are governed by no other Principles, then are we alive in God, and living Members of the mystical Body of his Son Jesus Christ.

This is our true Standard and Measure by which we are to judge of ourselves ; we are not true Christians unless we are born of God, and we are not born of God, unless it can be said of us in this Sense that we cannot commit Sin.

When by an inward Principle of Holiness we stand so disposed to all Degrees of Virtue, as the ambitious Man stands disposed to all Steps of Greatness, when we hate and avoid all Kinds of Sins, as the covetous Man hates and avoids all Sorts of Loss and Expense, then are we such Sons of God, as cannot commit Sin.

We must therefore examine into the State and Temper of our Minds, and see whether we be thus changed in our Natures, thus born again to a new Life, whether we be so spiritual, as to have overcome the World, so holy, as that we cannot commit

* 1 Ep. iii. 9.

Sin ; since it is the undeniable Doctrine of Scripture, that this State of Mind, this new Birth is as necessary to Salvation, as the believing in Jesus Christ.

To be eminent therefore for any particular Virtue, to detest and avoid several Kinds of Sins, is just nothing at all ; its Excellency (as the Apostle saith of some particular Virtues) is but as *sounding Brass and a tinkling Cymbal.*

But when the Temper and Taste of our Soul is entirely changed, when we are renewed in the Spirit of our Minds, and are full of a Relish and Desire of all Godliness, of a Fear and Abhorrence of all Evil, then, as St. *John* speaks, *may we know that we are of the Truth, and shall assure our Hearts before him, then shall we know, that he abideth in us by the Spirit, which he hath given us.**

We have already seen two Marks of those that are born of God, the one is, that they have overcome the World, the other, that they do not commit Sin.

To these I shall only add a third, which is given us by Christ himself, *I say unto you, love your Enemies, bless them that curse you, do good to them that hate you, and pray for them which despitefully use you, and persecute you, that you may be the Children of your Father which is in Heaven.*†

Well may a Christian be said to be a *new Creature,* and Christianity an entire Change of Temper, since such a Disposition as this, is made so necessary, that without it, we cannot be the Children of our Father which is in Heaven ; and if we are not his Children, neither is he our Father.

It is not therefore enough, that we love our Friends, Benefactors, and Relations, but we must love like God, if we will show that we are born of him. We must like him have a universal Love and Tenderness for all Mankind, imitating that Love, which would that all Men should be saved.

God is Love, and this we are to observe as the true Standard of ourselves, that *he who dwelleth in God, dwelleth in Love ;* and consequently he who dwelleth not in Love, dwelleth not in God.

It is impossible therefore to be a *true* Christian, and an *Enemy* at the same time.

Mankind has no Enemy but the Devil, and they who partake of his malicious and ill-natured Spirit.

There is perhaps no Duty of Religion that is so contrary to Flesh and Blood as this, but as difficult as it may seem to a worldly Mind, it is still necessary, and will easily be performed by such as are in Christ, new Creatures.

For take but away earthly Goods and Evils, and you take

---

* 1 Ep. iii. 19, 24.   † Matt. v. 44.

away all Hatred and Malice, for they are the only Causes of those base Tempers. He therefore that *hath overcome the World,* hath overcome all the Occasions of Envy and ill Nature ; for having put himself in this Situation, he can pity, pray for, and forgive all his Enemies, who want less Forgiveness from him, than he expects from his heavenly Father.

Let us here awhile contemplate the Height and Depth of Christian Holiness, and that god-like Spirit which our Religion requireth. This Duty of universal Love and Benevolence, even to our bitterest Enemies, may serve to convince us, that to be Christians, we must be *born again,* change our very Natures, and have no governing Desire of our Souls, but that of being made like God.

For we cannot exercise, or delight in this Duty, till we rejoice and delight only in increasing our Likeness to God.

We may therefore from this, as well as from what has been before observed, be infallibly assured, that Christianity does not consist in any partial Amendment of our Lives, any particular moral Virtues, but in an entire Change of our natural Temper, a Life wholly devoted to God.

To proceed,

This same Doctrine is farther taught by our blessed Saviour, when speaking of little Children, he saith, *Suffer them to come unto me, for of such is the Kingdom of God.* And again, *Whosoever shall not receive the Kingdom of God, as a little Child, shall in no wise enter therein.**

If we are not resolved to deceive ourselves, to have Eyes and see not, Ears and hear not, we must perceive that these Words imply some mighty Change in our Nature.

For what can make us more contrary to ourselves, than to lay aside all our manly Wisdom, our mature Judgments, our boasted Abilities, and become Infants in Nature and Temper, before we can partake of this heavenly State ?

We reckon it Change enough, from Babes to be Men, and surely it must signify as great an Alteration, to be reduced from Men to a State of Infancy.

One peculiar Condition of Infants is this, that they have everything to learn, they are to be taught by others what they are to hope and fear, and wherein their proper Happiness consists.

It is in this Sense, that we are chiefly to become as Infants, to be as though that we had everything to learn, and suffer ourselves to be taught what we are to choose, and what to avoid ; to pretend to no Wisdom of our own, but be ready to pursue

---

* Luke xviii. 16.

that Happiness which God in Christ proposes to us, and to accept it with such Simplicity of Mind, as Children, that have nothing of our own to oppose to it.

But now, is this Infant-temper thus essential to the Christian Life? Does the Kingdom of God consist only of such as are so affected? Let this then be added as another undeniable Proof, that Christianity requires a *new Nature*, and Temper of Mind ; and that this Temper is such, as having renounced the Prejudices of Life, the Maxims of human Wisdom, yields itself with a Child-like Submission and Simplicity to be entirely governed by the Precepts and Doctrines of Christ.

Craft and Policy, selfish Cunning, proud Abilities, and vain Endowments, have no Admittance into this holy State of Society with Christ and God.

The Wisdom of this World, the Intrigues of Life, the Designs of Greatness and Ambition, lead to another Kingdom, and he that would follow Christ, must empty himself of this vain Furniture, and put on the meek Ornaments of infant and undesigning Simplicity.

Where is the Wise? Where is the Scribe? Where is the Disputer of this World? saith the Apostle, *Hath not God made foolish the Wisdom of this World?**

If therefore we will partake of the Wisdom of God, we must think and judge of this World, and its most boasted Gifts, as the Wisdom of God judgeth of them ; we must deem them Foolishness, and with undivided Hearts labour after one Wisdom, one Perfection, one Happiness, in being entirely devoted to God.

This Comparison of the Spirit of a Christian, to the Temper of Children, may also serve to recommend to us a certain Simplicity of Manners, which is a great Ornament of Behaviour, and is indeed always the Effect of a Heart entirely devoted to God. .

For as the Tempers of Men are made designing and deceitful, by their having many and secret Ends to bring about, so the Heart that is entirely devoted to God, is at Unity with itself, and all others ; it being wholly taken up with *one great* Design, has no little Successes that it labours after, and so is naturally open, simple, and undesigning in all the Affairs of Life.

Although what has been already observed in the foregoing Pages might be thought sufficient to show, that Christianity requires a new Nature, a Life entirely devoted to God ; yet since the Scriptures add other Evidences of the same Truth, I must quote a Passage or two more on this Head.

---

* 1 Cor. i. 20.

The Holy Spirit of God is not satisfied with representing that Change which Christianity introduceth, by telling us, that it is a new Birth, a Being born of God, and the like, but proceeds to convince us of the same Truth by another Way of speaking, by representing it as a State of Death.

Thus saith the Apostle, *ye are dead, and your Life is hid with Christ in God.**

That is, you Christians are dead as to this World, and the Life which you now live, is not to be reckoned by any visible or worldly Goods, but is hid in Christ, is a spiritual Enjoyment, a Life of Faith, and not of Sight; ye are Members of that mystical Body of which Christ is the Head, and entered into a Kingdom which is not of this World.

And in this State of Death are we as Christians to continue till *Christ, who is our Life, shall appear, and then shall we also appear with him in Glory.*†

To show us that this Death begins with our Christian State, we are said to be *buried with him in Baptism ;* so that we entered into this State of Death at our Baptism, when we entered into Christianity.

Know ye not, says the Apostle, *that so many of us as were baptized into Jesus Christ, were baptized into his Death ? Therefore we are buried with him, by Baptism into Death.*‡

Now Christians may be said to be baptized into the Death of Christ, if their Baptism puts them into a State like to that, in which our Saviour was at his Death. The Apostle shows this to be the Meaning of it, by saying, *if we have been planted together in the Likeness of his Death,* that is, if our Baptism has put us into a State like that of his Death.

So that Christian Baptism is not only an external Rite, by which we are entered into the external Society of Christ's Church, but is a solemn Consecration, which presents us an Offering to God, as Christ was offered at his Death.

We are therefore no longer alive to the Enjoyments of this World, but as Christ was then nailed to the Cross, and devoted entirely to God, that he might be made *perfect through Sufferings,* and ascend to the Right Hand of God ; so is our old Man to be crucified, and we consecrated to God, by a Conformity to the Death of Christ, that *like as Christ was raised from the Dead by the Glory of the Father, even so we also should walk in newness of Life, and being risen with Christ, should seek those Things which are above.*

This is the true undeniable State of Christianity ; Baptism does

---

* Col. iii. 3.   † Ibid., 4.   ‡ Rom. vi. 4.

not make us effectually Christians, unless it brings us into a State of Death, consecrates us to God, and begins a Life suitable to that State of Things, to which our Saviour is risen from the Dead. This, and no other than this, is the Holiness, and spiritual Temper, of the Christian Life, which implies such a Resignation of Mind, such a Dedication of ourselves to God, as may resemble the Death of Christ. And on the other Hand, such a Newness of Life, such an Ascension of the Soul, such a holy and heavenly Behaviour, as may show that we are risen with Christ, and belong to that glorious State, where he now sits at the Right Hand of God.

It is in this Sense, that the holy Jesus saith of his Disciples, *they are not of this World, even as I am not of this World ;* being not left to live the Life of the World, but chosen out of it for the Purposes of his Kingdom, that they might copy after his Death, and Oblation of himself to God.

And this is the Condition of all Christians to the Consumma-tion of all Things, who are to carry on the same Designs, and by the same Means raise out of this corrupted State, a Number of Fellow-heirs with Christ in everlasting Glory. The Saviour of the World has purchased Mankind with his Blood, not to live in Ease and pleasurable Enjoyments, not to spend their Time in Softness and Luxury, in the Gratifications of Pride, Idleness, and Vanity, but to drink of his Cup, to be baptized with the Baptism that he was baptized with, to make War with their corrupt Natures, humble themselves, mortify the Desires of the Flesh, and like him be made perfect through Sufferings.

St. Paul so well knew this to be the Design and Spirit of Religion, that he puts his Title to the Benefits of Christ's Resur-rection upon it, when he says,

That *I may know him and the Power of his Resurrection, and the Fellowship of his Sufferings, being made conformable to his Death.**

It is his being made conformable to his Death, on which he founds his Hopes of sharing in the Resurrection of Christ. If Christians think that Salvation is now to be had on softer Terms, and that a Life of Indulgence and sensual Gratifications is consistent with the Terms of the Gospel, and that they need not now be made conformable to his Death, they are miserably blind, and as much mistake their Saviour, as the Worldly Jews who expected a temporal Messiah to deliver them.

Our Redemption is a Redemption by Sacrifice, and none are redeemed, but they who conform to it. *If we suffer with him we shall also reign with him.*

---

* Phil. iii. 10.

We must then, if we would be wise unto Salvation, die and rise again like Christ, and make all the Actions of our Life holy by offering them to God. *Whether we eat, or drink, or whatsoever we do, we must do all to the Glory of God.*

Since therefore, he that is called to Christianity, is thus called to an Imitation of the *Death* of Christ, to *forbear* from Sin, to overcome the *World*, to be born of the *Spirit*, to be born of God, these surely will be allowed to be sufficient Evidences, that Christianity requireth an *entire Change* of our Nature, a Life perfectly devoted to God.

Now if this is Christian Piety, it may serve to instruct two Sorts of People:

First, those who are content with an outward Decency and Regularity of Life: I don't mean such as are hypocritical in their Virtues; but all those who are content with an outward Form of Behaviour, without that inward Newness of Heart and Spirit which the Gospel requireth.

Charity, Chastity, Sobriety, and Justice, may be practised without Christian Piety: a *Jew*, a *Heathen*, may be charitable and temperate; but to make these Virtues become Parts of Christian Piety, they must proceed from a Heart *truly* turned unto God, that is full of an *infant* Simplicity, that is *crucified* with Christ, that is *born* again of the Spirit, that has overcome the *World*. Temperance or Justice without this *Turn* of Heart, may be the Temperance of a *Jew* or a *Heathen*, but it is not Christian Temperance till it proceed from a true Christian Spirit. Could we do and suffer all that Christ himself did or suffered, yet if it was not all done in the *same Spirit* and Temper of Christ, we should have none of his Merit.

A Christian therefore must be sober, charitable, and just, upon the same Principles, and with the same Spirit, that he receives the Holy *Sacrament*, for ends of Religion, as Acts of Obedience to God, as Means of Purity and Holiness, and as so many Instances of a Heart devoted to God.

As the bare eating of Bread, and drinking Wine in the Holy *Sacrament*, is of no use to us, without those religious Dispositions which constitute the true Frame of a pious Mind, so is it the same in all other Duties; they are mere outward Ceremonies, and useless Actions, unless they are performed in the *Spirit* of Religion: Charity and Sobriety are of no Value, till they are so many Instances of a Heart truly devoted to God.

A Christian therefore is to be sober, not only so far as answers the Ends of a decent and orderly Life, but in such a Manner as becomes one, who is *born* of the Holy Spirit, that is made one with Christ, who dwells in Christ and Christ in him. He must be

3

sober in such a measure as best serves the Ends of Religion, and practise such Abstinence as may make him fittest for the Holiness, Purity, and Perfection of the Christian Life.

He must be charitable, not so far as suits with Humanity and good Esteem amongst Men, but in such a Measure as is according to the Doctrines and *Spirit* of Religion.

For neither Charity, nor Temperance, nor any other Virtue, are Parts of Christian Holiness, till they are made holy and religious by such a Piety of Heart, as shows that we live *wholly* unto God.

This is what cannot be too much considered by a great many People, whose Religion has made no Change in their Hearts, but only consists in an external Decency of Life, who are sober without the Piety of Sobriety, who pray without Devotion, who give Alms without Charity, and are Christians without the Spirit of Christianity.

Let them remember that Religion is to *alter* our Nature, that Christian Piety consists in a *Change* of Heart, that it implies a new Turn of Spirit, a spiritual Death, a spiritual Life, a dying to the World, and a Living wholly unto God.

Secondly, This Doctrine may serve to instruct those who have lived Strangers to Religion, what they are to do to become true Christians.

Some People who are ashamed of the Folly of their Lives, and begin to look towards Religion, think they have done enough, when they either alter the outward Course of their Lives, abate some of their Extravagances, or become careful of some particular Virtue.

Thus a Man, whose Life has been a Course of Folly, thinks he has made a sufficient Change, by becoming temperate. Another imagines he has sufficiently declared for Religion, by not neglecting the public Worship as he used to do. A *Lady* fancies that she lives enough to God, because she has left off *Plays* and *Paint*, and lives more at home, than in the former Part of her Life.

But such People should consider, that Religion is no one particular Virtue ; that it does not consist in the *Fewness* of our Vices, or in any particular Amendment of our Lives, but in such a *thorough Change* of Heart, as makes Piety and Holiness the Measure and Rule of all our Tempers.

It is a miserable Error to be content with ourselves, because we are less vain, or covetous, more sober, and decent in our Behaviour, than we used to be ; yet this is the State of many People, who think they have sufficiently reformed their Lives, because they are in some Degree different from what they were. They think

it enough to be changed from what they were, without considering how thorough a Change Religion requires.

But let such People remember, that they who thus *measure
themselves by themselves are not wise.* Let them remember that
they are not Disciples of Christ, till they have like him offered
their whole Body and Soul as a reasonable and lively Sacrifice
unto God ; that they are not Members of Christ's mystical Body,
till they are united unto him by a *new Spirit ;* that they have
not entered into the Kingdom of God, till they have entered with
an *infant Simplicity* of Heart, till they are so born again as not to
commit Sin, so full of an heavenly Spirit, as to have *overcome the
World.*

Nothing less than this *great Change* of Heart and Mind can
give anyone any Assurance, that he is truly turned to God.
There is but this one Term of Salvation, *He that is in Christ, is
a new Creature.* How insignificant all other Attainments are, is
sufficiently shown in the following Words : *Many will say to me
in that Day, Lord, Lord, have we not prophesied in thy Name ?
And in thy Name have cast out Devils ? And in thy Name have
done many wonderful Works ? And then will I profess unto
them, I never knew you. Depart from me, ye that work Iniquity.**

So that there is no Religion that will stand us in any stead, but
that which is the *Conversion* of the Heart to God ; when all our
Tempers are Tempers of Piety, springing from a Soul that is *born
again of the Spirit,* that tends with one full Bent to a Perfection
and Happiness in the Enjoyment of God.

Let us therefore look carefully to ourselves, and consider what
manner of Spirit we are of : let us not think our Condition safe,
because we are of this or that Church or Communion, or because
we are strict Observers of the external Offices of Religion, for
these are Marks that belong to more than belong to Christ. All
are not his, that *prophecy* or even *work Miracles in his Name,*
much less those, who with worldly Minds and corrupt Hearts are
only baptized in his Name.

If Religion has raised us into a *new* World, if it has filled us
with new *Ends* of Life, if it has taken Possession of our Hearts,
and altered the whole Turn of our Minds, if it has changed all
our Ideas of Things, given us a new Set of Hopes and Fears, and
taught us to live by the *Realities* of an invisible World, then may
we humbly hope, that we are true Followers of the Holy Jesus,
and such as *may rejoice in the Day of Christ, that we have neither
run in vain, nor laboured in vain.*

---

* Matt. vii. 22.

Chapter III.

Christianity requireth a Renunciation of the World, and all worldly Tempers.

THE Christian Religion being to raise a *new*, spiritual, and as yet invisible World, and to place Man in a certain Order amongst *Thrones, Principalities*, and spiritual Beings, is at entire Enmity with this present, corrupt State of Flesh and Blood.

It ranks the present World along with the Flesh and the Devil, as an equal Enemy to those glorious Ends, and that Perfection of human Nature, which our Redemption proposes.

It pleased the Wisdom of God to indulge the *Jews* in worldly Hopes and Fears.

It was then said, *Therefore shall ye keep all the Commandments, which I command you this Day, that ye may be strong, and go in and possess the Land, whither you go to possess it.*

The Gospel is quite of another Nature, and is a Call to a very different State, it lays its first Foundation in the Renunciation of the World, as a State of false Goods and Enjoyments, which feed the Vanity and Corruption of our Nature, fill our Hearts with foolish and wicked Passions, and keep us separate from God, the only Happiness of all Spirits.

My *Kingdom*, saith our blessed Saviour, *is not of this World;* by which we may be assured, that no Worldlings are of his Kingdom.

We have a further Representation of the Contrariety, that there is betwixt this Kingdom and the Concerns of this World. *A certain Man*, saith our Lord, *made a great Supper, and bade many, and sent his Servant at supper-time, to say to them that were bidden: Come, for all Things are now ready; and they all with one Consent began to make Excuse. The first said, I have bought a Piece of Ground, and I must needs go and see it; another said, I have bought five Yoke of Oxen, and I go to prove them, I pray thee have me excused; another said, I have married a Wife, and therefore I cannot come.*

We find that the Master of the House was angry, and said, *None of those Men which were bidden, shall taste of my Supper.**

Our Saviour a little afterwards, applies it all in this Manner,

---

* Luke xiv. 16.

Whosoever he be of you, that forsaketh not all that he hath, he cannot be my Disciple. We are told, that *when the Chief Priests and Pharisees heard our Saviour's Parables, they perceived that he spoke of them.**

If Christians hearing the above-recited Parable, are not pricked in their Hearts, and don't feel that our Saviour speaks of them, it must be owned that they are more hardened than *Jews*, and more insincere than *Pharisees*.

This Parable teaches us, that not only the Vices, the Wickedness and Vanity of this World, but even its most lawful and allowed Concerns, render Men unable to enter, and unworthy to be received into the true State of Christianity.

That he who is busied in an honest and lawful Calling, may on that Account be as well rejected by God, as he who is vainly employed in foolish and idle Pursuits.

That it is no more pardonable to be less affected to the Things of Religion, for the Sake of any worldly Business, than for the Indulgence of our Pride, or any other Passion, it further teaches us, that Christianity is a Calling that puts an End to all other Callings; that we are no longer to consider it as our proper State, or Employment, to take care of Oxen, look after an Estate, or attend the most plausible Affairs of Life, but to reckon every Condition as equally trifling, and fit to be neglected, for the Sake of the *one thing needful*.

Men of serious Business and Management, generally censure those who trifle away their Time in idle and impertinent Pleasures, as vain and foolish, and unworthy of the Christian Profession.

But they don't consider that the Business of the World, where they think they show such a manly Skill and Address, is as vain as Vanity itself; they don't consider that the Cares of an Employment, an Attention to Business, if it has got hold of the Heart, renders Men as vain and odious in the Sight of God, as any other Gratification.

For though they may call it an honest Care, a creditable Industry, or by any other plausible Name, yet it is their particular Gratification, and a Wisdom that can no more recommend itself to the Eyes of God, than the Wisdom of an *Epicure*.

For it shows as wrong a Turn of Mind, as false a Judgment, and as great a Contempt of the true Good, to neglect *any* Degrees of Piety, for the Sake of Business, as for any the most trifling Pleasures of Life.

The Wisdom of this World gives an Importance, and Air of

---

* Matt. xxi. 45.

Greatness to several Ways of Life, and ridicules others as vain and contemptible, which differ only in their kind of Vanity; but the Wisdom from above condemns all Labour, as equally fruitless, but that which labours after everlasting Life. Let but Religion determine the Point, and what can it signify, whether a Man forgets God in his *Farm*, or a *Shop*, or at a *Gaming-Table?* For the World is full as great and important in its *Pleasures*, as in its *Cares;* there is no more Wisdom in the one, than in the other; and the Christian that is governed by either, and made less affected to Things of God by them, is equally odious and contemptible in the Sight of God.

And though we distinguish betwixt *Cares* and *Pleasures*, yet if we would speak exactly, it is Pleasure alone that governs and moves us in every State of Life. And the Man, who in the Business of the World would be thought to pursue it, because of its Use and Importance, is as much governed by his Temper and Taste for Pleasures, as he who studies the Gratification of his *Palate*, or takes his Delight in running *Foxes* and *Hares* out of Breath.

For there is no Wisdom or Reason in anything but Religion, nor is any Way of Life less vain than another, but as it is made serviceable to Piety, and conspires with the Designs of Religion to raise Mankind to a Participation and Enjoyment of the Divine Nature.

Therefore does our Saviour equally call Men from the *Cares* of Employments, as from the *Pleasures* of their Senses, because they are equally wrong Turns of Mind, equally nourish the Corruption of our Nature, and are equally *nothing* when compared to that high State of Glory, which by his Sufferings and Death he has merited for us.

Perhaps Christians who are not at all ashamed to be devoted to the Cares and Business of the World, cannot better perceive the Weakness and Folly of their Designs, than by comparing them with such States of Life, as they own to be vain and foolish, and contrary to the Temper of Religion.

Some People have no other Care, than how to give their *Palate* some fresh Pleasure, and enlarge the Happiness of *Tasting*. I desire to know now wherein consists the Sin or Baseness of this Care.

Others live to no other Purpose than to breed *Dogs*, and attend the Sports of the Field.

Others think all their Time dull and heavy, which is not spent in the Pleasures and Diversions of the *Town*.

Men of sober Business, who seem to act the grave Part of Life, generally condemn these Ways of Life.

Now I desire to know upon what Account they are to be condemned. For produce but the true Reason why any of these Ways of Life are vain and sinful, and the same Reason will conclude with the same Strength against every State of Life, but that which is entirely devoted to God.

Let the ambitious Man but show the Folly and Irregularity of *Covetousness*, and the same Reasons will show the Folly and Irregularity of *Ambition.*

Let the Man who is deep in worldly Business, but show the Vanity and Shame of a Life that is devoted to *Pleasures*, and the same Reasons will as fully set forth the Vanity and Shame of worldly *Cares*, So that whoever can condemn Sensuality, Ambition, or any Way of Life, upon the Principles of Reason and Religion, carries his own Condemnation within his own Breast, and is that very Person whom he despises, unless his Life be entirely devoted to God.

For worldly Cares are no more holy or virtuous, than worldly Pleasures, they are as great a Mistake in Life, and when they equally divide or possess the Heart, are equally vain and shameful, as any sensual Gratifications.

It is granted that some Cares are made necessary by the Necessities of Nature ; and the same also may be observed of some Pleasures ; the Pleasures of Eating, Drinking, and Rest, are equally necessary ; but yet if Reason and Religion do not limit these Pleasures by the Necessities of Nature, we fall from rational Creatures, into Drones, Sots, Gluttons, and *Epicures.*

In like Manner our Care after some worldly Things is necessary, but if this Care is not bounded by the just Wants of Nature, if it wanders into unnecessary Pursuits, and fills the Mind with false Desires and Cravings, if it wants to add an imaginary Splendour to the plain Demands of Nature, it is vain and irregular, it is the Care of the *Epicure*, a longing for *Sauces* and *Ragouts ;* and corrupts the Soul like any other sensual Indulgence.

For this Reason our Lord points his Doctrines at the most common and allowed Employments of Life, to teach us that they may employ our Minds as falsely, and distract us as far from our true Good, as any Trifles and Vanity.

He calls us from such Cares, to convince us, that even the Necessities of Life must be sought with a kind of Indifference, that so our Souls may be truly sensible of greater Wants, and disposed to hunger and thirst after Enjoyments that will make us happy for ever.

But how unlike are Christians to Christianity ! It commands us *to take no Thought, saying what shall we eat, or what shall we drink,* yet Christians are restless and laborious till they can eat in *Plate.*

It commands us to be indifferent about Raiment, but Christians are full of Care and Concern to be clothed in *Purple* and fine Linen; it enjoins us to take no Thought for the Morrow, yet Christians think they have lived in vain, if they don't leave Estates at their Death. Yet these are the Disciples of that Lord, who saith, *Whosoever he be of you, that forsaketh not all that he hath, he cannot be my Disciple.*

It must not be said that there is some Defect in these Doctrines, or that they are not plainly enough taught in Scripture, because the Lives and Behaviour of Christians are so contrary to them ; for if the Spirit of the World, and the Temper of Christians, might be alleged against the Doctrines of Scripture, none of them would have lasted to this Day.

It is one of the Ten Commandments, *Thou shalt not take the Name of the Lord thy God in vain ;* our Saviour has in the most solemn Manner forbid Swearing ; yet where more Swearing than amongst Christians, and amongst such Christians as would think it hard to be reckoned a Reproach to the Christian Name ?

The Scripture says of Christians, that they are born of God, *and have overcome the World;* can they be reckoned of that Number, who have not so much as overcome this flagrant Sin, and to which they have no Temptation in Nature ?

Well therefore may the Doctrines of Humility, Heavenly-mindedness, and Contempt of the World, be disregarded, since they have all the Corruptions of Flesh and Blood, all the innate and acquired Pride and Vanity of our Nature to conquer, before they can be admitted.

To proceed.

I know it is pretended by some, that these Doctrines of our Saviour, concerning *forsaking all,* and the like, related only to his first Followers, who could be his Disciples upon no other Terms, and who were to suffer with him for the Propagation of the Gospel.

It is readily owned that there are different States of the Church, and that such different States may call Christians to some particular Duties, not common to every Age.

It is owned also, that this was the Case of the first Christians, they differed from us in many Respects.

They were personally called to follow Christ ; they received particular Commissions from his Mouth, they were empowered to work Miracles, and called to a certain Expectation of Hatred and Sufferings from almost all the World.

These are Particulars in which the State of the first Church differed from the present.

But then it is carefully to be observed, that this Difference in the *State* of the Church, is a Difference in the *external State* of the Church, and not in the internal *inward State* of Christians. It is a Difference that relates to the Affairs and *Condition* of the World, and not to the *personal Holiness* and Purity of Christians.

The world may sometimes favour Christianity, at other Times it may oppose it with Persecution ; now this Change of the World makes two different States of the Church, but without making any Difference in the inward personal Holiness of Christians, which is to be always the same, whether the World smiles or frowns upon it.

Whatever Degrees therefore of personal Holiness or inward Perfection, were required of the first Followers of Christ, is still in the same Degree and for the same Reasons required of all Christians to the End of the World.

Humility, Meekness, Heavenly Affection, Devotion, Charity, and a Contempt of the World, are all *internal Qualities* of personal Holiness, they constitute that Spirit and Temper of Religion, which is required for its own Excellence, and is therefore of constant and eternal Obligation. There is always the same Fitness and Reasonableness in them, the same Perfection in practising of them, and the same Rewards always due to them.

We must therefore look carefully into the Nature of the Things, which we find were required of the first Christians ; if we find that they were called to Sufferings from other People, this may perhaps not be our Case ; but if we see they are called to Sufferings from themselves, to *voluntary Self-denials*, and renouncing their own Rights, we may judge amiss, if we think this was their particular Duty, as the first Disciples of Christ.

For it is undeniable, that these Instances of making themselves Sufferers from themselves, of voluntary Self-denial, and Renunciation of all worldly Enjoyments, are as truly Parts of personal Holiness and Devotion to God, as any Instances of Charity, Humility, and Love of God, that can possibly be supposed.

And it will be difficult to show, why all Christians are now obliged in Imitation of Christ to be *meek and lowly in Heart*, if they, like the first Christians, are not obliged to these Instances of Lowliness and Meekness, or if they are obliged still to imitate Christ, how can they be said to do it, if they excuse themselves from these plain and required Ways of showing it.

If therefore Christians will show that they are not obliged to those Renunciations of the World, which Christ required of his first Followers, they must show that such Renunciations, such voluntary Self-denials, were not Instances of personal Holiness and Devotion, did not enter into the Spirit of Christianity, or constitute that *Death* to the World, or *new Birth* in Christ, which the Gospel requireth. But this is as absurd to imagine, as to suppose that praying for our Enemies, is no part of Charity.

Let us therefore not deceive ourselves, the Gospel preaches the *same* Doctrines to us, that our Saviour taught his first Disciples, and though it may not call us to the same *external* State of the Church, yet it infallibly calls us to the same *inward* State of Holiness and Newness of Life.

It is out of all Question that this Renunciation of the World was then required, because of the Excellency of such a Temper, because of its Suitableness to the Spirit of Christianity, because of its being in some Degree like to the Temper of Christ, because it was a Temper that became such as were *born again* of God, and were made *Heirs* of eternal Glory, because it was a right Instance of their loving God *with all their Heart, and with all their Soul, and with all their Strength, and with all their Mind,* because it was a proper Way of showing their Disregard to the Vanity of earthly Comforts, and their Resolution to attend only to the one Thing needful.

If therefore we are not obliged to be like them in these Respects, if we may be less holy and heavenly in our Tempers, if we need not act upon such high Principles of Devotion to God, and Disregard of earthly Goods, as they did, we must preach a *new Gospel* of our own, we must say that we need not be *meek and lowly* as the first Christians were, and that those high Doctrines of Charity, of blessing and doing Good to our worst Enemies, were Duties only for the first State of the Church.

For this is undeniable, that if any Heights of Piety, any Degrees of Devotion to God, of Heavenly Affection, were necessary for the first Christians, which are not so now, that the same may be said of every other Virtue and Grace of the Christian Life.

All our Saviour's divine Sermon upon the *Mount,* may as well be confined to his first Disciples, as these Doctrines, and it is as sound in Divinity, as well founded in Reason, to assert, that our Saviour had only Regard to his first Disciples, when he said, *Ye cannot serve God and Mammon,* as when he saith, *Whosoever he be of you that forsaketh not all that he hath, he cannot be my Disciple.*

For let anyone think, if he can find the least Shadow of a Reason, why Christians should at first be called to higher

Degrees of Heavenly Affection, Devotion to God, and Disregard of the World, than they are now.

It will be as easy to show that they were obliged to a *stronger* Faith, a *more lively* Hope, than we are now.

But if Faith and Hope are Graces of too excellent a Nature, too essential to the Life and Spirit of a Christian, to admit of any Abatements in any Age of the Church, I should think, that heavenly Affection, Devotion to God, and dying to the World, are Tempers equally essential to the Spirit of Religion, and too necessary to the Perfection of the Soul, to be less required in one Age, than in another.

Besides, it is to be considered, that these Tempers are the natural and genuine Effects of Faith and Hope, so that if they are changed, or abated, Faith and Hope must have *so far* suffered Abatements, and failed in their most proper and excellent Effects.

All Men will readily grant, that it would be very absurd, to suppose, that more *Articles of Faith* should have been necessary to be believed by our Saviour's first Followers, than by Christians of After-ages.

Let it then be considered, why this would be absurd, and it will plainly appear, that the same Reason, which makes it absurd to suppose, that anything which was once necessary to be *believed*, should ever lose that Necessity, will equally show, that it is alike absurd to suppose, that anything that was once necessary to be *done,* should ever be lawful to be left undone.

For is it absurd to suppose, that *Articles of Faith,* should not have always the same Relation to Salvation? And is it not equally absurd to suppose the same of *any Graces* or Virtues of the Soul? That the Kingdom of Heaven should at such a time be only open to *such Degrees* of Piety, of heavenly Affection, and dying to the World, and at other Times make *no Demand* of them.

Again, I believe all Men will readily grant, that whenever the Church falls into such a State of Persecution as was in the Beginning, that we are then to suffer for the Faith as the first Christians did.

Now I ask why we are to do as they did, when we fall into the like Circumstances?

Is it because what they did was right and fit to be done? Is it because their Example is safe and agreeable to the Doctrines of Christ? Is it because we must value our Lives at no higher a Rate, than they valued theirs? Is it because suffering for the Faith, is always that same excellent Temper, and always entitled to the same Reward?

If these are the Reasons, as undoubtedly they are, why we must suffer as they did, if we fall into such a State of the Church as they were in, do not all the same Reasons equally prove that we must *use* the World as they did, because we are in the *same* World that they were in ?

For let us here put all the same Questions, in Relation to their Self-denials, and Renunciation of Riches, was not what they did in this Respect right and fit to be done ? Is not their Example safe and agreeable to the Doctrines of Christ ? Are we to value our worldly Goods, more than they valued theirs ? Is not the renouncing earthly Enjoyments for the Sake of Christ, always that *same excellent* Temper, and always entitled to the *same Reward ?*

Thus we see that every Reason, for suffering as the first Disciples of Christ did, when we fall into the *same State* of Persecution, that they were in, is as strong and necessary a Reason for our contemning and forsaking the World, as they did, because we are still in the *same World* that they were in.

If it can be shown, that the World is changed, that its Enjoyments have not that Contrariety to the Spirit of Christianity, that they had in the Apostles Days, there may be some Grounds for us Christians to take other Methods than they did. But if the World is the *same Enemy* it was at the first, if its *Wisdom* is still *Foolishness*, its *Friendship* still *Enmity with God*, we are as much obliged to treat this Enemy, as the first Disciples of Christ did, as we are obliged to imitate their Behaviour towards any other Enemies and Persecutors of the common Christianity.

And it would be very absurd to suppose, that we were to follow the Doctrines of Christ in renouncing the *Flesh* and the *Devil*, but might abate of their Enmity in Regard to the *World*, when it is by our Use of worldly Goods, that both the *Flesh* and the *Devil* gain almost all their Power over us.

Having said thus much to show that the Gospel belongs to us in *all* its Doctrines of Holiness and Piety, I shall proceed to enquire, what Heavenly Affection, what Renunciation of the World, and Devotion to God, is required of Christians in the Holy Scriptures.

We find in the Passage already quoted, with several others to the like Purpose, that our Saviour saith, as a common Term of Christianity, That *whosoever he be of you that forsaketh not all that he hath, he cannot be my Disciple.*

St. Mark tells us, *There came one running, and kneeled to him, and asked him, Good Master, what shall I do that I may inherit Eternal Life ? And Jesus said unto him, thou knowest the Commandments, do not commit Adultery, do not Kill, do not Steal, do* *not bear false Witness, defraud not, honour thy Father and Mother.**

And he answered and said unto him, Master, all these have I observed from my Youth.

Then Jesus beholding him, loved him, and said unto him, one thing thou lackest, go thy way and sell whatsoever thou hast, and give to the Poor, and thou shalt have Treasure in Heaven, and come take up the Cross and follow me.

And he was sad at that Saying, and went away grieved, for he had great Possessions.

In St. *Matthew* it is thus, *If thou wilt be perfect, go and sell that thou hast, &c.*

Some have imagined, that from our Saviour's using the Expression, *If thou wilt be perfect,* that this was only a Condition of some high uncommon Perfection, which Christians as such, were not obliged to aspire after; but the Weakness of this Imagination will soon appear, if it be considered, that the young Man's Question plainly showed what Perfection it was that he aimed at; he only asked what he should do that he might *inherit Eternal Life.* And it was in answer to this Question, that our Saviour told him, that though he had kept the Commandments, yet *one* thing he lacked.

So that when our Saviour saith, if *thou wilt be perfect,* it is the same thing as when he said, if thou wilt not be lacking in one thing, that is, if thou wilt practise all that Duty which will make thee inherit eternal Life, thou must not only keep the Commandments, *but sell that thou hast and give to the Poor.*

It plainly therefore appears, that what is here commanded is not in order to some exalted, uncommon Height of Perfection, but as a *Condition* of his being a Christian, and securing an Inheritance of Eternal Life.

This same thing is further proved from our Saviour's general Remark upon it; *How hardly shall they that have Riches enter into the Kingdom of God.*

By which it appears, that it was the bare entering into the State of Christianity, and not any extraordinary Height of Perfection, that was the Matter in question.

This Remark, and the other following one, where our Saviour saith, *It is easier for a Camel to go through the Eye of a Needle, than for a rich Man to enter into the Kingdom of God,* undeniably show us thus much, that what is here required of this young Man, is also required of *all* rich Men in *all* Ages of the Church, in order to their being true Members of the Kingdom of God.

* Chap. x. 17.

For how could this be said of rich Men, that they can hardly and with more Difficulty enter into the Kingdom of God, if they were not obliged to the same, that this rich Man was obliged to.

For if they may enjoy their Estates, and yet enter into the Kingdom of God, the Difficulty is vanished, and they may enter with Ease, though this young Man was put upon much harder Terms.

If therefore we will but use common Sense in understanding these Words of our Saviour, we must allow that they relate to *all* rich Men, and that the same Renunciation of all Self-enjoyment is required of them, that was required of this young Man.

His Disciples plainly understood him in this Sense, by their saying, *Who then can be saved?* And it appears by our Saviour's Answer, that he did not think they understood him amiss; for he seems to allow their Remark upon the Difficulty of the thing, and only answers, *That with God all things are possible;* implying that it was possible for the Grace of God to work this great Change in the Hearts of Men.

Those who will still be fancying (for there is nothing but Fancy to support it) that this Command related only to this young Man, ought to observe, that this young Man was very virtuous; that he was so eager after Eternal Life, as to *run* to our Saviour, and put the Question to him upon his *Knees*, and that for these things our Saviour *loved* him.

Now can it be imagined, that our Saviour would make Salvation more difficult to one who was thus disposed than to others?

That he would impose particularly hard Terms upon one whose Virtues had already gained his *Love?*

And such hard Terms, as for their Difficulty might justly be compared to a *Camel's* going through the Eye of a *Needle?* Would he make him lacking in one thing, which other Men might lack in all Ages, without any hindrance of their Salvation? Would he send him away sorrowful on the account of such Terms, as are no longer Terms to the Christian World?

As this cannot be supposed, we must allow, that what our Saviour required of that young man, was not upon any *particular* Account, or to show his *Authority* of demanding what he pleased; but that he required this of the young Man for the Sake of the *Excellency* of the Duty, because it was a Temper *necessary* for Christianity, and always to be required of all Christians; It being as easy to conceive, that our Saviour should allow of less *Restitution* and *Repentance* in some Sinners than in others, as that he should make more Denial of the World, more Affection for Heaven, necessary to some, than to others.

I suppose it cannot be denied, that an Obedience to this

Doctrine had shown an excellent Temper; that it was one of the most noble Virtues of the Soul; that it was a *right* Judgment of the Vanity of earthly Riches; that it was a *right* Judgment of the Value of heavenly Treasures; and that it was a *proper* Instance of true Devotion to God.

But if this was a Temper so absolutely, so excellently right then, I desire to know, why it has not the *same* Degree of Excellency still?

Hath Heaven or Earth suffered any Change since that time? Is the World become now more worth our Notice, or heavenly Treasure of less Value, than it was in our Saviour's Time? Have we had another Saviour since, that has compounded Things with this World, and helped us to an easier Way to the next?

Further, it ought to be observed, that when our Saviour commandeth the young Man to *sell all* and *give to the Poor*, he gives this Reason for it, *and thou shalt have Treasure in Heaven.*

This manifestly extends the Duty to *all* rich Men, since the Reason that is given for it, either equally obliges *all*, or obliges *none;* unless a Treasure in Heaven can be said to be a valuable Consideration to some, but not to others.

The Matter therefore evidently comes to this, either we must say that our Saviour did not make a reasonable Proposal to the young Man, that what he required of him, was not sufficiently Excellent in itself, and advantageous to him, or we must allow that the same Proposal is as Reasonable for us to accept of now, as it was in the first Ages of the Church.

We must Observe too, that if all the Reasons which pressed this Duty upon the young Man, equally recommend it to us, that if we neglect it, we are equally Unreasonable with him, who went away Sorrowful.

Let those who are startled at this Doctrine, and think it *unnecessary* now, deal Faithfully with their own Hearts, and ask themselves, whether they should not have had the same Dislike of it, had they lived in our Saviour's Days, or whether they can find any one Reason, why they should have been so Spiritual and Heavenly then, which is not as good and as strong a Reason for their being as Spiritual and Heavenly now.

Let them consider, whether if an *Apostle* was to rise from the Dead, calling *all* rich Men to this Doctrine, they would not drive their Coaches from such a Preacher, rather than be saved at such a Price.

To proceed, if this selling all, this Renunciation of worldly Wealth, was not required for the Excellency of the Duty, and its Suitableness to the Spirit of Christianity, it will be hard to show a Reason, why such voluntary Self-denial, such Renunciation of one's own Enjoyments, such Persecution of one's self, should be required at a Time, when Christianity exposed its Members to such uncommon Hatred and Persecution from other People.

Our Saviour allowed his Disciples when they should fall under Persecution, to flee from one City to another, though they were to be as *harmless* as *Doves*, yet he commanded them to be as *wise* as *Serpents*.

If therefore the Enjoyment of Riches had been a thing that had suited with his Religion ; was not a Renunciation of all worldly Wealth, a Temper necessary and never to be dispensed with, one would suppose, that it would least of all have been imposed, at a Time when there were so many other unavoidable Burdens to be undergone.

Since therefore this forsaking and renouncing all by our own Act and Deed, since this Degree of Self-denial and Self-persecution was commanded at a Time, when all the World were Enemies to Christians, since they were not then spared or indulged in any pleasurable Enjoyments of their worldly Wealth, but were to add this Instance of Suffering, to all the Sufferings from their Enemies, we may be sure, that it was required because it was a *necessary* Duty, because it was a proper Behaviour of such as were *born of God*, and made *Heirs* of eternal Glory.

If this be true, then it must be owned, that it is still the same *necessary* Duty, and is now as well that proper Behaviour of those who are Sons of God, as ever it was.

For Christianity is just that same spiritual heavenly State, that it was then, the Dignity of Christians has suffered no Alteration since that Time, and a Treasure in Heaven, an Eternal Happiness are still the same great and important Things.

Chapter IV.

A Continuation of the same Subject.

ANYONE that is at all acquainted with Scripture must Observe, that the Doctrine of the foregoing Chapter, is not barely Founded on those particular Texts there considered, but that the same Spirit of renouncing the World, is the most common and repeated Subject of our Saviour's heavenly Instructions.

A certain Man said unto him Lord, I will follow thee whitherso-

*ever thou goest. And Jesus said unto him, the Foxes have Holes, and the Birds of the Air have Nests, but the Son of Man hath not where to lay his Head.**

Another also said Lord, I will follow thee, but let me first go bid them farewell, that are at Home at my House.

And Jesus said unto Him, no Man having put his Hand to the Plough, and looking back, is fit for the Kingdom of God.

These Passages are all of a kind with what our Saviour said to the young Man, they directly teach that same Renunciation of the World, as the first and principal Temper, the very Soul and Essence of Christianity.

This Doctrine is pressed, and urged upon us by various Ways, by every Art of Teaching, that it might enter into the Heart of every Reader.

The Kingdom of God, saith our Saviour, *is like unto a Merchant-Man seeking goodly Pearls, who when he had found one Pearl of great Price, he went and sold all that he had and bought it.*†

The Doctrine of this Parable needs no Interpretation, it is plain and strong, and presses home the Advice that our Saviour gave to the rich young Man.

When it says, that the Kingdom of God *is a Pearl of great Price,* I suppose it means, that a great deal is to be given for it, and when it says, that the Merchant went and sold *all* that he had and bought it, I suppose this is to teach us, that it cannot be bought at any *less* Price.

The modern *Jews* would be upon much easier Terms than those who lived in our Saviour's Days ; if we can now tell them that the Kingdom of God is no longer like *one Pearl of great Price,* and that they need not sell *all* that they have and buy it ; but may go on seeking Pearls as they used to do, and yet be good Members of the Kingdom of God.

Now if we may not preach such a *new* Gospel as this to the present *Jews,* I don't know how we can preach it to Christians.

This Parable does not suppose, that the Merchant went to Trading again, after he had sold *all,* and bought this Pearl of great Price. He was content with that, and did not want any other Riches.

If the Kingdom of God, is not Riches sufficient for us, but we must add another Greatness, and another Wealth to it, we fall under the Condemnation of this Parable.

To proceed. The peaceful, pleasurable Enjoyments of Riches, is a State of Life everywhere condemned by our Blessed Saviour.

---

* Luke ix. 57, 58.   † Matt. xiii. 45.

*Woe unto you that are Full, for ye shall Hunger, woe unto you that Laugh now, for ye shall Weep and Mourn.**

If we can think that for all this, the Joys of Prosperity, and the gay Pleasures of Plenty, are the allowed Enjoyments of Christians, we must have done wondering at the Blindness and Hardness of the *Jews'* Hearts.

Woe unto you that are Rich, for ye have received your Consolation ! It is not said woe unto you that are Rich, for ye have Enriched yourselves by *evil* Arts, and *unlawful* Means, but it is the *bare Enjoyment*, the Consolation that is taken in Riches, to which this Woe is threatened.

This same Doctrine is pressed upon us by a remarkable Parable, so plain and lively, that one would think that every Christian that has heard it, should be afraid of everything that looked like Self-indulgence, or Expense in his own Pleasures and Pride.

There was a certain rich Man, which was clothed in Purple and fine Linen, and fared sumptuously every Day.

And there was a certain poor Beggar named Lazarus, which was laid at his Gate full of Sores, and desiring to be fed with the Crumbs which fell from the rich Man's Table : moreover the Dogs came and licked his Sores.

It came to pass, that the Beggar died, and was carried by the Angels into Abraham's Bosom. The rich Man also died, and was buried, and in Hell he lifted up his Eyes, being in Torments, and seeth Abraham afar off, and Lazarus in his Bosom.†

This Parable teacheth neither more nor less than what our Saviour taught, when he commanded the young Man to sell all that he had. For it is the bare pleasurable Enjoyment, the living in the usual Delights of a great Fortune, that the Parable condemneth. Here is no Injustice, no Villanies or Extortions laid to his Charge, it is only a Life of Splendour and Indulgence, that leaves him in Hell.

This we are further taught, by *Abraham's* Answer to him, *Son, remember that thou in thy Life-time receivedst thy good Things :* This is alleged as the sole Reason of his being in Torments.

It is to be Observed, that nothing is mentioned of *Lazarus*, but his low and afflicted State, and then it is, *he is comforted, and thou art tormented.*

Can anything more plainly show us the Impossibility of enjoying *Mammon* while we live, and God when we die ? A rich Man enjoying the Pleasures of Riches, is for that Reason found in Torments, a Beggar patiently bearing Want, is for that Reason made the Care of Angels, and conducted to *Abraham's* Bosom.

* Luke vi. 25.   † Luke xvi.

Does not this manifestly teach us that same Renunciation of worldly Enjoyments, as if we had been expressly required to part with all that we have?

For if a Life of Splendour, and Pleasure, and sensual Gratifications, is the Portion of those who choose to enjoy it, if it exposes us to so much *Woe* and Wrath hereafter, well might our Blessed Saviour tell the rich Man, that he lacked *one Thing*, that he was to *sell all* that he had and give to the Poor.

If therefore this Parable contains the Doctrine that it first taught, if Time has not worn away its Meaning, it contains a Doctrine that concerns *all* rich Men; it speaks as home to them, and calls as loudly for a Renunciation of all worldly Indulgences, as our Saviour did to the rich Man.

So that there is no Advantage got by considering our Saviour's Command, as a *particular* Charge, and given to a particular young Man; since it appears by other express Passages and Parables, that the *same* is required of all other rich Men, as they expect any other Consolation, than what is to be found in Riches.

If we will here also appropriate this Parable to this particular rich Man, we shall judge as reasonably, as if we should maintain that the *Hell* in which he was tormented was made only for him, and is a State which no one else has any Occasion to fear.

We must therefore, unless we will set aside the Gospel, and think ourselves not concerned in its Doctrines, take this as an undeniable Truth, that Christianity is still that same opposite State to the World that it was in our Saviour's Days; that he speaks to us the same Language that he spoke to the young Man in the Gospel; that if we will not hear his Voice, but indulge ourselves in the proud sensual Delights of Riches and Grandeur, our Fate is taught us in the rich Man in Torments; and to us belongs that dreadful Threatening, *Woe unto you that are rich, for you have received your Consolation.*

I know it has been said by some, that all that we are taught by the Command given to the young Man to *sell all*, is this, that whenever we cannot keep our Possessions without violating some essential Duty of a Christian, that then, and not till then, need we think that we are called upon by Christ to quit all and follow him.

I have, in Answer to this, already shown, that the Thing required of this young Man, was no *particular* Duty, but that our Saviour pressed it upon *all*, and by a Reason which made it equally conclusive for all People, namely, a *Treasure in Heaven.*

I have shown that the same Doctrine is taught in general, by comparing the Kingdom of God to *one Pearl* of great Price, which the Merchant could buy at no less a Price, than by selling *all* that he had ; by the Parable of the *rich* Man in Torments, on the Account of his living in the State and Pleasures of a Fortune ; and lastly, by a general Woe that is threatened to all who are rich, as having received their *Consolation :* So that this seems a full Answer to this Interpretation.

But I shall however consider it further.

Now if this be all that is taught us Christians, by the Case of the young Man in the Gospel, that we are to part with our Enjoyments and Possessions, when we cannot keep them without renouncing some great Truth of our Religion, and that till such a time happens, we may peacefully and pleasurably enjoy the Delights and State of Plenty.

If this be the Case, I ask how a good Christian is to be assured that this is a safe and just Interpretation ? How shall he be satisfied that there is no Danger in following it ?

It is plainly an interpretation of our own making, it is not the *open expressed* Sense of the Words, it is an Addition of something to them, for which we have no Authority from the Passage itself. So that it may well be asked, how we can be sure that such an Interpretation may be safely complied with.

The Text saith, *Sell all* that thou hast ; this Interpretation saith, Ye need not sell yet, nay, that you need not sell *at all*, but that you may go on in the pleasurable Enjoyment of your several Estates, till such time as you cannot keep them without denying the Faith.

So that the Interpretation seems to have *nothing* to do with the Text, and only teaches a Doctrine, that might as well be asserted without this Text, as with it.

I ask therefore for what Reason we allow this Passage to teach us no more than this ? Is there any other Part of Scripture that requires us to make this Interpretation ? Does it better suit with the Spirit and Temper of the Christian Religion ? Is it more agreeable to its heavenly Designs, its Contempt of the World, than to take them in their apparent Sense ?

If this were true, then the first Followers of Christ, who observed this Doctrine in its literal Sense, and renounced all, acted less suitably to the Spirit of Christianity, than those who now enjoy their Estates.

This Absurdity is enough to expose any pretended Necessity of this Interpretation, which Absurdity must be granted, if we say that this new Interpretation is more suitable to the Spirit of Christianity, than to take the Words as still obliging in their first Sense.

But to cut off all Pretence of any Necessity from any other

Part of Scripture, I have made it plainly appear, that the same Doctrine is certainly taught by many other express Passages of Scripture.

This Interpretation therefore is as contrary to many other Parts of Scripture, as to this Text; it is contrary to the Spirit of Christianity, and is only brought in to soften the Rigours of Religion, that People may with quiet Consciences enjoy the Pleasures of Plenty, and those who want it, spend their Time in the Ways and Means of acquiring it.

If therefore there be not an *entire Change* in the Way to Heaven, if the once *strait Gate* be not now a wide and open Passage to all full, fat, and stately Christians; if there is still any Meaning in these Words, *Blessed are the Poor in Spirit, for theirs' is the Kingdom of God*, the sober Christian may as well doubt of this Allowance of enjoying the Pleasures and Plenty of his Estate, till Persecution for the Faith drives him out of it, as if he was told, that he need not *resist* the Devil, till such time as he tempted him to *deny* the Faith, or give up some Truth of his Religion.

When our Saviour gave this Command to the young Man, and afterwards observed, upon his Refusal, that it was easier for a *Camel* to go through the Eye of a Needle, than for a rich Man to enter into the Kingdom of God, the Apostles took that Command to signify the common Conditions of entering into Christianity, and immediately declared that they had *left all and followed him.*

And our Saviour answered them in such a Manner, as showed, that the Doctrine then delivered, related to all Mankind in the same Sense, and had nothing particular in it, that related to one Man, or one Age of the Church, more than another.

Verily I say unto you, there is no Man that hath left House or Brethren, or Sisters, or Father, or Mother, or Wife, or Children, or Lands, for my Sake, or the Gospel's, but he shall have an hundred fold now in this present time, and in the World to come Eternal Life.*

Let it now be considered, that supposing it was barely lawful, to enjoy our Estates, and as the World says, live up to them, is this a State of any Merit? Is there any Reward annexed to it? If it is not our Sin, it is at best a losing our Time, and as unrewardable as Sleeping.

But on the other Side we are infallibly assured, that if we come up to the Doctrine of the Text, if we part with our worldly

---

* Mark x. 29.

Enjoyments and Gratifications for the Sake of Christ, that in this Life we shall receive an *hundred fold,* and in the World to come Eternal Life.

Now if such Persons as these, are to be thus blessed in this Life, and also so rewarded in the next, it is certain that they who are not such Persons, will not be so doubly blessed both in this Life and that which is to come.

But now what an Interpretation must that be, which leads Men from being an *hundred* times as happy as they might be in this Life, and from such an Height of Reward in the next?

Is not this enough to show us, that the Wisdom of this Interpretation, is not a Wisdom from above, that it savoureth not the Things that be of God?

For who can be so wise unto Eternal Life, who can make so much of his Plenty, as by thus parting with it?

Who that was governed by a Wisdom from above, would seek for an Evasion, where the open Sense, is not only safe, but entitled to so vast a Recompense both now and hereafter?

It is to me no small Argument, that our Saviour meant no such Allowance, as this Interpretation has found out, because it is so contrary to the Perfection of the Soul, and is so disadvantageous to those that follow it.

Our blessed Saviour and his Apostles both in Doctrine and Practice are on the Side of renouncing the Enjoyments of Riches, and who is he that dare preach up a worldly Peace and Indulgence, without either Text or Precedent from Scripture, and such a Peace as leads Men from such high Rewards both in this Life, and that which is to come?

When our Saviour told *Peter* of his Sufferings, *Peter took him and began to rebuke him, saying, Be it far from thee, Lord, this shall not be unto thee. But Jesus turned and said to Peter, Get thee behind me, Satan, thou art an Offence unto me, for thou savourest not the Things that be of God, but those that be of Men.*

But after all, this Enjoyment of worldly Riches which this Interpretation pleads for, cannot be shown to be barely lawful, this I say cannot be shown, without showing at the same time, that this Passage, *It is easier for a Camel to go through the Eye of a Needle, than for a rich Man to enter into the Kingdom of God,* is so old as to be of no Significancy now, for if the Difficulty still continues, the rich Man must have as much to part with now, as he had then.

The same must be said of all those other Passages abovementioned, concerning the Kingdom being compared to *one great Pearl,* the Case of the *rich* Man in Torments, and the general *Woe* that is denounced against such as are rich, as having received their *Consolation ;* all these, with a great Variety of other Texts, must have quite lost their first natural Meaning, if this Interpretation be admitted as barely lawful.

So that it is an Interpretation that runs away from the plain open Sense of the Words, and leads from those great Rewards that belong to it ; it is an Interpretation made without any Necessity, not supported by any Doctrine, or Practice of Scripture, contrary to the Practices of the first Christians, contrary to the heavenly Spirit of our Religion, and so contrary to various plain Passages of Scripture, that they must have lost their true Meaning, if this Interpretation be admitted.

Lastly, If all that can be concluded from this Command of our Saviour, is only this, that we are obliged to part with our Estates, when we cannot keep them, without selling the Truth ; if *sell all thou hast and give to the Poor, and thou shalt have Treasure in Heaven,* only means, when applied to us, *thou mayest keep and enjoy thy Estate, till some wicked Terms of keeping it are imposed upon thee,* this is no higher a Perfection, no greater Degree of Heavenly-mindedness, or Disregard to the World, than a *Jew* or honest *Heathen* would maintain.

For who does not know that it is better to be *just* and *faithful,* than to be *rich,* and that a Man is rather to part with his Estate, than to keep it at the Expense of his Virtue and Integrity ? This is only the Virtue of choosing rather to be poor, than a Thief.

But if Christians can think that this is the highest Renunciation of the World, the highest Degree of heavenly Affection, to which they are called, if they can think that this is all that is meant by their being *crucified* and *dead* to the World, by their being in Christ *new Creatures,* by their being *born of God, and having overcome the World,* they may be justly said to treat the Scriptures, as the *Jews* treated our Saviour, when they said, *We will not have this Man to reign over us.*

I have, I think, sufficiently shown that our Saviour required an entire Renunciation of the World, a forsaking all its Enjoyments, in order to be his true Disciples, and that the same is as certainly required of us, as he is the same Christ, and we Heirs of the same Glory.

It will now therefore, I know, be asked, whether all Christians are obliged to *sell* their Estates and give to the Poor, in order to inherit eternal Life ?

The Absurdity and Ridiculousness of such a thing, and the Disorder it must occasion in Life, will be thought sufficient to expose and confute all the foregoing Doctrine.

As to the Absurdity and Ridiculousness of this Doctrine in

the Eyes of worldly Wisdom, that is far from being any Objection against it, since we are assured by God himself, that the *Wisdom* of this World is *Foolishness* with God, and that the Spirit of Christianity, and the Spirit of the World, are as contrary to one another, as the Kingdom of Light, and the Kingdom of Darkness.

What can be more contrary to worldly Greatness and Wisdom, than the Doctrine of the *Cross*, a crucified Saviour ? Which way could anyone expose himself to more Jest and Ridicule, than by being too meek and humble to resent an Affront, and accept a *Challenge* ?

Not only *Rakes* and *Libertines*, but the grave, the religious part of the World, talk of the Necessity of defending their Honour, and reckon it a Shame not to resent and fight when the Affront is given.

This makes the Spirit of the World, though it be as consistent with our Religion, to honour the Memory of *Cain* for killing his Brother, as to make it a part of Honour to give or accept a *Challenge*.

This may serve to show us, that we must disregard the Maxims and Wisdom of this World, and not form our Judgments of Christian Virtues with any Regard to it, since by it, Patience and Meekness may be reckoned shameful, and Revenge and Murder as Instances of Honour.

But I give now a direct Answer to the foregoing Question, and venture to affirm, upon the Proofs I have already produced, that all Christians are really and effectually obliged to do that, which our Saviour required of the young Man.

Our Saviour bid him sell all that he had and give to the Poor, that he might have Treasure in Heaven : that is, he required him to renounce the Self-enjoyment of his Estate, to live no longer in the Gratifications of his Plenty, but offer it all to God in Works of Charity and Relief of others.

Now the *selling all*, is only a Circumstance of parting with the Enjoyment of his Riches from himself, to all such Objects and Uses as are worthy of it in the Sight of God.

If our Saviour had told Sinners that they must repent in *Sackcloth and Ashes*, I should have thought, that *Sackcloth and Ashes* were only mentioned as a *particular* way of expressing a general Duty ; and that though the Circumstance of *Sackcloth and Ashes* might be omitted, yet the *Thing* intended, the Degree of Humiliation and Sorrow, was always to be performed in the same Degree.

I take it to be the same in the Case before us. It is not necessary that a Man should *sell all* that he hath, because that was the Expression used to the young Man, but it is necessary that he comply with the *Thing* signified, and practise all that Disregard of the World, and heavenly Affection which is there taught.

He sufficiently selleth all, who parteth with the Self-enjoyment of it, and maketh it the Support of those that want it.

This seems to me to be the true and plain Meaning of the Passage. The Words *sell all*, are only used as a *Form of Speech*, as a general Way of expressing the parting with the Enjoyment of an Estate, as *Sackcloth and Ashes* were a general Way of expressing Repentance, and not as laying any direct Obligation of parting with an Estate in that *particular* Way, any more than *Sackcloth* is always necessary to a true Repentance.

A Person that was to give away his Estate, would surely comply with the Doctrine of the Text, which shows that it is the *Thing* signified. and not the *particular* Manner of doing it, that is required.

Yet it is the keeping to this *literal Sense* of the Words, as if the *selling all*, was the particular Thing enjoined, that has taught People to excuse themselves from the Doctrine there delivered.

For there was some Pretence to think, that so particular an Action as the *selling all*, could only relate to him, to whom it was enjoined.

But if Men would consider, that this *selling all*, is only a Circumstance of the Thing, as *Sackcloth* is a Circumstance of Repentance, and that the Thing required is *heavenly Affection*, and Devotion to God, they would find themselves as much concerned in the Doctrine there delivered, as in any other Doctrine of Scripture.

When our Saviour related the good *Samaritan's* Charity, and said unto the Man that talked with him, *Go and do thou likewise,* he is not exhorted to stay for an Opportunity of doing the same Action, but to do the same Thing which was implied by that Action.

Taking therefore the Words in this plain Sense, as an Exhortation to such a Degree of heavenly Affection, and disclaiming all Self-enjoyment of Riches, and not as to any particular Action of *selling all*, it must be affirmed, that they equally concern *all* rich Men to the End of the World, as that young Man to whom they were spoken.

For as he was called to that Temper of Mind, because it was a *right* Temper for a Christian, a *proper* Instance of his Faith and Hope, and Devotion to God, and a *right* Way of using the Things of this World; how can it be thought, that the same Temper is not equally *right* and *Christian* in every rich Man now ? Or how can it be thought that the rich Men of this Age, are not equally obliged to act conformably to the Temper and Spirit of Religion now, as well as in the Days of Christ?

Are not Humility and Meekness to be practised in the *same Fulness*, that they were in our Saviour's Time ? But if they are, it will be impossible to show, why any other Virtues should admit of any Abatement.

Or can anyone show a better Instance of Humility and Meekness, than in departing from the splendid Enjoyments of his Fortune, to make it the Support and Relief of poor and distressed People ?

It ought also to be considered, whether it is not impossible to show that Meekness and Humility which was then required, unless he practises them in these Instances. Let it also be considered, that this Use of worldly Things is not only commanded, as suitable to the Graces and Virtues of the Christian Life, but that the Case of the *rich* Man in Torments, with the other Passages above-mentioned, are so many express Threatenings against our Disobedience.

So that it must be affirmed, that we are as much obliged to labour after the same Degrees of Faith, Hope, heavenly Affection, and Disregard of the World, as after the same Degrees of Humility, Charity, and Repentance, that ever were required of any Christians.

Let it also be considered, that the Command of selling all, is only particular in the Expression, but that Thing required, is the general Temper of Christianity ; as is expressed by being *dead* to the World, having our *Conversation* in Heaven, being *born of God*, and having *overcome* the World ; these Expressions have no proper Meaning, if they don't imply all that heavenly Affection, and Disregard of Riches, to which our Saviour exhorted the young Man.

God forbid, saith St. *Paul, that I should glory, save in the Cross of our Lord Jesus Christ, whereby the World is crucified unto me, and I unto the World.**

Now I desire to know why any Christian should think it less dreadful, not to be crucified and dead to the World, than St. *Paul* thought it ? Is not the Temper and Spirit which the Apostle shows here, as much to be aspired after, as in any other Part of Scripture ?

But can those who spend their Estates in their own Indulgences, who live in the Pomp and Pleasures of Riches, can they

---

* Gal. vi. 14.

without Profaneness say that of themselves, which the Apostle here saith of himself?

Or can they be said to have the Spirit of Christ, who are directed by a Spirit so contrary to that of the Apostle? Yet the Scripture says expressly, that *if any Man hath not the Spirit of Christ, he is none of his.*

Thus we see that this Renunciation of the World, which is thought too great an Extreme, to be taken from the Command given to the young Man in the Gospel, is the Common Temper of Christianity, and a Doctrine the most universally taught of any other. It is indeed the very Heart and Soul of Christian Piety, it is the natural Soil, the proper Stock from whence all the Graces of a Christian naturally grow forth, it is a Disposition of all others the most necessary and most productive of Virtue. And if we might now be *more earthly,* than in the Days of Christ, we must of necessity be proportionably wanting in all other Virtues. For heavenly Affection enters so far into the being of all Christian Virtues, that an Abatement in that, is like an Alteration in the first Wheel that gives Motion to all the rest.

I will now a little appeal to the Imagination of the Reader.

Let it be supposed, that rich Men are now enjoying their Riches, and taking all the common usual Delights of Plenty, that they are labouring for the Meat that perisheth, projecting and contriving Scenes of Pleasure, and spending their Estates in proud Expenses.

After this Supposition, let it be imagined, that we saw the Holy Jesus, who had not where to lay his Head, with his twelve Apostles, that had left all to follow him ; let us imagine that we heard him call all the World to take up the *Cross* and follow him, promising a *Treasure in Heaven,* to such as would quit all for his Sake, and rejecting all that would not comply with such Terms, denouncing *Woe* and eternal Death, to all that lived in Fulness, Pomp, and worldly Delights. Let it be imagined that we heard him commanding his Disciples to take no Thought, saying what shall we Eat, or what shall we Drink, or where-withal shall we be Clothed, and giving this Reason for it, because *after all these Things do the Gentiles seek.*

Let it be imagined that we saw the first Christians, taking up the Cross, renouncing the World, and counting all but Dung, that they might gain Christ.

I do not now appeal to the *Judgment* or *Reason* of the Reader, I leave it with his *Imagination,* that wild Faculty, to determine, whether it be possible for these two different Sorts of Men, to be true Disciples of the same Lord.

To proceed.

Let us suppose that a rich Man was to put up such a Prayer as this to God.

'O Lord, I thy sinful Creature, who am born again to a lively 'Hope of Glory in Christ Jesus, beg of thee, to grant me a '*thousand* times more Riches than I *need*, that I may be able to 'gratify Myself and Family in the Delights of Eating and 'Drinking, State and Grandeur, grant that as the little Span of 'Life wears out, I may still abound more and more in Wealth, 'and that I may see and perceive all the best and surest Ways of 'growing Richer than any of my Neighbours: this I humbly and 'fervently Beg in the Name, *&c.*'

Such a Prayer as this should have had no Place in this Treatise, but that I have Reason to hope, that in proportion as it offends the *Ear*, it will amend the *Heart*.

There is no one, I believe, but would be ashamed to put up such a Prayer as this to God, yet let it be well Observed, that all are of the Temper of this Prayer, but those who have *overcome* the World.

We need not go amongst Villains and People of scandalous Characters, to find out those, who desire a *thousand* times more than they want, who have an Eagerness to be every Day richer and richer, who catch at all Ways of Gain that are not scandalous, and who hardly think anything enough, except it equals or exceeds the Estate of their Neighbours.

I beg of such that they would heartily condemn the profane and unchristian Spirit of the foregoing Prayer, and that they would satisfy themselves, that nothing can be more odious and contrary to Religion than such Petitions.

But then let them be assured also of this, that the same Things which make an unchristian Prayer, make an unchristian Life.

For the Reason why these Things appear so odious in a Prayer, is because they are so contrary to the Spirit of Religion. But is it not as bad to live and act contrary to the Spirit of Religion, as to pray contrary to it?

At least must not that Manner of Life be very blamable, very contrary to Piety, which is so shocking when put into the Form of a Prayer?

But indeed whatever we may think, as we live, so we really pray, for as Christ saith, *where our Treasure is, there will our Heart be also ;* so as the Manner of our Life is, so is our Heart also, it is continually praying, what our Life is acting, though not in any express Form of Words,

To pursue this Argument a little, is this Prayer too shocking?

Dare we not approach God with such a Spirit? How dare we then think of approaching him with such a Life?

Need we any other Conviction, that this Manner of Life is contrary to the Spirit of Christianity, than this, that the praying according to it in Christ's Name, comes near to Blasphemy?

Does not this also sufficiently convince us of the Reasonableness of Christ's Command, to forsake the Fulness, the Indulgence, and Pride of Estates, since it is a State of Life, that our Reason dare not ask God to give us?

Let it be considered how we should abominate a Person, whom we knew to use such a Prayer, and let that teach us how abominable a Life that is like it, must make us to appear in the Eyes of God, and with this Addition of Folly joined to it, that we call the Prayer *Profane*, but think the Life, that answers to it, to be *Christian.*

Perhaps there cannot be a better way of judging of what Manner of Spirit we are of, than to see whether the Actions of our Life are such, as we may safely commend them to God in our Prayers.

For it is undeniable, that if they are such as we dare not mention to God in our Prayers, we ought in all Reason to be as fearful of acting them in his Presence.

We may indeed do several innocent Things, which on account of their Littleness, are unfit to be put into our Devotions, but if the chief and main Actions of our Life are not such, as we may justly beg the Assistance of God's Holy Spirit in the Performance of them, we may be assured, that such Actions make our Lives as unholy, as such Petitions would make our Prayers.

From all that has been above observed, I think it is sufficiently plain, that the present Disciples of Jesus Christ are to have no more to do with worldly Enjoyments, than those that he chose whilst he himself was on Earth, and that he expects as much Devotion to God, and heavenly Affection from us, as from any that he conversed with, and speaks the same Language, and gives the same Commands to all rich Men now, that he gave to the rich young Man in the Gospel.

Chapter V.

A further Continuation of the same Subject.

THE Subject of the two preceding Chapters is of such Importance, that I cannot leave it, without adding some further Considerations upon it.

For, notwithstanding the Scriptures are so clear and express on the side of the Doctrine there delivered, yet I must expect to encounter the Prejudices of Men, who are settled in other Opinions.

I know it will still be asked, Where can be the Impiety of getting or enjoying an Estate?

Whether it be not honourable, and Matter of just Praise, to provide an Estate for one's Family?

It will also be asked, What People of *Birth* and *Fortune* are to do with themselves, if they are not to live suitably to their Estates and Qualities?

Anyone who has taken the trouble to read this Treatise, must have found, that the Doctrine here taught is none of mine, and that therefore I have no occasion to support it against such Questions as these.

The same Persons may as well ask, why the little Span of Life is made a State of Trial and Probation, in which Men of all Conditions are to *work out their Salvation with Fear and Trembling.*

But however to the first Question let it be answered:

Take no thought, saying, what shall we eat, or what shall we drink, or wherewithal shall we be clothed; for after all these things do the Gentiles seek.

If to be careful and thoughtful about the Necessaries of Life, be a Care that is here forbidden, and that because it is such a Care as only becomes *Heathens,* surely to be careful and thoughtful how to raise an Estate, and enrich one's Family, is a Care that is sufficiently forbidden Christians. And he that can yet think it lawful and creditable to make it the Care and Design of his Life to get an Estate, is too blind to be convinced by Arguments. He may with as much Regard to Scripture say, that it is lawful to *swear* falsely, though it forbids him to *speak* falsely.

Our Saviour saith, *Labour not for the Meat that perisheth, but* *for that Meat which endureth unto Everlasting Life.** He commands us not to lay up for ourselves Treasures on Earth ; he assures us that we cannot serve God and *Mammon.*

Now these Places have no meaning, if it is still lawful for Christians to heap up Treasures, to labour for great Estates, and pursue Designs of enriching their Families.

I know it is easy to evade the Force of these Texts, and to make plausible Harangues upon the Innocency of labouring to be rich, and the Consistency of serving God and *Mammon.*

I don't question but the rich young Man in the Gospel, who had kept the Commandments of God from his Youth, could have made a very good Apology for himself, and have shown how reasonable and innocent a thing it was, for so good and so young a Man to enjoy an Estate.

The *rich* Man in Torments could have alleged how much Good he did with his Fortune, how many Trades he encouraged by his *Purple* and *fine Linen,* and faring *sumptuously* every Day, and how he conformed to the Ends and Advantages of Society by so spending his Estate.

But to return : The Apostle saith, *Having Food and Raiment, let us be therewith content, that they who will be rich fall into a Temptation and a Snare, and into many foolish and hurtful Lusts, which drown Men in Destruction and Perdition.*†

We may perhaps by some Acuteness of reasoning find out, that this Doctrine still leaves us at our liberty, whether we will labour to be rich or not, and if we do, we are as much enlightened as the *Quakers,* who find themselves at liberty from the use of the Sacraments.

We may pretend, that notwithstanding what the Apostle says, of a *Snare,* a *Temptation,* and foolish *Lusts,* yet that we can pursue the Means, and desire the Happiness of Riches, without any Danger to our Virtue.

But if so, we are as prudent as those Christians, who think they can secure their Virtue without *Watching and Prayer,* though our Saviour has said, *Watch and pray that ye enter not into Temptation.*

He therefore that neglects Watching and Prayer, though the appointed Means of avoiding Temptation, may show that he lives as much according to Scripture, as he that is careful and desirous of Riches and Wealth, though they are the declared Occasions of *Sin, Snares,* and *Destruction.*

If we will not be so humble and teachable, as to conform to Scripture in the Simplicity and Plainness of its Doctrines, there

---

* John vi. 27.   † 1 Tim. vi. 8.

will be no End of our Errors, but we shall be in as much Darkness as where the Light of Scripture never appeared.

For if we could submit to its plain and repeated Doctrines, it would never be asked, what People of *Birth* and *Fortune* are to do with themselves, if they are not to live up to the Splendour and plenty of their Estates.

The rich Man in the Gospel was a *Ruler*, a *young* Man, and a *good* Man ; if therefore there are any amongst us that are neither young nor good, it can hardly be thought that they have less to do to inherit Eternal Life, than the young Man in the Gospel.

And as for those who like him have kept the Commandments of God from their Youth, I dare not tell them that they are not under a necessity of offering all their Wealth to God, and of making their Estates, however acquired, not the Support of any foolish vain Indulgences, but the Relief of their distressed Brethren.

Suppose great People by Means of their Wealth could throw themselves into a *deep Sleep* of pleasant Dreams, which would last till Death awaked them, would anyone think it lawful for them to make such Use of their Riches ?

But if it was asked why this is not as lawful, as a Life of high Living, vain Indulgences, and worldly Pleasures, it could not be easily told.

For such a Life as this, is no more like a State of *Probation*, than such a *Sleep* is like it ; and he that has done nothing but sleep and dream to the Time of his Death, may as well say that he has been *working out his Salvation with Fear and Trembling*, as he that has been living in such Luxury, Splendour, and vain Gratifications, as his Estate could procure him.

The Gospel has made no Provision for Dignity of *Birth*, or Difference in *Fortune*, but has appointed the same *strait Gate*, the common Passage for all Persons to enter into Glory.

The Distinctions of civil Life have their Use, and are in some Degree necessary to Society, but if anyone thinks he may be less devoted to God, less afraid of the Corruptions of Pleasures, the Vanities of Pride, because he was born of one Family rather than another, he is as much mistaken, as he that fancies he has a Privilege to steal, because he was born of a Father that was poor.

Why may not poor People give themselves up to *Discontent*, to *Impatience* and *Repining ?* Is it not because Christianity requires the same Virtues in all States of Life ? Is it not because the Rewards of Religion are sufficient to make us thankful in every Condition ?

But who sees not, that these same Reasons equally condemn

the Gratifications, the sensual Indulgences of the Rich, as the Discontents and Repinings of the Poor?

So that a great Man taking his Swing in worldly Pleasures, in the various Gratifications, which his Plenty can furnish, is as good a Christian, as careful of his Duty to God, as the poor Man who resigns himself up to Discontent, and spends his Time and Spirits in restless Complaints and Repinings.

And if the Joys of Religion, our Hopes in Christ, are sufficient to make us rejoice in Tribulation, and be thankful to God in the Hardships of Poverty, surely the same Hopes in Christ must be equally sufficient to make us forbear the Luxury and Softness, and all other Pleasures of imaginary Greatness.

If therefore the rich or great Man can find out a Course of Pleasures, that support no wrong Turn of Mind, a Luxury and Indulgence which don't gratify Sensuality, Delights, and Entertainments, which indulge no vain and weak Passions, if they can find out such Self-enjoyments of their Riches, as show that they love God with all their Strength, and their Neighbours as themselves; if they can find out such Instances of Splendour and Greatness, as gratify neither the *Lust of the Flesh, the Lust of the Eyes, nor the Pride of Life,* Religion has no Command against such Enjoyments.

But if this cannot be done, let it be remembered, that the Rich have no more Permission to live in sensual Pleasures, and vain Indulgences, than the Poor have, to spend their Time in anxious Complaints and unthankful Repinings.

Let it also be remembered, that if any Distinctions of Life make Men forget, that Sin is their only Baseness, and Holiness their only Honour, if any Condition makes them less disposed to imitate the low, humble Estate of their suffering Master, or forget that they are to return to God by Humiliation, Repentance, and Self-denial, instead of being of any real Advantage, it is their Curse, their Snare, and Destruction.

Had there been any other lawful Way of employing our Wealth, than in the Assistance of the Poor, our Saviour would not have confined the young Man in the Gospel to that *one* Way of employing all that he had.

Was there no Sin in pampering ourselves with our Riches, our Saviour had not said, *Woe unto you that are rich, for ye have received your Consolation!*

Had a Delight in the Splendour and Greatness of this Life, been an innocent Delight for People of Birth and Fortune, he had never said, *Blessed are the poor in Spirit, for theirs is the Kingdom of Heaven.*

Had worldly Mirth, and the noisy Joys of Splendour and

5

Equipage, been any part of the Happiness of Christians, he had never said, *Blessed are they that mourn, for they shall be comforted.*

Thus does it appear, from almost every Part of Scripture, that a Renunciation of the World and all worldly Enjoyments, either of Pleasure or Pride, is the necessary Temper of all Christians of every State and Condition.

I know that to all this, it will still be objected, that the different *States* of Life, are Things *indifferent* in themselves, and are made good or evil, by the Tempers of the Persons who enjoy them. That a Man is not necessarily vain and proud, because he lives in great Show and Figure, any more than another is necessarily humble and lowly in Mind, because he lives in a low Estate.

It is granted, that Men may be of a Temper contrary to the State in which they live, but then this is only true of such as are in any State by Force, and contrary to their Desires and Endeavours.

A Man in a low Estate may be very vain and proud, because he is in such a State by Force, and is restless and uneasy till he can raise himself out of it. If the same can be said of any Man that lives in all the Splendour and Figure of Life, that he is in it by Force, and is restless and uneasy till he can lay all aside, and live in a humble lowly State, it may be granted that such a Man, though in the Height of Figure, may be as humble, as another in starving Circumstances may be proud.

But nothing can be more false, than to conclude, that because a Man may be in a low Estate, without having Lowliness of Mind, which Estate he is in by Force, that therefore another may live in all the Height of Grandeur, the Vanity of Figure which his Fortune will allow, without having any Height or Vanity of Mind, though the State of Life be according to his Mind, and such as he chooses before another that has less of Figure and Show in it.

Nothing can be more absurd than such a Conclusion as this; it is as if one should say, that because a Man may be an *Epicure* in his Temper, though he is forced to live upon Bread and Water, therefore another who seeks after all Sorts of Dainties, and lives upon Delicacies out of Choice, may be no *Epicure.*

Again, Who does not know that a Man may give all his Goods to feed the Poor, and yet want Charity? But will anyone therefore conclude, that another may keep all his Goods to himself, and yet have Charity?

Yet this is as well argued, as to say, that because a Man has nothing to spend, he may yet be proud; therefore though another may lay out his Estate in vain Expenses, he may yet have true Humility of Mind.

For as the Man in a low Estate, would be truly what his Estate is, if he liked it, and had no Desires that it should be otherwise than it is, so for the same Reason, if those who live in Pleasures, in Show and vain Expenses, live in such a State out of Choice, we must talk Nonsense, if we do not say, that their Minds are as Vain as the Vanity of their State.

Again, those who talk of People being Humble in a State, that has all the Appearance of Pride and Vanity, do not enough consider the Nature of Virtue. Humility and every other Virtue is never in a complete state, so that a Man can say, that he has finished his task in such or such a Virtue.

No Virtues have any Existence of this Kind in human Minds, they are rather continual Struggles with the contrary Vices, than any finished Habits of Mind.

A Man is humble not for what he has already done, but because it is his continual Disposition to oppose and reject every Temptation to Pride. Charity is a continual Struggle with the contrary Qualities of Self-Love and Envy.

And this is the State of every Virtue, it is a progressive Temper of Mind, and always equally labouring to preserve itself.

Those therefore who suppose, that People may be so finished in the Virtue of Humility, that they can be truly Humble in the Enjoyments of Splendour and Vanity, do not consider that Humility is never finished, and that it ceases to Exist when it ceases to oppose and reject every Appearance of Pride.

This is the true State of every Virtue, a resisting and opposing all the Temptations to the contrary Vice.

To suppose therefore a Man so truly Humble, that he may live in all the Appearances of Pride and Vanity, is as Absurd, as to suppose a Man so inwardly Sober, that he need refuse no strong *Liquors*, so inwardly Charitable that he need not avoid Quarrels, or so Holy that he need not resist Temptations to Sin.

Lastly, The Necessity of renouncing the World in whatever Condition of Life we are, besides what appears from particular Commands, may be proved from those great Degrees of Holiness, those divine Tempers, which Christianity requires.

Christians are to love God, with *all their Heart, with all their Soul, with all their Mind, and with all their Strength, and their Neighbour as themselves.*

Now it is absolutely impossible in the Nature of the Thing, that we should practise either of these Duties in any Christian Sense, unless we are so born of God, *as to have overcome the World.*

A Man that has his Head and his Heart taken up with worldly Concerns, can no more love God with all his Soul and with all his Strength, than a Man who will have his Eyes upon the Ground, can be looking towards Heaven with all the Strength of his Sight.

If therefore we are to love God with all our Heart and with all our Soul, it is absolutely necessary, that we be first persuaded, that we have no Happiness but in him alone, and that we are capable of no other good, but what arises from our enjoyment of the divine Nature.

But we may be assured that we never believe this Truth till we resign or renounce all Pretensions to any other Happiness. For to desire the Happiness of Riches, at the same time that we know that all Happiness is in God, is as impossible as to desire the Happiness of Sickness, when we are assured that no bodily State is happy but that of Health.

It is therefore certain in an absolute Degree, that we are as much obliged to renounce the World with all our Heart and all our Strength, as we are obliged to love God with all our Heart and all our Strength.

It being as impossible to do one without the other, as to exert all our Strength two different ways at the same time.

It is also certain in the same absolute Degree, that we unavoidably love everything in proportion, as it appears to be our Happiness, if it appears to be half of our Happiness, it will necessarily have half the Strength of our Love, and if it appears to be all our Happiness we shall naturally love it with all our Strength.

The Christian Religion therefore which requires the whole Strength of our Nature to aspire after God, lays this just Foundation of our Performing this Duty, by Commanding us to renounce the Happiness of the World, knowing it impossible to have two Happinesses, and but one Love.

And indeed what can be more ridiculous, than to fancy, that a Man who is labouring after Schemes of Felicity, that is taken up in the Enjoyments of the World, is loving God with *all his Soul* and *all his Strength?*

Is it not as absurd as to suppose a Man that is devoted to the Sports of the Field, is at the same time contemplating Mathematical Speculations with all the Ardour of his Mind?

Let anyone but deal faithfully with himself, consult his own Experience, the inward Feeling of his Mind, and consider, whether whilst his Soul is taken up with the Enjoyments of this Life, he feels that his Soul is loving God with all its Force and Strength ; let any Man say, that he feels this strong Tendency of his soul towards God, whilst it tends towards earthly Goods, and I may venture to depart from all that I have said.

Nothing therefore can be more plain than this, that if we are to fill our Soul with a new Love, we must empty it of all other Affections, and this by as great a Necessity as any in Nature.

The Love of God, as I have said of every other Virtue, is never in any complete State, but is to preserve and improve itself by a continual Opposition and Resistance of other Affections.

It is as necessary therefore continually to renounce the World, and all its Objects of our Affections, in order to form the Love of God in our Hearts; as it is necessary to renounce and resist all Motives of Self-love and Envy, to beget the Habit of Charity.

And a Man may as well pretend, that little Envies are consistent with true Charity, as that little Desires after the Vanities of the World, are consistent with an entire Love of God with all our Hearts.

It may be said, that though this Appears true in the Reason of the Thing, as considered in Speculation, yet that this is a Love for *Angels,* and not suited to the State of Man.

I answer, it is what God has required, and the same Objection may be made against all other Christian Virtues, for they are all required in a perfect Degree.

Secondly, if it is a Degree of Affection hardly attainable, this makes for the Doctrine, which I have delivered, and shows the absolute Necessity of having no more Enjoyments in the World than such as *Necessity* requires.

For if it is so hard to raise the Soul to this Degree of Love, surely it must be stupid to add to the Difficulty, by foolish and contrary Affections.

Thirdly, If this is the proper Love of Angels, this proves that it is as proper for us, who are taught by God to pray, that his Will may be done on Earth as it is in Heaven.

At least, if this is the Love of Angels, it shows us, that we are to imitate it as far as our Nature will allow, and to stop at no Degrees short of it, but such as we cannot possibly reach.

But can he be said to be doing his utmost to Love like an Angel, that is building Schemes of Felicity on Earth, and seeking Satisfaction in its imaginary Enjoyments?

As sure therefore as this is the Love of Angels, as sure as we are called to an Angelical State of Life with God, so surely are we obliged to lay aside every hindrance, to part with every Enjoyment, that may stop or retard the Soul in its Rise and Affection towards God.

We differ from Angels, as we are in a State of Probation, and loaded with Flesh ; and though till the Trial be over, we must bear with Infirmities and Necessities, to which they are not subject, yet we must no more choose Follies, or find out false Delights for ourselves, than if we were, like them, free from all Infirmities.

The Love of Enemies, is said to be a Love that becomes the Perfection of God, but yet we see, that we are so far from being excused from this Manner of Love, because it is Divine, and suits the Nature of God, that we are for that Reason expressly called to it, that we may be *Children of our Father which is in Heaven.*

If therefore we are called to that Spirit of Love, which becomes the Perfection of God, surely the manner of angelic Love is not too high for us to aspire after.

All therefore that we are to learn from this Matter is this, that a Renunciation of the World is necessary, that this holy Love cannot be attained, unless we only use the World so far as our *Needs* and *Infirmities* require, and think of no Happiness but what is prepared for us at the right Hand of God.

Fourthly, this entire Love of God is as possible, as the Attainment of several other Duties, which still are the Rules of our Behaviour, and such as we are obliged to aspire after in the utmost Perfection.

The sincere Love of our Enemies, is perhaps of all other Tempers the hardest to be acquired, and the Motions of Envy and Spite the most difficult to be entirely laid aside, yet without this Temper, we are unqualified to say the Lord's Prayer. We see Examples of this Love of God in the first Followers of our Saviour ; and though we cannot work Miracles as they did, yet we may arrive at their personal Holiness, if we would but be so Humble as to imitate their Examples.

Our Saviour told them the infallible Way of arriving at Piety, which was by renouncing the World, and taking up the Cross and following Him, that they might have Treasure in Heaven. This was the only way then, and it would still be as Successful now, had we but the Faith and Humility to put it in Practice.

But we are now it seems become so *Wise* and *Prudent*, we see so much further into the Nature of Virtue and Vice, than the Simplicity of the first Christians, that we can take all the Enjoyments of the World along with us in our Road to Heaven.

They took Christ at his word and parted with all, but we take upon us to Reason about the Innocency of Wealth, and stately Enjoyments, and so possess everything, but the Spirit of our Religion.

It is sometimes said in defence of the Dulness of our Affections towards God, that Affections are Tempers which we
cannot command, and depend much upon Constitution, so that
Persons who are possessed of a true Fear of God, may yet by
Reason of their Constitution, feel less Vehemency of Love than
others, who are less piously disposed.

This is partly true and partly false.

It is true, that our Affections are very much influenced by
our Constitutions, but then it is false, that this is any Defence
of our want of Affection towards God.

Two Persons that equally feel the want of something to
quench their Thirst, may show a different Passion after Water,
by a difference in their Constitutions, but still, thirst after Water
is the ruling Desire in both of them.

Two *Epicures,* by a difference in their Constitutions, may
differ in the manner of their Eagerness after Dainties, but still,
it is the Love of Dainties, that is the governing Love in both of
them.

It is the same thing in the case before us, two Persons may
equally look upon God as their sole Happiness, by Reason of
their different Tempers, one may be capable of greater Fervours
of Desire of him than the other, but still, it is the ruling Desire
of the other.

Therefore though good Men may content themselves, though
they have not such Flames of Desire, as they may see or hear
of in other People, yet there is no Foundation for this content,
unless they know, that they seek and desire no other Happiness
than God, and that their Love, though not so fervent as some
others, is still the ruling and governing Affection of their Soul.

Notwithstanding the Difference in Constitution, we see all
People are affected with what they reckon their Happiness: If
therefore People are not full of a Desire of God, it is because
they are full, or at least engaged with another Happiness; it is
not any Slowness of Spirits, but a Variety of Enjoyments that
have taken hold of their Hearts, and rendered them insensible of
that Happiness that is to be found in God.

When any Man has followed the Counsels of our Blessed
Saviour, when he has renounced the World, rejected all the
flattering Appearances of worldly Happiness, emptied himself of
all idle Affections, and practised all the Means of fixing his
Heart upon God alone, he may be pardoned if he still wants
such Warmth of Affection, as so great a Good might justly
raise.

But till all this be done, we as vainly appeal to our Constitutions, Tempers, and Infirmities of our State, as the unprofitable

Servant appealed to the Hardness of his Master, and therefore hid his Talent in the Earth.

And it is there said, *Out of thine own Mouth will I Judge thee, thou wicked Servant, thou knewest that I was an austere Man, &c., wherefore then gavest not thou my Money into the Bank, &c.*

So we may justly fear, that we shall be Judged out of our own Mouths, for if we know, the loving God with all our Heart and Soul, to be so difficult to the Temper and Infirmities of our Nature, why therefore do we not remove every Hindrance, renounce every vain Affection, and with double Diligence practise all the Means of forming this divine Temper? For this we may be assured of, that the seeking Happiness in the Enjoyments of Wealth, is as contrary to the entire Love of God, as wrapping up the Talent in a *Napkin*, is as contrary to improving it.

He that has renounced the World, as having nothing in it that can render him Happy, will find his Heart at liberty to aspire to God in the highest Degrees of Love and Desire; he will then know what the *Psalmist* means, by those Expressions, *My Heart is athirst for God, when shall I appear before the Presence of God?*

And till we do thus renounce the World, we are Strangers to the Temper and Spirit of Piety, we do but *act* the Part of Religion, and are no more affected with those Devotions which are put into our Mouths, than an *Actor* upon the *Stage* is really angry himself, when he speaks an angry Speech.

Religion is only what it should be, when its Happiness has entered into our Soul, and filled our Hearts with its proper Tempers, when it is the settled Object of our Minds, and governs and affects us, as worldly Men are affected with that Happiness which governs their Actions.

The ambitious Man naturally rejoices at everything that leads to his Greatness, and as naturally grieves at such Accidents as oppose it.

Good Christians that are so wise as to aim only at *one* Happiness, will as naturally be affected in this Manner, with that which promotes or hinders their Endeavours after it.

For Happiness in whatever it is placed, equally governs the Heart of him that aspires after it.

It is therefore as necessary to renounce all the Satisfactions of Riches and Fortune, and place our sole Happiness in God, as it is necessary to love him with all our Heart, and all our Soul, with all our Mind, and all our Strength.

Another Duty which also proves the Necessity of this Doctrine, is the Love of our Neighbour. *Thou shalt love thy Neighbour as thyself.*

Now he that thinks he can perform this Duty, without taking our Saviour's Advice of forsaking all and following him, is as much mistaken, as if he imagines that he loves his Neighbour as himself, though he heaps up Treasures for his own Self-enjoyments, and Self-gratifications.

If a Man would know what this Love of his Neighbour implies, let him look impartially into his own Heart, and see what it is that he wishes to himself, and then turn all those same Wishes to his Neighbour, and this will make him feel the just Measure of his Duty, better than any other Description.

This will also teach him, that this true Love of his Neighbour is as inconsistent with the Love of the World, as Duelling is inconsistent with Meekness and Forgiveness of Injuries.

This Love is a Temper of Mind that suits only such Beings, as have *one common undivided* Happiness, where they cannot be Rivals to one another; now this is the State of Christians, who have as truly *one common* Happiness, as they have one common God; but if we put ourselves out of this State, and project for ourselves other Felicities in the uncertain Enjoyments of this Life, we make ourselves as incapable of this neighbourly Love, as *Wolves* and *Bears* that live upon Prey.

Now one common undivided Happiness being the only possible Foundation for the Practice of this great Benevolence, it is demonstrable, that if we seek any other Happiness than this, if we don't renounce all other Pretensions, we cannot keep clear of such Tempers, as will show, that we do not love our Neighbour as ourselves.

This Love, as has been said of the entire Love of God, is suited to the State of Angels, it being not to be imagined that they have more Benevolence than this for one another; they can readily perform this Duty, because they never vary from their *one true* Happiness; and as this makes it easy to them, so nothing can make it *possible* for us, but by imitating them, in placing our *only* Happiness in the Enjoyment of our true Good.

If our Happiness depends upon Men, our Tempers will necessarily depend upon Men, and we shall love and hate People in Proportion, as they help or hinder us in such Happiness.

This is absolutely necessary, and we can never act otherwise, till we are governed by a Happiness where no Men can make themselves our Rivals, nor prevent our Attainment of it.

When we are in this State, it will be no harder to help our Neighbour as ourselves, than it is to wish them the Enjoyment of the same Light, or the same common Air; for these being Goods, which may be enjoyed equally by all, are not the Occasions of Envy.

But whilst we continue eager Competitors for the imaginary Enjoyments of this Life, we lay a necessary Foundation for such Passions, as are all directly contrary to the Fruits of Love.

I take it for granted, that when our Saviour delivered this Doctrine of Love, he intended it should be a governing Principle of our Lives; it concerns us therefore, as we have any Regard to our Salvation, to look carefully to ourselves, and to put ourselves in such a State, as we may be capable of performing it.

Now in this State we cannot be, till we are content to make no more of this World, than a Supply of our Necessities, and to wait for *one only* Happiness in the Enjoyment of God.

I don't appeal to Niggards and Worldlings, to the Proud and Ambitious; let those who think themselves *moderate* in their worldly Desires and Enjoyments, let such deal faithfully with their own Breasts, and see whether their Prosecution of worldly Affairs, permits them to love all Christians as themselves.

Their Moderation may perhaps keep them from the bitter Envyings and Hatred, to which ambitious Worldlings are subject, but still they have as certainly in their Degree, and in Proportion to their Love of the World, their Envyings, and Hatreds, and Want of sincere Love, as other Men.

If anyone's Heart can bear him Witness, that in Thought, Word, and Deed, he treats all Men with that Love which he bears to himself, it must be one, whose Heart fervently cries out with the Apostle, *God forbid that I should glory, save in the Cross of Jesus Christ, by which the World is crucified unto me, and I unto the World.*

Any other Glory than this, any other Use of the World, than being thus crucified to it, is inconsistent with this Degree of brotherly Love.

For a further Proof of this Truth, we need only look into the World, and see the Spirit that appears amongst almost all Christians.

We need not go to wicked and loose People, let us go into any virtuous Family whatever, we shall find that it has its particular *Friendships* and *Hatreds*, its *Envyings* and *Evil-speakings*, and all founded in the Interests and Regards of the World.

Now all this necessarily proceeds from hence, that all Christians are busy in attending to their worldly Interests, intending only to keep clear of dishonest and scandalous Practices; that is, they use the World as far as honest *Heathens*, or *Jews* would do, and so consequently have such Tempers as *Jews* and *Heathens* have.

For it is not only Cheating and unlawful Practices, but the

bare Desire of worldly Things, and the placing Happiness in them, that lays the Foundation of all these unchristian Tempers ; that begets particular Friendships and Enmities, and divides Christians into more Parties, than there are Families amongst them.

Were there no dishonest Persons amongst us, yet if Christians give themselves up to the Happiness and Enjoyments of this World, there would be still almost the same Want of the loving our Neighbours as ourselves.

So that it is purely the engaging so far in the World, as sober Christians do, it is their false Satisfaction in so many Things that they ought to renounce, it is their being too much alive to the World, that makes all, even the Devout and Religious, subject to Tempers so contrary to the Love of their Neighbour.

How comes it that most People find it so easy to love, forgive, and pray for all Men at the Hour of their Death ? Is it not because the Reason of Enmity, Envy, and Dislike, then ceases ? All worldly Interests being then at an End, all worldly Tempers die away with them.

Let this therefore teach us that it is absolutely necessary to die to the World, if we would live and love like Christians.

I have now done with this Subject of *renouncing the World and all worldly Tempers.* I hope I have been so plain and clear upon it, as is sufficient to convince any serious Reader, that it is a Doctrine of Jesus Christ, that it is the very Foundation of his Religion, and so necessary, that without it we can exercise no Christian Temper in the Manner that we ought.

Some People have imagined, that they only renounce the World, as it ought to be renounced, who retire to a *Cloister*, or a *Monastery ;* but this is as unreasonable, as to make it necessary to lay aside *all* Use of *Clothes*, to avoid the Vanity of *Dress*.

As there is a sober and reasonable Use of particular Things, so there is a sober reasonable Use of the World, to which it is as lawful to conform, as it is lawful to eat and drink.

They only renounce the World as they ought, who live in the midst of it without worldly Tempers, who comply with their Share in the Offices of human Life, without complying with the Spirit that reigneth in the World.

As it is right to go thus far, so is it wrong as soon as we take one Step further.

There is nothing right in eating and drinking, but a strict and *religious* Temperance. It is the same thing in other Compliances with the State of this Life ; we may *dress*, we may *buy* and *sell*, we may *labour*, we may provide for ourselves and our Families ; but as these Things are only lawful for the same

Reason that it is lawful to eat and drink, so are they to be governed by the same *religious* Strictness, that is to govern our Eating and Drinking; all Variation from this Rule, is like *Gluttony* and *Intemperance*, and fills our Souls with such Tempers, as are all contrary to the Spirit of Christ and his Religion.

The first Step that our Desires take beyond Things of Necessity, ranks us amongst *Worldlings*, and raises in our Minds all those Tempers, which disturb the Minds of worldly Men.

You think yourself very reasonable and conformable to Christianity, because you are moderate in your Desires; you don't desire an immense Estate, you desire only a *little* Finery in Dress, a *little* State in Equipage, and only to have Things *genteel* about you.

I answer, if this be your Case, you are happy in this, that you have but little Desires to conquer; but if these Desires have as *fast* hold of you, as greater Desires have of other People, you are in the same State of Worldly-mindedness that they are, and are no more *dead* to the World, than they that are the *fondest* of it. A Fondness for three or four Hundred Pounds a Year, is the same Slavery to the World, as a Fondness for three or four Thousand; and he that craves the Happiness of *little Fineries*, has no more renounced the World, than he that wants the Splendour of a large Fortune.

You hate the Extravagance of *Dress*, but if you cannot depart from your own *little Finery*, you have as much to alter in your Heart, as they that like none but the *finest* of Ornaments.

Consider therefore, that what you call moderate Desires, are as great Contrarieties to Religion, as those which you reckon immoderate; because they hold the Heart in the same State of false Satisfactions, raise the same vain Tempers, and do not suffer the Soul to rest wholly upon God.

When the Spirit of Religion is your Spirit, when Heavenly-mindedness is your Temper, when your Heart is set upon God, you will have no more Taste for the Vanity of one sort of Life than another.

Further, imagine to yourself, that this Pretence in Favour of moderate Desires, and *little Fineries*, had been made to our blessed Saviour, when he was upon Earth, preaching his Doctrines of renouncing the World and denying ourselves.

I dare say your own Conscience tells you, that he would have rebuked the Author of such a Pretence with as much Indignation, as he rebuked *Peter, Get thee behind me, Satan, for thou savourest not the Things that be of God.*

Now the Spirit of Christianity is the same Spirit that was in Christ, when he was upon the Earth; and if we have Reason to think, that such a Pretence would have been severely condemned by Christ, we have the same Reason to be sure, that it is as severely condemned by Christianity.

Had our blessed Saviour a little before he left the World, given Estates to his Apostles, with a Permission for them to enjoy *little Fineries*, and a moderate *State* in *genteel Show* and *Equipage*, he had undone all that he had said of the Contempt of the World, and Heavenly-mindedness; such a Permission had been a Contradiction to the most repeated and common Doctrines that he had taught.

Had his Apostles lived in such a State, how could they have gloried only in the *Cross* of Christ, by which the World was crucified unto them, and they unto the World? How could they have said, *Love not the World, nor the Things in the World, for all that is in the World, the Lust of the Flesh, the Lust of the Eyes, and the Pride of Life, is not of the Father, but is of the World?*

Had they lived in a *little State*, in a moderate Show of Figure, Equipage, and worldly Delights, how could they have said, that *She that liveth in Pleasure, is dead whilst she liveth?*

How could they have said, that *They who will be rich, fall into a Temptation, and a Snare, and into many foolish and hurtful Lusts, which drown Men in Destruction?*

For it is not the Desire of *great* Riches, but it is the Desire of Riches, and a Satisfaction in the Pleasures of them, that is the *Snare*, and the *Temptation*, and that fills Men's Minds with foolish and hurtful Lusts, that keeps them in the same State of worldly Folly, as they are whose Desires are greater.

Lastly, Had the Apostles lived in that Manner, how could they have said, that *Whatsoever is born of God, overcometh the World?*

For certainly he who is happy in the *Pleasure* and *Figure* of a small Estate, has no more overcome the World, than he who is happy in the *Splendour* of one that is greater.

Thus therefore Matters stand with Relation to our blessed Saviour and his Apostles; the Doctrines they taught made it impossible for them to take any Part, or seek any Pleasure in the *Show*, and *Figure*, and *Riches*, of this World.

One would think that this one Reflection, was alone sufficient to show us, what Contempt of the World, what heavenly Affection we are to aspire after.

For how blind and weak must we be, if we can think that we *may* live in a Spirit and Temper, which could not *possibly* be the Spirit and Temper of Christ and his Apostles?

Another Pretence for worldly Care, and Labour after Riches, is to provide for our Families.

You want to leave Fortunes to your Children, that they may have their Share in the *Figure* and *Show* of the World. Now consider, do you do this upon Principles of Religion, as the wisest and best Thing you can do, either for yourself, or your Children?

Can you be said to have chosen the *one Thing needful* for yourself, or the *one Thing needful* for them, who make it your chief Care, to put them in a State of Life, that is a *Snare*, and a *Temptation*, and the most likely of all others, to fill their Minds with *foolish and hurtful Lusts?*

Is it your Kindness towards them, that puts you upon this Labour? Consider therefore what this Kindness is founded upon; perhaps it is such a Kindness, as when *tender* Mothers carry their Daughters to all *Plays* and *Balls;* such a Kindness, as when *indulgent* Fathers support their Sons in all the Expense of their Follies; such kind Parents may more properly be called the *Tempters* and *Betrayers* of their Children.

You love your Children, and therefore you would leave them rich. It is said of our blessed Saviour, that he loved the *young rich* Man that came unto him, and as an Instance of his Love, he bid him *sell all* that he had, and give to the Poor. What a Contrariety is here? The Love which dwelleth in you, is as contrary to that Love which dwelt in Christ, as Darkness is contrary to Light.

We have our Saviour's express Command to love one another, *as he hath loved us*, and can you think that you are following this Love, when you are giving those Things to your Children, which he took away from his Friends, and which he could not possibly have given them, without contradicting the greatest Part of his Doctrines?

But supposing that you succeed in your Intentions, and leave your Children rich, what must you say to them when you are dying? Will you then tell them, that you have the same Opinion of the Greatness and Value of Riches that you ever had, that you feel the Pleasure of remembering how much Thought and Care you have taken to get them? Will you tell them, that you have provided for their Ease and Softness, their Pleasure and Indulgence, and Figure in the World, and that they cannot do better, than to eat and drink, and take their Fill of such Enjoyments as Riches afford? This would be dying like an *Atheist*.

But on the other Hand, if you will die like a *good Christian*, must you not endeavour to fill their Minds with your dying Thoughts? Must you not tell them, that they will soon be in a State, when the World will signify no more to them, than it does to you, and that there is a Deceitfulness, a Vanity, a Littleness, in the Things of this Life, which only dying Men feel, as they ought.

Will you not tell them, that all your own Failings, the Irregularity of your Life, your Defects in Devotion, the Folly of your Tempers, the Strength of your Passions, and your Failure in Christian Perfection, has been all owing to wrong Opinions of the Value of worldly Things; and that if you had always seen the World in the same Light that you see it now, your Life had been devoted to God, and you would have lived in all those holy Tempers and heavenly Affections, in which you now desire to die?

Will you not tell them, that it is the Enjoyment of the World, that corrupts the Hearts, and blinds the Minds of all People, and that the only Way to know what Good there is in *Devotion*, what Excellence there is in *Piety*, what Wisdom in *Holiness*, what Happiness in *heavenly Affection*, what Vanity in this *Life*, and what Greatness in *Eternity*, is to die to the World, and all worldly Tempers?

Will you not tell them, that Riches spent upon ourselves, either in the Pleasures of *Ease* and *Indulgence*, in the Vanity of *Dress* or the Show of *State* and *Equipage*, are the Bane and Destruction of our Souls, making us blindly content with *Dreams* of Happiness, till Death awakes us into *real* Misery?

From this therefore it appears, that your Kindness for your Children, is so far from being a good Reason why you should so carefully labour to leave them rich, and in the Enjoyment of the *State* and *Show* of the World, that if you die in a Spirit of Piety, if you love them, as Christ loved his Disciples, your Kindness will oblige you to exhort them to renounce all Self-enjoyment of Riches, as contrary to those holy Tempers, and that heavenly Affection, which you now find to be the only Good and Happiness of human Nature.

Chapter VI.

Christianity calleth all Men to a State of Self-denial and Mortification.

CHRISTIANITY is a *Doctrine of the Cross*, that teaches the Restoration of Mankind to the Favour of God, by the Death and Sacrifice of Jesus Christ. This being the Foundation of the Christian Religion, it shows us, that all Persons who will act conformably to the Nature and Reason of Christianity, must make themselves Sufferers for Sin.

For if there is a Reasonableness between Sin and Suffering, every Christian acts against the Reason of Things, that does not endeavour to pay some part of that Debt which is due to Sin.

Indeed it would be strange to suppose, that Mankind were redeemed by the Sufferings of their Saviour, to live in Ease and Softness themselves; that Suffering should be the *necessary* Atonement for Sin, and yet that *Sinners* should be excused from *Sufferings*.

Such an High Priest became us, says the Apostle, *who is holy, harmless, undefiled, separate from Sinners.*

Now if the *Holiness* of Christ rendered his Sacrifice acceptable to God, does not this teach us that we must labour to be *holy* in order to be accepted of God?

But is there not the same Reason, and the same Example in the Sufferings of Christ, if they made God more propitious to Sin, must we not as well take this Way of Suffering, to make ourselves fitter Objects of Divine Pardon?

There is therefore the same Reason in the Nature of the Thing, for us Sinners to endeavour to conform ourselves to the *Sufferings*, as to labour after the *Holiness* of Christ; since they both jointly conspired to recommend the great Atonement for Sin, and must jointly conspire to render us proper Objects of the Benefits of it.

Nor is the sinless State of Christ a better Reason for us to avoid and flee from Sin, than his suffering State is a Reason for our renouncing all Softness and Indulgence in Pleasures.

Had Christ wanted either Holiness or Sufferings, his Sacrifice had been wanting in an essential Part. If therefore we think to be accepted of God by Holiness, without Suffering, we seem to contradict the Nature of our Religion as much, as if we thought to be accepted through Sufferings without Holiness.

It may perhaps be said, in the Words of our *Liturgy*, *That Christ having by his one Oblation of himself once offered, made a full, perfect, and sufficient Sacrifice, Oblation, and Satisfaction, for the Sins of the whole World*, that Christians have no Occasion to make any Suffering for Sin.

To this it may be answered,

That the Sacrifice of Christ is full and sufficient, first, as it takes away the Necessity of all the *legal Sacrifices*: Secondly, as it has no Need to be repeated again: And thirdly, as it fully reconciles God to accept of us upon the Terms of the New Covenant.

Now there is no Occasion to suffer for Sin, in order to make the Sacrifice of Christ *more complete*, or to add a further Value to the Atonement for Sin; but then it is to be considered, that if

Self-suffering for Sin be a good and reasonable Duty in itself, and proper for a Sinner, that the Fulness of Christ's Sacrifice has no more taken away the Necessity of it, than it has taken away the Necessity of Humility, or any other Virtue.

Christ is as well said to be our *Sanctification*, our *Holiness* and *Righteousness*, as our Atonement for Sin, yet we should much mistake the Scripture, if we should think, that because he is our Holiness, therefore we need not endeavour to be Holy ourselves.

Yet this is as good a Conclusion, as to imagine, that we need not suffer for our Sins ourselves, because Christ's Sufferings are a full Atonement for Sin.

For they are no otherwise a *sufficient Atonement* for Sin, than as Christ is our *sufficient Holiness*, so that we may as well trust to his Holiness, without labouring to be Holy ourselves, as trust to his Sufferings, without making ourselves also Sufferers for Sin.

Let it now therefore be observed, that were there no particular Precepts or Doctrines, that expressly called us to a State of Self-denial, and Self-suffering, the very Nature of Religion, is an undeniable Argument, that the Way of Suffering, is the right and certain Way for Sinners to find God more Propitious to their Sin.

He that can doubt of this, must suppose, that God required a Way of Atonement in Jesus Christ, that had nothing of Atonement in it ; for if it had, it must be undeniable, that all, who, as far as their Natures will allow, conform themselves to the Similitude of Christ's Sacrifice, must make themselves more acceptable to God.

That Christ's Sufferings have not made all other Sufferings for Sin needless, is plain from hence, that all Christians are still left subject to *Death.* For surely it may with Truth be affirmed, that Death is a Suffering for Sin.

Now since all Christians are to offer up their Bodies at Death, as a *Sacrifice* or *Suffering* for Sin, this plainly teaches us that a State of Self-denial and Suffering is the proper State of this Life. For surely it must be proper to make every Part of our Life suitable to such an *End.*

Does God unmake us, and dash our very Form into pieces ? and can we think that a Life of Pleasure and Self-indulgence, can become us under such a Sentence ?

What plainer Proof can we have, that we are *devoted* Sufferers for Sin, than that we are devoted to Death ? for Death hath no place in a State of allowed Pleasure and Enjoyment. When the Suffering for Sin is over, there will be no more Death ; but so long as Death lasts, so long are all Beings that are subject to Death, in a State that requires Humiliation and Suffering ; and

6

they rebel against God, if they do not make their Lives conformable to that Mark of divine Displeasure, which death signifies.

Thus as the *Mortality* of our Condition, is a certain Proof that our Life is in *Disorder*, and *unacceptable* to God, so is it also a Proof, that we ought to refuse Pleasures and Satisfactions, which are the Pleasures of a State of Disorder, and stay for Joy and Delights till we are removed to such a State of Perfection, as God will delight to continue to all Eternity.

The Apostle tells us that *Flesh and Blood cannot enter into the Kingdom of God*, must we not therefore be very unreasonable, if we can cast about for Mirth in such a Condition, or give up ourselves to the vain Pleasures and Indulgences of a Flesh and Blood, which are too corrupt, too unholy to enter into the Kingdom of God?

This may suffice to show us the Excellency and Reasonableness of our Saviour's Doctrine.

He said unto them all, if any Man will come after me, let him deny himself, take up his Cross daily and follow me.

For whosoever will save his Life, shall lose it, and whosoever will lose his Life for my sake, the same shall save it.

Here is a common Condition proposed to all that would be Christ's Disciples, they are called to deny themselves, and take up their Cross daily. To show us that this belongs to all Christians, the Apostle saith, *He said unto them* all; St. *Mark* hath it thus, *And when he had called the People unto him, with his Disciples also, he said unto them.*

The Church of *Rome* refuses to give the *Cup* in the Holy Sacrament to the Laity. We reckon it a very good Argument against that Custom, that our Saviour when he delivered the Cup, said unto them, *Drink ye all of this.*

Now if it be an Argument that *all Christians* are to receive the Cup, because in the Institution of the Sacrament it is said, *Drink ye all of this*, is it not as good an Argument that all Christians are here called to deny themselves, and take up their Cross daily, because it is delivered in the same Manner, *He said unto them* all, and again, *When he called the People unto him with his Disciples also, he said unto them?*

To me this Place seems as general a Call to all Christians, as *Drink ye all of this*, is a general Command to all Christians.

Let anyone try to evade the Obligation of this Text, and he will find, that he must use such Arguments, as will equally serve to get rid of any other Part of Holy Scripture.

If this Passage only called the first Disciples of Christ to an external State of Sufferings, and Persecutions from other People, it might with some Pretence be supposed only to relate to People, when they are in such a State of Persecution.

But as it calls them to *deny themselves,* to take up their Cross daily, it is plain, that it calls them to a Suffering and Self-denial, which they were to inflict upon themselves.

Now if they are called thus to deny themselves, and subject themselves to a voluntary Cross in order to be Christ's Disciples, it will be hard to show, that Self-denials are not as lasting Terms of Christianity, as Baptism and the Lord's Supper.

Water-Baptism is Necessary because our Saviour has Insti-tuted it, and the Reason for continuing it, is the same as for observing it at first. But still, it is but an external Rite, or Sacrament, which in its own Nature hath nothing relating to Holiness and Purification of the Soul, but has all its Excellency from the Institution of Christ.

This cannot be said of these Sort of Sufferings, for they have an *internal* and *essential* Relation to Holiness and Purification in the *present State* of Man.

I say in the *present State* of Man, because though these Self-denials or Mortifications, are proper only to Man whilst he is in this State of Corruption, yet they are as true Parts of Holiness, and as essential Virtues, as those which will last for ever.

Charity to the Poor is founded in the Necessities and Infir-mities of this Life, yet it is as real a Degree of Holiness, and as much to be performed for its own Sake, as that Charity which which will never have an End.

It is the same in these Self-denials, they only belong to a State of Sin, but whilst such a State continues, they are the indispensable Duty of Sinners, and as necessary and acceptable to God as relieving the Poor.

This must be allowed, or we must deny, that there was any real Atonement for Sin in the Sufferings and Death of Christ ; for if there were any real Atonement in the Sufferings of Christ, if his Sufferings rendered God propitious and reconciled to Sinners, it is undeniable, that all who suffer with the *same Spirit* that Christ suffered, must in their Degree recommend themselves to the Favour of God, on the same Account, and for the same Reasons that the Sufferings of Christ procured Peace and Recon-ciliation.

If Christ the Lord of all, and Head of the Church, is still making Intercession for us at the Right Hand of God, does not this plainly teach us, that we cannot be accepted by God, unless we live in a State of Supplication and Prayer for ourselves ?

And if he who had no Sin of his own, was obliged to such Sufferings to make himself be heard as an *Advocate* for Sin :

6—2

surely Sinners themselves cannot presume to sue for their own Pardon, without putting themselves in the *like State* of Humiliation and Suffering. For since the Atonement is made by Sufferings, this as truly recommends Sufferings to Sinners, as if it had been made by Prayer, that would have shown the Way of Prayer to have been the Way of finding Pardon.

Self-denial therefore and Sufferings are Duties essential to the present State of Sin, and recommend us to God, as Holiness and Purity recommend us, by their own Nature and intrinsic Fitness, that is, they are good, as Prayer, Humility, and Charity are good.

When we shall be removed to a State that is free from Sin, Self-Denial and Mortification will then be no Part of our Duty; but so long as this State of Sin lasts, so long does the Necessity and Reason of Self-denial and Mortification last; they are as necessary, as Prayers and Devotion, and are as truly essential Parts of Holiness, as Chastity and Humility.

For Repentance and Sorrow for Sin is as necessary to a being in a State of Sin, as necessary on its own Account, and from the Nature of the Thing, as the Love of God is necessary from a Being that receives all his Happiness from God.

For to express our Indignation, and inflict Punishment on that which displeases God, is as reasonable in itself, and as much an Act of Holiness, as to love and cherish that which God loves. So that all our Self-denials as Punishments of Sin, as Expressions of Sorrow for Guilt, and as Preventions of Temptation, may be considered as so many Instances of our Love of Purity.

Whilst therefore we continue in a State of Corruption, it is as necessary that we continue in a State of Repentance, Self-denial, and Sorrow, as it is necessary to continue our Desires and Endeavours after Purity.

If we can find a Time when we have no Sin to lament, no Occasion for the Severities of Repentance, it may be granted, that that would be a Time for the abstaining from Self-denial, and voluntary Sufferings.

But if human Life knows of no such Season, if we can never look at ourselves, but under the Weight of Sin, it is a Demonstration that Indignation at ourselves, and a voluntary Suffering for Sin, is the necessary constant State of Christians.

Indeed if it be allowed that Repentance and Sorrow for Sin is necessary, and that it ought to be the constant Habit of a Christian's Mind, till this Life be at an End, we need no stronger Proof of the constant Necessity of Self-denial and Mortification.

For what Reason can there be for Sorrow and Grief for Sin, which is not the same Reason for Self-denial, and the daily Cross? Is not Grief and Sorrow for Sin, a *Suffering and Punishment* for Sin? Or can we grieve and afflict ourselves for our Sins, unless we express that Grief by a hearty Indignation, and real Self-denial?

If therefore we consider the Reason and Fitness of Repentance, we see the Reason and Fitness of Self-denial, and voluntary Sufferings, and consequently we must acknowledge, that these Self-denials are not less necessary, nor less recommended to us, than Repentance and Sorrow for Sin.

For since they are of the same Nature, and for the same End, and also essential to true Repentance, it follows, that all Christians are obliged to be as constant in their Self-denials, and Mortifications, as they are to be constant in their Repentance.

Because such voluntary Sufferings have the same essential Relation to Holiness, that Charity and the Love of God have.

For though Charity and the Love of God will never cease, but this Self-denial will have an End, yet is this Self-denial during this State of Sin, as essential to the Holiness of Persons in such a State, as any other Virtue.

It being the same Degree of inward Purity, and as right a Spirit and Temper to *mourn and afflict* ourselves for our Sins, as to *love* that which God *loves*, or be thankful for his Mercies.

Now if a Person was to give himself up to *Sorrow* in a *State* of *Happiness*, or to Unthankfulness, though in the Midst of Mercies, he would act just as unreasonably, just as contrary to the Nature of Things, as he that gives himself up to Pleasures and Indulgences in a State of Corruption and Sin.

Let it therefore be carefully observed, that Self-denial and Mortification, are only other Words for Repentance and Sorrow for Sin, and he that can distinguish them from one another, may distinguish Grief from Sorrow.

He therefore that can doubt, whether Christians are called to a daily Practice of Self-denial, seems to know as little of true Religion, as if he doubted whether they were called to a daily Repentance. For when we may live in a State contrary to *Repentance*, then, and then only, may we live in a State contrary to *Self-denial.*

Let a Christian ever cease from Self-denial, let him ever forbear the Mortification of his Appetites, and at that Time he ceases to consider himself as a *Sinner*, and behaves himself as though he were then free from the *Guilt* and *Danger* of Sin.

But as he never is in this State of Freedom, so if he acts as if he were so, he acts as falsely, as if he took himself to be an *Angel*.

There is therefore as much Reason that the *daily Cross,* or Self-denial, should be imposed upon Christians, as a daily Prayer, or Repentance; and there is the same Impiety, the same false Judgment in refusing a daily Self-denial, as in refusing or ceasing from a daily Devotion and Sorrow for Sin.

For a Man may as well imagine that he prays or gives Thanks to God, when he only repeats the Words of a Prayer or Thanksgiving, as that he repents for his Sins, unless his Repentance be a *real* Punishment, a *true State* of Mortification.

We may now observe, that this Doctrine of Self-suffering is founded upon the most important fundamental Articles of our Religion.

If we consider our Redemption as an Atonement made by Suffering, does not this show us the Necessity of seeking Pardon by a Fellowship in the Sufferings of Christ?

Need we any other Argument, that there is no State so suitable to a Sinner as that of Suffering, when God has appointed Sufferings as the Atonement for Sin?

If we consider that we are devoted to *Death,* and under a Necessity of falling into Dust, as a *Sacrifice* for Sin, does not this teach us the Necessity of making our Life conformable to the Intention of such a Death?

For could there be any *Necessity* that we should die as a *Sacrifice* for Sin, if we might lead a Life of a *contrary* Nature? Or could we act more contrary to God, than by making that Life a State of Pleasure and Indulgence, which he has laid under the *Curse* of Death? Ought we to indulge a Life which God considers as too unholy to continue in Being?

Lastly, If we consider that Repentance is the chief, the most constant and perpetual Duty of a Christian, that our Holiness has hardly any other Existence, than what arises from a perpetual Repentance, can it be doubted, that Mortification and Self-denial are essential, perpetual Parts of our Duty?

For to suppose a Repentance without the Pain of Mortification, and the Punishment of Self-denial, is as absurd, as to suppose a Labour after Holiness, which takes not one Step towards it.

For if Repentance be not an Exercise of Mortification and Self-denial, it is no more a State of Repentance, than the lifting up our Hands, without our Hearts, is a State of Prayer and Devotion.

Repentance is a hearty Sorrow for Sin, Sorrow is a Pain or Punishment, which we are obliged to raise to as high a Degree as we can, that we may be fitter Objects of God's Pardon.

So that Self-denial and Mortification is only another Word, for a *real Repentance*.

If Christians will still so far forget the Nature and Design of their Religion, as to imagine that our Saviour's Call to a daily Cross and Self-denial was only a Call to his first Disciples to expect Sufferings and Death from their Enemies, they are governed by as little Reason, as if they should think, *Repent ye, for the Kingdom of Heaven is at Hand,* only obliged those to Repentance, who first entered into the Kingdom of God.

For there is nothing in the Nature of Repentance, that shows it to be a more constant Duty, or more essential to the Christian Life, than there is in this Mortification and Self-suffering.

It is also very absurd to suppose, that a Command to deny themselves and take up their own Cross daily, should mean only the enduring and expecting of Sufferings from others.

Let us now suppose the contrary, that Christians are not called to this State of Mortification, or Denial of their Appetites. Let us suppose that Christian *Churches* are full of *fine gay* People, who spend their Days in all the Pleasures and Indulgences which the Spirit of the World can invent.

Can it in any Sense be said of such, that they live in a *State of Repentance and Sorrow* for Sin? May they not with as much Regard to Truth, be said to live in *Sackcloth and Ashes?* Can their Hearts feel any Sorrow, or be mourning for the Weight and Misery of Sin, who live only to the studied Enjoyments of Ease and Pleasure? Can they be said to grieve at Guilt, or be afraid of Sin, who pamper all their Appetites, and seek all the Enjoyments that lead to Temptation? Can they who live in the Gratifications of the Flesh, and Scenes of Pleasure, be said to be working out their Salvation *with Fear and Trembling?* May they not as justly be said to be walking barefoot to *Jerusalem?*

If therefore we will not destroy the whole State of Religion, if we will but own it to be a State of *Trial and Probation,* we must also allow, that Self-denial and Abstinence from Pleasures are daily essential Duties of it.

For a Life of Sorrow for Sin, and mourning for the Guilt of it, and a Life of Pleasure and Indulgence, are inconsistent States, and as necessarily destroy one another, as Motion puts an End to Rest.

Repentance will have no Place in Heaven, because that will be a State of Perfection, and for the same Reason it ought never to be laid aside on Earth, because there is no Time, when we are not under the Guilt, and subject to the Danger of Sin.

This does not suppose, that we are always to be uttering

Forms of Confession from our Mouths, but it supposes, that we are always to live with so much Watchfulness, as becomes penitent Sinners, and never do anything, but what highly suits with a *State of Repentance.*

So that whenever we can abate our Self-denials, without abating our Sorrow for Sin, when we can find Pleasures that neither *soften* the Mind, nor make it *less fearful* of Temptation, then, and so far only, may we seek our Ease.

For Repentance whilst it is only a Lipwork at stated Times is nothing, it has not had its Effect, till it has entered into the State and Habit of our Lives, and rendered us as fearful of Sin in every Part of our Lives, as when we are making our Confessions.

Now this State of Penitence, which alone is suited to a State of Corruption and Infirmity, can no more exist without constant daily Self-denial, than we can daily govern our Appetites, without daily looking after them.

To proceed. Our Saviour saith, *Blessed are they that mourn for they shall be comforted.*

Now this is another direct Call to Self-denial and Abstinence from Pleasures, as must appear to everyone, that knows Mourning to be different from Pleasure and Indulgence.

The Blessedness that is here ascribed to Mourning, must be understood in relation to Mourning, as it is a *State of Life,* and not as to any transient Acts, or particular Times of Mourning.

For no Actions are valuable, or rewardable, but as they arise from a *State or Temper* of Mind that is constant and habitual.

If it had been said blessed are the Charitable, it must have meant, blessed are they who live in a *State and Habit* of Charity. For the same Reason, are we to understand the Blessedness which is due to Mourning, to be only due to a State and Life of Mourning.

Secondly, *Blessed are they that mourn,* shows us that this Mourning concerns all Men as such, without any Distinction of *Time* or *Persons,* so that its Excellency and Fitness must be founded upon something that is common and constant to all times and all Persons. For if there was any time, when we might change this State of Mourning, or were there any Persons that might be excused from it, it could not be said in general, *Blessed are they that mourn.*

If therefore this Mourning be a reasonable and excellent Temper, that equally leads *all Orders* of Men to Blessedness, its Reasonableness must be founded in the common State and Condition of Man; that is, if Mourning be good for all Men, it must be, because the State and Condition of all Men as such, requires Mourning.

But if this Mourning be founded in the present State of Man, as suitable to his Condition in this Life, it must be always the same excellent and proper Temper, till Death changes his State, and puts him in a Condition, that requires another Temper.

Now what can this State of Mourning be, but a godly Sorrow founded upon a true Sense and Feeling of the Misery of our State, as it is a State of *fallen Spirits*, living in Sin and Vanity, and *Separation* from God?

What can it be, but a ceasing to enjoy and rejoice in the false Goods and Enjoyments of this Life, because they delude and corrupt our Hearts, increase our Blindness, and sink us deeper in our Distance from God?

What Mourning can be blessed, but such as mourns at that which displeases God, which condemns and rejects what the Wisdom of God rejects, which loosens us from the Vanity of the World, lessens the Weight of our Corruption, and quickens our Motions and Aspirings towards Perfection?

This is not a Mourning that shows itself in *occasional Fits* of Sorrow, or Dejection of Mind, but it is a *regular Temper*, or rather a *right Judgment*, which refuses Pleasures, that are not only the Pleasures of a corrupted State, but such as also increase and strengthen our Corruption.

One constant Property of a true Mourning, is Abstinence from Pleasures; and we generally reckon a Sorrow very near its End, when Diversions and Amusements begin to be relished.

This Mourning therefore to which this Blessedness is ascribed, must be a constant Abstinence from vain Joys; it must preserve itself by rejecting and disrelishing all those worldly Delights and Satisfactions, which if admitted, would put an end to its State of Mourning.

Now what is all this, but that State of *Self-denial* and *Daily-cross* to which our Saviour called his Disciples?

For we may imagine anything, if we can imagine, that a State of religious Mourning is not a State of religious Self-denial.

Unless therefore we will say, that the Blessedness of Mourning, was also only preached to Christ's first Followers, we must allow, that *all Christians* are equally called to that *Daily-cross* and *Self-denial*, which was then required.

It ought also here to be observed, that we are called to these Duties upon our Hopes of Happiness.

For *Blessed are they that mourn, for they shall be comforted*, is the same thing as saying, Miserable and cursed are they that do not mourn, for they shall not be comforted. Again,

Blessed are the poor in Spirit, for theirs' is the Kingdom of Heaven.

Nothing can carry a greater Denial and Contradiction to all the Tempers and Ways of the World than this Doctrine ; it not only puts an end to all that we esteem wicked and immoderate Desires of worldly Satisfactions, but calls us from all worldly Satisfactions, which anyway fasten the Soul to any false Goods, and make it less ardent after true Happiness. As the Christian Religion regards only the Salvation of our Souls, and restoring us to a Life with God in Heaven, it considers everything as ill, that keeps us in a State of any false Enjoyment, and nothing as good, but what loosens us from the World, and makes us less Slaves to its Vanities. *Blessed are the poor in Spirit*, because it is a Spirit of Disengagement and Disrelish of the World, that puts the Soul in a State of Liberty and Fitness, to relish and receive the Offers of true Happiness.

The Doctrine of this Text, is purely the Doctrine of *Self-denial* and *Daily-cross*, to which our Saviour called his Disciples.

For let anyone consider, how it is possible for a Man to be *poor in Spirit*, but by renouncing those Enjoyments, which are the proper Delights of such as are *high*, and *rich* in Spirit. Now a Man is *high* in Spirit, when his own State and Dignity give him a Pleasure, he is *rich* in Spirit who seeks and delights in the Enjoyments and Felicities which Riches afford, he is therefore *poor in Spirit*, who mortifies all vain Thoughts, rejects every Self-pleasure, and avoids and dislikes the empty Satisfactions which Riches and Fortune give.

Now this, which is undoubtedly the Doctrine of this Passage, is the very Essence and Soul of all Self-denial and Mortification, which is nothing else but a constant checking all our vain Tempers, and a denying ourselves such Enjoyments, as naturally strengthen and support them. So that the Blessedness of Poverty of Spirit, is the Blessedness of Self-denial and Mortification.

For surely if we are called to a constant Poverty of Spirit, we are called to a constant Refusal of all Enjoyments, but such as Poverty of Spirit requires.

For it is to be observed, that when it is said, *Blessed are the poor in Spirit*, that the Meaning is, *Blessed* are they that are governed by this Spirit, for that is only a Man's Spirit and Temper, which rules and directs his Actions.

An ambitious Man, is one that is governed by his Spirit of Ambition, so a Man is poor in Spirit, when that is the Spirit which governs his Actions.

As the rich in Spirit, are such as seek the Felicity and Gratifications of Riches, so the poor in Spirit is he, who avoids and dislikes all such Gratifications, and seeks such Things as properly suit with such a mortified Habit of Mind.

So that no one is to reckon himself *poor in Spirit*, till it makes him not only reject all Instances of Pride and Self-enjoyment, but till he seeks and desires things that are as proper to a Poverty of Spirit, as *Food* is proper to Hunger, or *Water* to Thirst.

For as Hunger is known by its being a Desire of *Food,* and Thirst by its Desire of *Liquor,* so Poverty of Spirit can only be known, by its seeking such things, as are as *true Signs* of it, as the seeking of Water, is a Sign of Thirst.

For this is undeniable, that every Spirit or Temper must only be known, by the Nature of the Things it covets.

If we are High-minded, our Care will be exercised about high Things, and if we are lowly in Heart, we shall as certainly not only condescend, but seek after things that are lowly. Let a Man therefore, who would deal faithfully with himself, consider not only whether he is *Proud, Luxurious, Indulgent* of himself, and devoted to the Pleasures and Satisfactions of this Life, but let him consider whether he is *poor in Spirit*, whether the Things that he seeks, the Designs he has on foot, the Happiness he aims at, and the Course of his Life, be such as is really directed by a true Poverty of Spirit.

For he ought not to think that he is governed by this Spirit, till he finds himself an Enemy to every Pleasure, every Care, and every Labour that is contrary to it. When he hates Self-indulgence, as the *Epicure* hates Self-denial, when he studies Humility, as the *ambitious* Man aims at *Greatness,* when he avoids the Vanities of the World, as the *Sailor* avoids *Rocks,* then may he reckon himself entitled to that Blessedness, which belongs to those who are *poor in Spirit.*

This is that Self-denial, Holy-discipline, Daily-cross, to which all Christians are called ; that by thus losing their Lives, that is, thus ceasing to live the Life of this World, they may purchase to themselves a Life of endless Happiness in another State.

I believe there are few Christians, who do not acknowledge that Christianity is still in some Degree a *Doctrine of the Cross ;* and that the Texts above cited, have still some meaning with regard to all Christians ; but then they believe this in some such loose and general Way, or live with so little regard to what they do believe of it, that they feel no Condemnation of themselves, whatever their Lives are, from hearing these Doctrines.

But notwithstanding all this, it is certain that Christians are as much obliged to conform exactly to these Doctrines of the Cross, as to the Observance of the Ten Commandments. For the Ten Commandments were not more certainly Laws to the

Jews, than the Doctrines of Self-denial and Poverty of Spirit are Laws to *all Christians*.

Another plain and remarkable Instance of Self-denial, is to be seen in the following Words.

Ye have heard that it hath been said, an Eye for an Eye, and a Tooth for a Tooth, but I say unto you, that ye resist not Evil, but whosoever will smite thee on thy right Cheek, turn to him the other also. And if any Man will sue thee at Law and take away thy Coat, let him have thy Cloak also. And whosoever shall compel thee to go with him a Mile, go with him twain.

Our Blessed Saviour's first Proposal was this, *If any Man will come after me, let him deny himself, take up his Cross daily, and follow me.*

In the Text before us, he instructs them in several Instances, wherein this Self-denial and Daily-cross consisted, which are now the common Terms of Salvation to all Christians.

We are to deny ourselves, in not demanding a *Tooth for a Tooth*, we are to take up our *Daily-cross* by turning our Cheek to the Smiter, and suffering such ill Usage, as we could prevent by Resistance.

We are to deny ourselves, in not defending ourselves by Suits at Law; and must take up the Cross of one Injury after another, rather than appeal to the Contention of a Trial. This is sufficiently taught, by our being required to expose ourselves to the farther Loss of our *Cloak*, rather than have recourse to Law to secure our *Coat*.

The Words which deliver this Doctrine are so very plain and express, that they need no Illustration, it is as plain also, that they equally belong to all Christians of all Ages. The Manner of our Saviour's delivering himself upon these Points, puts it out of all question, that they were Doctrines of the *Cross*, which were to be perpetual Marks of his Followers.

Ye have heard that it hath been said, an Eye for an Eye, &c. But I say unto you, that ye resist not Evil, &c.

It was not possible for our Saviour to express himself in a more authoritative Manner than he has here done, or to show us more plainly, that he was here acting as the *great Law-giver* of Christians, and delivering Doctrines which should be *perpetual Laws* to all his Disciples, and such as should constantly distinguish them from all the World. Nor is it possible for anyone to evade the literal and open Meaning of these Doctrines, but in such a way as must destroy the Sense of any other Part of Scripture.

If it could be shown, that we are not obliged by the plain and express Doctrine of these Passages, it might as well be shown, that the next Doctrine, *But I say unto you, love your Enemies, bless them that curse you,* does not oblige us in the plain and literal Sense of the Words.

For both the Passages are equally supported by the same Authority of our Saviour, expressed in the same manner, *I say unto you.* This Degree also of Love which we are to show to our Enemies, is as much a Doctrine of the *Cross,* as contrary to all our natural Tempers, and worldly Interests, as that of Patience, Meekness, and Submission to those who treat us injuriously. These Virtues are also necessary to one another ; we cannot thus Love and do good to our Enemy, unless we are thus patient under Sufferings, and deny ourselves all Instances of Anger and Uneasiness at them.

It is pretended by some that these Passages only forbid our Prosecution of *spiteful* and *malicious* Suits at Law.

But such People might as well pretend, that the Eighth Commandment only forbids *wanton* and *spiteful* Stealing, but allows it, when it is done Soberly and with no spiteful Intention.

For the Case which our Saviour put, is directly intended against such a Pretence as this.

It is the Case of a Man, who has a Suit commenced against him for his *Coat,* he is not allowed to consider that it is his *own* Coat, and that he enters no further into the Trial, than to secure his *Coat ;* he is not allowed to show this Degree of Contention or Anger at Injustice, or Impatience under Suffering, but is patiently to permit his Coat to be taken from him, though that Patience be the Means of losing his Cloak also.

It is not therefore spiteful Prosecutions, but the most seemingly reasonable Self-defence that is here forbidden. Further, *Malice* and *Revenge* were not allowed to the *Jews,* yet we are here commanded to deny ourselves such Methods of Self-defence, and Rules of Justice as were allowed to them.

If Christians will still think that they may defend *all* their Rights, and enter into all *such Contentions* for them, as the *Laws* of the Land will support them in, if they will think that they need bear *no other* Injuries, but such as Courts of *Law* cannot redress, they are as much mistaken, as if they imagine, they need Practise no other Charity or Worship of God, but such as humane Laws Demand.

For Christian *Meekness, Self-denial,* and *Patience* under Sufferings, are no more to be formed by the Standard of human Laws, than our Devotion to God.

In these Things Jesus Christ is our *only Lawgiver,* and his Laws are to be complied with as the certain Terms of our Salvation.

Notwithstanding therefore we may be able either by personal Power or legal Contention to repel Injuries, return Evil for Evil, and demand a *Tooth* for a *Tooth*, yet as Disciples of Christ we are to turn our Cheek to the Smiter, let him that would take our Coat, have our Cloak also, and be rather content to suffer many Injuries, than by defending ourselves, raise our Passions, embitter our Tempers, and destroy that Charity which we owe to our Neighbour.

Now this *Meekness* and *Self-denial* is highly suitable to the Spirit and Temper of Christianity.

It is highly suitable to a Religion that restores Sinners to God by *Sufferings*, it is suited to such as have *forsaken all* to follow Christ, it is suited to such as are to be *dead* and *crucified* to the World, to such as are to be *meek* and *lowly* as Christ, it is suited to such as are commanded to *love* and do all Good to their most violent Enemies, and who are to love their Neighbour as themselves.

And whatever Pride, Self-love, or *humane Wisdom* may suggest against this Doctrine, may with equal Strength be Objected against all those other Doctrines, which are thus of a Spirit like unto it.

But let Christians consider, that it is of these Doctrines of the *Cross*, that our Saviour saith, *Whosoever shall be ashamed of me and of my Words, of him shall the Son of Man be ashamed, when he shall come in his own Glory and in his Father's, and of the holy Angels.* Further,

This is my Commandment, saith Christ, *that ye love one another, as I have loved you.* Now this as plainly forbids all Strife and angry Contentions with others, as when we are commanded to part with our Coat rather than contend for it. For it is as impossible to love our Adversary whilst we are contending with him, as Christ loved us, as to follow Christ, and at the same time depart from him.

His Love towards Mankind (which is the Example for our Love) knew of no Enemies, nor refused any Sufferings, but was a continual Labour for the Salvation of all Men. If therefore we treat *any* Persons as our *Enemies*, or fly in the Face of those who injure us, and are impatient under Sufferings, we are fallen from that Love which is to govern all our Actions.

Men may fancy what they please of the Charity of their Temper, whilst they are resisting Evil, and carrying on the Contentions of Law, as others may think they *have their Conversation in Heaven*, whilst they are labouring after Riches on Earth; but if they would consider, that Christian Charity is to be like the Charity of Christ, who died for his Enemies, they would soon find, that it must be a Charity of another Kind, that allows them to *contend* with their Enemies.

Every Resistance or Contention of any Kind, is a Quarrel, and necessarily begets some Degrees of Spite and Ill-will, and though they may often be carried on with some Show of *external Decency*, yet the *inward Temper* partakes of the Contention, is tainted with some *little* and *ill-natured* Resentments, and destroys that divine Spirit of Love to which we are called.

So that to talk of the Charity of resisting, and contentious Suits at Law, is almost like talking of the Charity of *Duels*.

The only Way therefore to preserve our Christian Spirit, and show ourselves more like Christ than those who injure us, is to act as he did under Injuries, and bear them with Patience, for such Reasons as rendered him patient. We are sure that whilst we follow him, we follow the *Way, the Truth, and the Life*, but as soon as we resent and form Designs of conquering our Oppressor, we partake of his Spirit, and offend against Meekness and Charity, as he offended against Justice.

We must therefore bear with Injuries and Wrongs, not because it is difficult to redress them, but because it is difficult, and next to impossible, to resist and contend with our Adversaries, without forfeiting that Humility, Meekness, and Divine Love, to which we are called.

We must suffer with Patience, because such Patience is an Exercise of our Self-denial, that renders us more like our Lord and Master.

This cannot be doubted of, since we are told of our blessed Saviour, *That though he were a Son, yet learned he Obedience, by the Things which he suffered.*

Now if this be true, is it not true in the same Degree, that we are not only to bear Sufferings with Patience, but even receive them with Thankfulness, as proper Means to teach us Obedience to the Laws of God?

For if he who was a Son, who was without Sin, and so full of Divine Knowledge, yet received *Instruction* from Sufferings, surely we who are poor infirm Creatures, must want that Instruction which is to be learnt from them.

For to suppose, that we can be obedient to God without Sufferings, is to suppose, that we can do our Duty without such Helps as the Son of God had. Sufferings are therefore to be considered amongst the Graces of God, which *purify* our Souls, *enlighten* our Minds with Divine Knowledge, and prepare us *to perfect Holiness in the Fear of God.*

But how contrary to the Spirit of Christ do we act, if our Sufferings provoke us into Methods of *Retaliation*, and instead of teaching us Obedience to God, lead us into a State of *Enmity* towards our Brethren.

Further; It became him, saith the Apostle, *for whom are all Things, and by whom are all Things, in bringing many Sons unto Glory, to make the Captain of their Salvation perfect through Sufferings.**

We are here plainly taught not only that Christ was made perfect through Sufferings, but that it was fit he should be made perfect that Way, as the only Way that could bring *many Sons unto Glory.*

So that we see one End of Christ's Sufferings before his being crowned with Glory and Honour, was to teach us, that Sufferings is the *Way* to arrive at Glory, and that those who desire to be Sons of Glory, must first be made perfect through Sufferings.

We therefore forget the Nature of our Religion, we mistake the one great Design of Christ's Sufferings, we go out of the Road to Glory, if we do not patiently submit to Sufferings, if we are not thankful that we *suffer with Christ, that we may reign with him.*

Men in vain pretend that they only defend themselves against *Injustice.* For these are the very Hardships which Christ suffered, and which they are, if they would be guided by his Spirit, to suffer with Patience.

St. Peter speaking to Servants, saith, *This is thank-worthy, if a Man for Conscience toward God endure Grief suffering wrongfully. If when ye do well and suffer for it, ye take it patiently, this is acceptable with God. For even hereunto were ye called, because Christ also suffered for us, leaving us an Example, that ye should follow his Steps.*

Here the Apostle founds the Duty of Servants being subject to Masters, who treat them *injuriously*, upon the *common Doctrine* of Christianity; because to suffer *wrongfully* is thank-worthy before God, and because Christ's Example has called us to bear with Patience those injurious and wrongful Hardships.

Let it therefore be carefully observed, that as sure as the Apostle here speaks by the Spirit of God, so sure is it that our Behaviour is not thank-worthy or acceptable with God, unless we endure wrongful Sufferings with Patience, and that if we lay aside this Meekness, we leave the Example of Christ, who only saves such as follow his Steps.

I have now gone through several Instances of that Mortification, Self-denial, and Suffering, to which the Christian World are called.

---

* Heb. ii. 10.

If the Doctrines of this Chapter seem hard and grievous, they can only seem so to such, as have wrong Notions of human Life.

Too many People imagine this Life to be something, that is substantial in itself, and valuable for its own Goods, and look upon Religion as something that is added to it, to make a worldly Life more easy, regular, and happy ; and so embrace Religion with no other Spirit, nor to any further Degree, than as it complies with the Ease, Order, and Happiness, of that Way of Life in which they live.

Our blessed Saviour has fully confuted this Opinion, by teaching us, that there is but *one Thing needful.* If therefore we are but so far Christians, as to believe that what our Saviour has here taught, is strictly true, then all the pretended Grievances of Self-denial and Suffering are all struck off at once.

For what though Meekness, Patience, and Humility, may often make us Sufferers, yet if such Sufferings make us only lose such Things as are *not needful* for us, where is any Ground for Complaint ?

But further, such Sufferings are not only without any real Hurt, but they promote our Happiness, and become Matter of real and solid Joy.

Blessed are ye, when Men shall revile you, and persecute you, and shall say all manner of Evil of you falsely for my Sake, rejoice and be exceeding glad, for great is your Reward in Heaven.*

Christ does not endeavour to comfort us in this State, as if it were a *hard* or *melancholy* State, which we must bear because it is made easier with Patience, or because God has pleased to impose it upon us, but he looks at it in quite another View, not as needing Comfort, but as having Matter fit for Congratulation.

What Christians are they therefore, what Strangers to the Spirit of Christ, who reckon those Things amongst the Hardships of Religion, which Christ recommends to us as Reasons of *rejoicing,* and being *exceeding* glad ?

The whole Matter therefore plainly comes to this, if our Sufferings, our Injuries, or Hardships, be such as we undergo, because we dare not depart from that Meekness, and Patience, and Charity, which Christ has taught, because we had rather love our Enemies than be revenged on them, rather suffer like Christ, and be full of his Spirit, than avoid Sufferings by a contrary Temper, such Sufferings are our greatest Gains.

If on the contrary, you know of any Meekness and Patience which is not after the Example of Christ, any Injuries or Suffer-

---

* Matt. v. 11.

ings which you can resist, and yet show that you follow the Example of Christ's Patience, and Meekness, and Charity, the Doctrine of this Chapter has no Recommendation of such Sufferings.

You are only here exhorted to bear such Injuries and Sufferings as make you more like Christ, such as are true Instances of that Meekness, Patience, and Charity, which were the principal Tempers of his Spirit.

Now be the Hardships or Self-denials what they will, if they make us more like to Christ, they have done more for us, than all the Prosperity in the World can do ; and he that defends himself at the Expense of any Temper, that was the Temper of Christ, has done himself an Injury, greater than the worst and most powerful of his Enemies can bring upon him.

And all this is founded upon this one Reason, because there is but *one Thing needful*, the Salvation of our Souls. It is this that changes the Natures of all human Things, and makes everything good or evil only so far as it promotes or hinders this *one End* of Life. The Salvation of the World is the only Happiness of the World, and he that has secured his Share in that, has secured to himself all the Joy and Gladness that can befall human Nature.

A Christian therefore that is not content with Salvation, that wants to add a worldly Joy and Pleasure to the great Things of Religion, is more senseless than the Man, who should think he had hard Usage to be saved from a *Shipwreck*, unless he were carried off upon a *Cedar Plank*.

Chapter VII.

Some further Considerations upon the Reasonableness of Self-denial.

BEFORE I proceed any further in other Instances of Self-denial, it may be proper to show in what the Duty of Self-denial is founded, or wherein the Reasonableness and Necessity of it consists.

Every Duty or Virtue of the Christian Life is founded in Truth and Reason, and is required because of its Fitness to be done, and not because God has Power to command what he pleases.

If we are commanded to be meek and humble, it is because Meekness and Humility are as true Judgments, and as suitable to the Truth of our State, as it is a true Judgment and suitable to the State of every dependent Being to be thankful for Mercies.

If we are bid to rejoice, it is at something that is truly joyful; if to fear, it is to fear something that is really dreadful. Thus we are called to no Tempers but such as are so many true Judgments, and as truly founded in the *Nature* and *Reason* of Things, as if we were bid to believe *two* to be the half Part of *four*.

God is Reason and Wisdom itself, and he can no more call us to any Tempers or Duties, but such as are strictly reasonable in themselves, than he can act against himself, or contradict his own Nature.

As we can say with Assurance, that God cannot lie, so we may with the same Certainty affirm, that he cannot enjoin anything to rational Creatures, that is contrary to the Reason of their Nature, no more than he can enjoin them to love Things that are not lovely, or hate Things that are in their Nature not hateful.

When God speaks, we are as sure that infinite Reason speaks, as we are sure there is a God.

A little Reflection upon this Matter, will give us the utmost Assurance in such Reasonings as this.

As sure therefore as there is a God, so sure is it that a Religion from God has only reasonable Commands to reasonable Creatures. No Tempers can be imposed upon us by Way of *Task* and *Imposition*, which we might as reasonably be without, if it were not required of us. God can only will, that reasonable Creatures should be more Reasonable, more Perfect, and more like Himself, and consequently can enjoin us no Duties, or Tempers of Mind, but such as have this Tendency. All his Commands are for our Sakes, founded in the Necessities of our Natures, and are only so many Instructions to become more Happy, than we could be without them.

A good Man who enjoys the Use of his Reason, is offended at *Madmen* and *Fools*, because they both act contrary to the Reason of Things. The *Madman* fancies himself, and everything about him, to be different from what they are; the *Fool* knows nothing of the Value of Things, is ridiculous in his Choices, and prefers a *Shell* before the most useful Things in Life.

Now a good Man merely through the Love of Reason, is offended at their Conduct, and would do all that he could to abate the *Frenzy* of the one, and the *Stupidity* of the other.

Let this a little represent to us the Conduct of God towards fallen Man. God is *Reason* itself, how highly therefore must he be offended at the Follies and Stupidity of Mankind? If a *Madman* seems so unreasonable a Creature to us, because he fancies himself to be *something* that he is not, how unreasonable must fallen Man, who is fallen from all true Knowledge of himself, appear to him who is infinite Reason?

Again, God is *Goodness* itself, if therefore human Goodness is inclined to endeavour the Cure of *Madmen* and *Fools*, must not Goodness itself be much more inclined to correct the Madness and Folly of fallen Man?

We see that Men are said to be *Mad*, when they fancy themselves and the things about them to be different from what they are; they are said to be *Fools*, when they mistake the *Value* of Things. Now if this be true, as it most certainly is, it may serve to show us, that Man in his present State of Disorder and Ignorance, must appear to God, both as *Fool* and *Mad*; for every Sinner is truly *Mad*, as he imagines himself, and all things about him, to be what they are not; he is really a *Fool*, as he is ridiculous in his Choices, and mistakes the *Value* of Things.

Now Religion is our *Cure*, it is God's merciful Communication of such Rules and Discipline of Life, as may serve to deliver us from the *Infatuation* and *Ignorance* of our fallen State. It is to teach us the Knowledge of ourselves, and all things about us, that we may no longer act like Madmen; it is to teach us the true *Value* of Things, that we may know our good and evil, and not be as *Idiots* in the Choice of Things.

Now Fools and Madmen have their Paradise, and are pleased with their imaginary Happiness; this makes them averse from all Methods of Cure.

For this Reason, God presses his Instructions upon us with Terrors and Threatenings, and makes those Virtues which are the natural Good and Cure of our Souls, such Duties to him, as he will punish the Neglect of them.

So that the Power of God is mercifully employed to move us to such a reasonable Way of Life, as is necessary for our Happiness.

Some People are so weak, as to wonder, what we call Sin should be so odious to God, or what it can signify to God, whether we are *Wise* or *Foolish.*

Let such consider, that God is *Wisdom* and *Reason* itself, and consequently everything that is contrary to Reason and Wisdom, is contrary to his Nature; so that a State of Sin, is a State of Contrariety to God. To ask therefore why God hates all Sin, is the same thing as to ask, why God cannot tell any Sort of *Lie*, it is because every Deviation from Truth is contrary to his Nature, which is Truth itself, so every Instance of Sin, as it is an unreasonable Act, is contrary to his Nature, who is *Reason* itself.

There is therefore a necessity from the Nature of Things, that every Creature be delivered from Sin, before it can enter into the beatific Presence of God; for if God could reward wicked Beings, and make them Happy by the Enjoyment of his Presence, he would as much cease to act according to the Nature of Things, as if he should punish a Being that lived in Innocence, for to punish Innocence, and to reward Sin, are equally contrary to the *Nature* and *Reason* of Things.

This Observation may teach us to admire the Excellency of the Christian Religion, which restores Sinners to God by so *great an Atonement* for Sin, and which only admits the *Repentance* and Devotion of fallen Man, through the *Merits* and *Mediation* of the Son of God.

To return, Let such People also consider, that even reasonable Men have a necessary Dislike of Fools and Madmen, they cannot possibly make them the Objects of their Pleasure and Affection.

But now if some things are so odious in themselves, that even the Reason of Man cannot but abhor them, how much more odious, how much more contrary to the Perfection of the divine Nature, must the Folly and Madness of Sin be?

Thus if we consider what Reason is in ourselves, that it necessarily dislikes unreasonable Persons as well as Things, we may have some Notion, how all Sin and Sinners, that is, all Beings which act contrary to *Reason*, must be in a State of the utmost Contrariety to God, who is the *highest Reason.*

God is Love, yet it is certain, that he can only love such Things as are Lovely; so God is *Goodness,* yet he cannot make Sinners Happy, because there is as much Contradiction to Reason and Perfection in making Sinners Happy, as in loving things that are not truly Lovely, or in hating things, that are not Hateful. This may serve to give us in some Measure a true Idea of the Nature of Religion and the Nature of Sin.

That Religion is God's gracious Method of delivering us from the Unreasonableness and Corruption of our Natures, that by complying with its Rules and Discipline, we may be so altered in our Natures, so restored to Reason, as to be fit for the Rewards of an infinitely Wise and Perfect Being.

That *Sin* is the Misery and Disorder, the Madness and Folly of our Nature, which as necessarily separates us from God, as God is contrary to all Unreasonableness.

I have just mentioned these things, to help us to conceive rightly, what is meant by the Reasonableness and Necessity of those Tempers which Religion requires. As I hope this is sufficient to give anyone a positive Assurance, that Religion is so far from being an Imposition upon us, consisting of needless Duties, that it is founded in the Nature and Reason of Things, and is as necessary to restore us to the Enjoyment of God, as it is necessary that God should love things according as they are Lovely.

For let anyone carefully consider this Proposition, whether it be not absolutely certain, that God loveth all things, accordingly as they are Lovely. Is not this as certain as that God is Reason itself? Could he be infinitely Reasonable, or Reason in Perfection, if he did not regard things according to their Natures? hating only those things that are truly Hateful, and loving things so far as they are Lovely? To act by any other Rule, than the Reason and Nature of Things, is to act by Humour and Caprice.

Let this therefore teach us, that as we are in ourselves, so we are necessarily either odious, or acceptable to God.

So far as we cease from Sin, and suffer ourselves to be made Wise and Reasonable, by the Wisdom and Reason of Religion, so far we make ourselves Objects of the Love of that infinitely perfect Being, who necessarily loves Beings as they are lovely in their Nature.

And so far as we continue in the Madness and Folly of Sin, and neglect the Rules of Religion which would deliver us from the Guilt and Slavery of it, so far we make it necessary for that perfect Being to hate us, who cannot but hate things accordingly as they are in themselves Hateful.

Some People, either through Self-love, or some confused Opinion of God and Themselves, are always fancying themselves to be *particular* Favourites of God, imagining all their little Successes, or Blessings in their Health and Circumstances above other People, to be distinguishing Marks of God's *particular* Kindness towards them.

But such Persons must consider that God is *Reason* itself, that he is subject to no *particular* Fondness, no more than he is capable of Weakness, and that he can no more love them, with any *particular* Love, that is not an Act of the highest Reason, than he can lie, or act contrary to the Truth.

They should consider that the Things of this Life, its Successes and Prosperities, are so far from being Marks of God's particular Favour, that Afflictions have a much better Claim to it, *for whom the Lord loveth he chasteneth, &c.*

When such People fancy themselves in the *particular* Favour of God, they should consider, that to be loved by God, is to be loved by *infinite Reason* and Wisdom, and that Reason can only love or approve Things as they are conformable to it. To be approved by Reason, we must act conformably to Reason, and to be approved by the highest Reason, we must act conformably to the highest Reason.

So that when our Lives are conformable to the highest Reason, then may we believe that so far as they are such, so far are they in the Favour of God, who is the highest Reason. To fancy that anything else can make us Favourites of God, is mere Ignorance and Pride, and owing to the same Vanity and Self-love, which makes some People think that they are admired and esteemed by all that know them.

For so sure as God is Reason itself, so sure is it, that to be loved by God, and to be approved by the highest Reason, is the same thing ; so that if he whose Life is not conformable to the highest Reason, imagines that he is particularly beloved by God, he is guilty of the same Absurdity, as if he believed that God is not the highest Reason, or Reason in Perfection.

It is not more certain that there is but one God, than it is certain that there is but one Way of making ourselves Objects of his Love, namely, by conforming and acting according to the highest Reason. When our Lives are agreeable to Reason, and the Nature of Things, then are our Lives agreeable to God.

Now so far as we act conformably to Religion, so far we act according to the highest Reason, and draw near to God, by a Wisdom that comes from God, and was revealed unto us, that it might make us such reasonable Beings, as to be fit Objects of his eternal Love.

For a Religion from God must be according to the Nature of God, requiring no other Change of Thoughts or Actions, but such as is conformable to Truth and Reason.

Now the Reasonableness of Actions consists in their Fitness to be done ; there is a Reasonableness in being thankful for Mercies, there is a Reasonableness in rejoicing at Things that are joyful, and so in all other Actions or Tempers they are either reasonable or unreasonable, as they are agreeable or contrary to the Nature of Things.

This is what I would have understood by the Reasonableness of all religious Duties or Tempers ; they are all required, because they are as suitable to the Nature and Reason of Things, as it is suitable to the Reason of Things, to be thankful for Mercies, or fear Things that are truly dreadful.

Thus for Instance, Humility is nothing else but a *right Judg-*

ment of ourselves, and is only so far enjoined, as it is suitable to the Truth of our State ; for to think worse of ourselves than we really are, is no more a Virtue, than to take *five* to be less than *four*.

On the contrary, he that is proud, offends as much against Truth and Reason, and judges as falsely of himself, as the *Madman* who fancies himself to be a King, and the *Straw* to which he is chained, to be a *Throne* of State.

Having observed thus much concerning the Reasonableness of Tempers or Duties, which Religion demands, I proceed now to show, wherein the Reasonableness and Necessity of Self-denial consists.

If a Person was to walk upon a *Rope* across some great River, and he was bid to deny himself the Pleasure of walking in *silver Shoes*, or looking about at the Beauty of the Waves, or listening to the Noise of Sailors, if he was commanded to deny himself the Advantage of *fishing* by the Way, would there be any Hardship in such Self-denial ?   Would not such Self-denials be as reasonable, as commanding him to love Things that will do him good, or to avoid Things that are hurtful ?

Strait is the Gate, and narrow is the Way that leadeth unto Life, saith our blessed Saviour.   Now if Christians are to walk in a *narrow Way that leadeth to Eternal Life*, the chief Business of a Christian must be, to deny himself all those Things which may either stop or lead him out of his narrow Way.   And if they think that Pleasures and Indulgences are consistent with their keeping this narrow Way, they think as reasonably, as if the Man upon the Rope should think, that he might safely use silver Shoes, or stop in his Way to catch Fish.

Again, If a Man that was a Slave to Sottishness, and stupefying Pleasures, that rendered him averse from all Exercises of the Mind, was yet obliged in order to save his Life, to attain to such or such a Degree of mathematical Knowledge, must it not be as necessary for such a one to deny himself those Indulgences which increased his Stupidity, as it would be necessary to study the Relations of Figures ?

Now this is the Foundation of all Christian Self-denial; we are born and bred in Slavery to Sin and corrupt Tempers, and are only to be saved by putting off this old Man, and being renewed in Holiness and Purity of Life. The Denials therefore of Religion, are only the necessary Means of Salvation, as they are necessary to lessen the Corruption of our Nature, destroy our old Habits, alter the Taste and Temper of our Minds, and prepare us to relish and aspire after Holiness and Perfection.

For since our Souls are in a State of Corruption, and our Life is a State of Probation, in order to alter and remove this Corruption, it is certain, that every Thing and every Way of Life which nourishes and increases our Corruption, is as much to be avoided, as those Things which beget in us Purity and Holiness, are to be sought after.

A Man who wants his Health, is as well and for the same Reasons to avoid such Things as nourish his Illness, as he is to take Medicines that have a healing Quality. Self-denial is therefore as essential to the Christian Life, as Prayer is, it being equally necessary to deny ourselves such Things as support our Corruption, as it is necessary to pray for those Things which will do us good, and purify our Natures.

The whole of the Matter is this, Christians are called from a State of Disorder, Sin, and Ignorance, to a State of Holiness, and Resemblance of the Divine Nature. If therefore there are any Things, or any Ways that corrupt our Minds, support our Vanity, increase our Blindness, or nourish Sensuality, all these are as necessarily to be avoided, as it is necessary to be holy.

If there are any Denials or Mortifications that purify and enlighten the Soul, that lessen the Power of bodily Passions, that raise us to a heavenly Affection, and make us taste and relish the Things that be of God, these are as necessarily to be practised, as it is necessary to believe in Jesus Christ.

So that the Matter comes to this, if there are no Indulgences in *eating* that do us Harm, then *fasting* is of no Use, but if there are, if they enslave the Soul, and give it a sensual Taste, then we are as much obliged to abstain from what does us this Harm, as we are obliged to pray for anything that can do us good.

No Christian who knows anything of the Gospel, can doubt whether *fasting* be a common Duty of Christianity, since our Saviour has placed it along with secret Alms, and private Prayer. *When thou fastest, anoint thy Head, and wash thy Face, that thou appear not unto Men to fast, but to thy Father which is in secret, and thy Father which seeth in secret shall reward thee openly.**

So that the same Instructions and the same Reasons are given for *private fasting*, as for *secret Alms* and private *Prayer*, that thy Father who seeth in secret, may reward thee openly. Now as it is manifestly entitled to the same Reward, it is manifestly put upon the same Foot, as private Prayer, and as equally acceptable to God.

Eating and Drinking are the common Support of Life, but then as they are the Support of a corrupt Life, the Nourish-

---

* Matt. vi. 17, 18.

ment of a disordered Body that weighs down the Soul, whose Appetites and Tempers are in a State of Enmity with the Life and Purity of the Soul, it is necessary that we take care so to support the Life of the Body, as not to occasion the Sickness and Death of the Soul.

The Fall of Man consists very much in the Fall of the Soul into the Dominion and Power of the Body, whose Joy, and Health, and Strength, is often the Slavery, Weakness, and Infirmity, of the Soul.

How far our Bodies affect our Habits, or Ways of Thinking, may be seen by the Difference between Sickness and Health, Youth and Old Age. These different States of the Body, alter the whole Turn of our Minds, and give us new Ways of Thinking, all owing to the different Strength of bodily Appetites and Tempers. No sooner is the Body weakened by any Occasion, but the Soul is more at Liberty, speaks higher for itself, and begins to act more reasonably.

What is the Reason that a *Midnight* Reflection goes generally deeper than a Thought at any other time? No Reason can well be assigned, but the Peace and Tranquillity of the Body, which gives the Soul a Liberty of seeing further into Things, than at any other time.

The Difference between the same Man full and fasting, is almost the Difference of two Persons ; a Man that in the Morning finds himself fit for any Meditations, is after a full Meal changed into another Creature, fit only for idle Amusements, or the Yawnings of an Animal.

He has not only created a Dulness in his Soul, but has perverted its Taste; for he can be pleased with a *Romance* or *impertinent* History, at the same time that he has no Relish for a Book of Devotion, that requires less Attention.

I mention this to show, that *fasting* has a nearer Relation to all *religious* Tempers, than is generally thought, and that indulgent or full Feeding does not only dull the Mind, but more particularly gives it a Dullness towards the Things of Religion. If it were not thus, a Book of religious Reflections would be as acceptable at such Times, as those other Books which require as much, or more Attention.

And the Reason of this is plain, because all our Tempers and Desires are always suitable to the State we are in ; if we are in a State of sensual Joy, feeling the Happiness of a *full Stomach* and *heated Blood*, we relish or desire nothing but what suits with it. For this Reason *Plays*, and *Romances*, and vain Diversions, can entertain a Man that has eat as long as he could, but Lectures upon *Morality*, or Discourses upon *Death* and *Judgment*, would tire him into Sleep. What we observe of the *Jaundice,* that it makes us see all things *yellow,* is in a certain Degree true of every *State* of the Body; it makes us conceive things with some Degree of Likeness to the Condition it is then in. Every Alteration in the Body, gives some Alteration to our way of conceiving the same Things.

As he therefore that would see things in their proper Colours, must first cure himself of the *Jaundice,* so he that would apprehend things according to their Natures, must take care that his Body be so ordered, as to have as little a Share as possible in his Judgments.

When a Man has his Stomach full of Wind, and feels no pleasant Enjoyment of his Body, you can hardly propose anything to him, that will appear reasonable : Do but stay till his Stomach is altered, till he has had a full and cheerful Meal, and he will be as naturally in a better Temper, as any other Animal that has filled its Belly.

When Men have been unreasonably out of Temper, through the mere Motions of the Body, I believe they often condemn themselves afterwards, but then they do not consider, that the contrary State, is a State of the same Slavery to the blind Motions of the Body, and liable to the same Condemnation. For if a *full* and *pleasant* Meal, makes us so *gay* and *cheerful,* as to laugh and be pleased with the *vainest Things,* we are then as unreasonable, and as mere Slaves to our Bodies, as when a *cold* or *empty* Stomach shall make us angry at everything.

For it is as great a Contradiction to Reason and Wisdom, to be pleased with Things or Persons, because our Body is in a State of Joy, as it is to be Angry and Displeased at Things or Persons, because an easterly Wind, or an undigested Meal has soured our Spirits.

Now both these States, are equally States of Slavery to the Body, equally expose our Folly, and have the same Contrariety to Religion. A Man is as far from religious Wisdom, when *full feeding* has made him merry, *vain,* and *trifling,* as when a *contrary State* of Body makes him *sour, angry* and *fretful.*

It is the Business therefore of Religion, to put an end to these States of Slavery, to deliver Man from these blind Laws of *Flesh* and *Blood,* and give him a Wisdom and Constancy, a Taste and Judgment suitable to the Reason and Wisdom of the Laws of God. To fill our Souls with such Principles of Peace, as may give us Habits of Tranquillity, superior to the changeable Tempers of our Bodies.

Now *Fasting,* as it is a Denial of *bodily Indulgences,* as it disciplines the Body into a State of Obedience, and contradicts its Appetites, is the most constant and universal Means of pro-curing Liberty and Freedom of Mind.

For it is the Love of our Body, and too much Care of its Enjoyments, that makes us too sensible of its Demands, and subject to its Tempers. Whatever we nourish and cherish, so far gains an Interest in us, and rules us in the same Degree, that it has got our Affections. Till therefore Religion has entered us into a State of Self-denial, we live in a State that supports the Slavery and Corruption of our Natures.

For every Indulgence of the Body in Eating and Drinking, is adding to its Power, and making all our Ways of Thinking subservient to it.

A Man that makes every Day, a Day of *full* and *cheerful* Meals, will by Degrees make the Happiness of every Day depend upon it, and consider everything with regard to it.

He will go to *Church* or stay at home, as it suits with his *Dinner*, and not scruple to tell you, that he generally eats too heartily to go to the Afternoon Service.

Now such People are under a worse Disorder of Body, than he who has the *Jaundice*, and have their Judgment more per-verted, than he who sees all Things *yellow*.

For how can they be said to perceive the Difference of Things, who have more Taste for the Preparations of the *Kitchen*, than for the Joys and Comforts of the House of God, who choose rather to make themselves *unfit* for Divine Service, than to balk the Pleasure of a *full Meal*? And this not by Chance, or upon some unusual Occasion, but by a constant intended Course of Life.

Let such People deal faithfully with themselves, and search out their Spirit. Can they think that they are *born again of God*, that they have the *Spirit of Christ*, who are thus subject to the Pleasures of *Gluttony*? Can they be said to treat their Bodies as *Temples* of the Holy Ghost, who make them *unfit* for the holy Service of public Worship? Can they be said to offer their Bodies unto God, as a *reasonable, holy*, and *living* Sacrifice? Can they be said to *love God with all their Heart, and all their Soul*, or to have *forsaken all* to follow Christ, who will not so much as forsake *half a Meal* for the sake of Divine Worship?

I know it will be thought too severe that I have called this *Gluttony*, because it is the Practice of Numbers of People of Worth and Reputation ; but I hope they will turn their Dislike of the Name, into a Dislike of the Thing, for it is as certainly *Gluttony*, as picking of Pockets is stealing.

The Sin of *Gluttony* is the Sin of Over-eating, of being too much given to full Meals. Now this may be difficult in some

Instances to state exactly, yet he who owns he eats so much as renders him *indisposed* for the public Worship of God, has determined against himself, and put his own Case out of all Question. For if there be such a Sin, as the Sin of Over-eating, it must surely then be committed when we eat too much to attend upon the Service of the Church.

Men may fancy that they are only chargeable with *Gluttony*, who eat till they *surfeit* their Bodies ; they may think those only guilty of *Drunkenness*, who drink till they have lost their Senses. But there is a much surer Rule to go by, given them by the Spirit of God. *Whether ye eat or drink, or whatsoever ye do, do all to the Glory of God.* All therefore in Eating and Drinking that is not within the Bounds of the Glory of God, is offered to something that is not the Glory of God, it is offered to the Corruption and Sensuality of our Natures, it is the Sin of Intemperance, and has the Sin of Indevotion added to it, when it is indulged at a time, that keeps us from the public Worship of God.

Let such People examine their own Hearts, and see what Opinion they have of Divine Service. Can they look upon it, as doing God's Will on Earth as it is done in Heaven? Can they look upon it, as entering into the Presence of God, as approaching the Throne of Grace? Can they esteem it to be the Nourishment and Support of their Souls, a necessary Means of securing the Divine Assistance, as a most acceptable Way of pleasing God, and securing their eternal Happiness, who are not afraid to eat and drink till they are indisposed and unwilling to attend at it? If they still have just Notions of the Nature of Divine Service, let them think of these Words of our blessed Saviour, *If ye know these Things, happy are ye if ye do them.*

But if they look upon it as of less Concern than a *full Meal*, if they think that there is no Occasion for *Exactness* in it, it is time they were told, that they have *not the Love of God abiding in them.*

For if they did really *hunger and thirst after Righteousness*, which is the true Love of God, they would rejoice at every Opportunity of entering further into his Favour ; they would go to the House of God, the Abode of his Presence, with more Joy than to any other Place, and think those Days the most happy, that were most devoted to the Cares and Joys of a Life with God to all Eternity.

They would cut off a *right Hand*, or pluck out a *right Eye*, rather than be hindered from those Helps, which are to raise their Hope, enliven their Faith, and form their Souls to a Delight and Joy in God.

If they want this Zeal towards God, they want a Zeal which is the Life and Spirit of a Christian, which distinguishes a Disciple of Christ from those who live without God in the World.

I have spoken the more home to this Point, because it is so allowed a Practice, which as unavoidably destroys the true Spirit and Temper of Religion, as any Things that are notoriously sinful.

Indeed a constant Course of full Feeding is the Death of the Soul, and every Day that is a Day of such Happiness, is a Day lost to Religion.

When a Man has rejoiced himself with full Eating and Drinking, he is like any other *Animal*, disposed only to *Play* or *Idleness*. He has no more Feeling of Sin than he has of *Hunger*, can no more perceive himself to be a *miserable fallen* Creature, than he can perceive himself to be a *Beggar*, and consequently is no more affected with any *Forms of Confession* or Repentance, than if he was every Day to confess, that he was a *starving Beggar*.

For this Course of *Self-enjoyment* is as contrary to Humility, Contrition, and a true Sense of Sin, as it is contrary to a State of *Beggary and Want*, and consequently a Man in such Happiness, can no more sincerely deplore the *Weight of Sin,* than he can feel himself in the *Misery of Poverty.*

If therefore Religion is to be the State and Temper of our Minds, if it is to be the ruling Taste and Relish of our Souls, if its Goods and Evils are to govern our Actions, it is as necessary to renounce Sensuality, and mortify our Bodies, as it is necessary to resist Temptations. For Abstinence or Self-denial is not only a good, advisable, and reasonable Practice, but is a constant, necessary, and universal Duty, and enters further into the Cure of our Souls, than any other Practice. It is as necessary for a Christian who would get rid of the Disorders of his Nature, and lessen the Weight of Sin, as it is necessary for a Man in a *Dropsy* to abstain from *Drink*, or a Man in a *Fever* to refrain from such Things as *inflame* his Blood.

Indeed this Self-denial is the chief and most general Exercise of the Christian Life, and is the very *Form* and *Substance* of every Virtue; for so far as we deny our natural Tempers, so far we seem to be advanced in Virtue.

We are so far humble, as we deny ourselves in the Instances of Pride, so far heavenly-minded, as we deny our earthly Inclinations, so far charitable, as we deny our Tempers of Self-love and Envy; and so in every Virtue, it seems to have its chief Foundation in the Denial of some corrupt Temper of our Natures.

I know some People object, that *Fasting* is not an *universal* Duty, that it is rather like some particular *Medicine* or *Remedy*, that is only necessary for some particular Cases, and particular Constitutions.

To this it may be answered, that if by *Fasting*, is meant an entire Abstinence from all Food for such or such a certain Space of Time, that Fasting in that Sense, is not an universal and constant Duty. But then it ought to be observed, that this is no more the Nature of Fasting, than any *particular Form* of Confession of such or such a Length, is the precise Nature of Repentance.

For as Repentance does not consist in any stated fixed Degrees of Sorrow and Pain for Sin, which is to be the *common* Repentance for *all* Men, in *all* States, and at *all* Times, but is such an Exercise of Grief and Contrition, as is suited to everyone's particular State, so *Fasting* is not any *fixed Degree* of Abstinence from *all* Food, which is to be the *common* Measure of Fasting to *all* Men, in *all* States, and at *all* Times, but is such an Exercise of Abstinence and Self-denial, as is proper to everyone's particular State.

Now if we understand Fasting in this Sense in which it ought to be understood, as an Abstinence from such Food and such Pleasures and Degrees of Feeding as are proper in every State of Life, to destroy Sensuality, lessen the Corruption of our Natures, and make us relish and taste spiritual Enjoyments, in this Sense Fasting is as *constant and universal* a Duty, as Repentance.

For as Repentance is an universal Duty, because the Reason of it is common to all Men, so this Fasting is necessary to all Men, because Sensuality, fleshly Lusts, and the Corruption of bodily Tempers, is the *universal* Corruption of all Men.

It is sometimes also objected, that Fasting cannot be an universal Duty, because some People's Constitutions will not suffer them to eat enough for their Health.

To this it may be answered, that some People may be so infirm, that they cannot attend at the *public Worship* of God, yet surely public Worship is an *universal* Duty, though some People's Constitutions may make them incapable of going to it.

Secondly, This Objection is only of Weight against Fasting, as it signifies an entire Abstinence from all Food for a certain Space of Time, but is of no Force against such an Abstinence, as I have shown to be the *common Duty* of all Christians.

Thirdly, Persons of weak and infirm Constitutions, have often as much Necessity of Self-denial, as others of the most healthful Bodies; for their very State, it may be, has taught them Indulgence, by being accustomed to so much Care of themselves, they become no better than perpetual Nurses of themselves, and consequently are too much devoted to that, which is not the *one Thing needful.*

Weakly People may as well be *Epicures*, and have the same *Sensuality* to conquer, as other People, and consequently have the same Necessity of their Degree of Abstinence and Denial, that others have.

Let such People have recourse to the Example of *Timothy*, who was an apostolical Bishop.   His History teaches us, that he was weakly, and subject to frequent Infirmities, who notwithstanding he may be supposed to have enjoyed the *extraordinary* Gifts of the Holy Ghost, yet in this state of Divine Greatness, and Bodily Weakness, he wanted the *Authority* and *Advice* of an Apostle to persuade him to drink anything besides Water.   This we are sufficiently taught, by the Apostle's giving this Advice in his Epistle to him, *Drink no longer Water,* that is, nothing but Water, *but use a little Wine for thy Stomach's Sake, and thine often Infirmities.*

Lastly, The World abounds with People who are weakly and tender merely by their Indulgences ; they have bad Nerves, low Spirits, and frequent Indispositions through Irregularity, Idleness, and Indulgence.

Now these People, it is true, are not *fit for Fasting*, and, perhaps if they were to deal faithfully with themselves, they would find that they are as unfit for most other Exercises of Religion ; and consequently if their Condition might be pleaded as an Objection against the Necessity of Fasting, it might as well be pleaded against the Necessity of half the Duties of Christianity.

Upon the whole Matter it appears, that Fasting is a constant universal Duty, and that it is liable to no other Exceptions, than such as are common to several other great Duties of Religion.

It is no *fixed Degree* of Sorrow that is the common Repentance of all Men, it is no *particular Sum* of Money that is the common Charity of all Men, it is no *fixed Form*, or *Length*, or *Hour* of Prayer, that is the common Devotion of all Men, yet all these are *constant* and *universal* Duties.

In like Manner, though *Fasting* may be subject to all the same Variations, yet is it a *constant* and *universal* Duty.

Justus is a grave sober Man, he is very angry at those People who neglect or ridicule *Fasting;* he thinks they know nothing of Religion.

Thus far *Justus* is very right, and knowing thus much, one would wonder that he is so inconsistent with himself, for presently after this, *Justus* will tell you, that he never fasts but upon *Good-Friday* and the *Thirtieth of January*.

If *Justus* had lived before the Murder of King *Charles*, he had had but one Fast in the Year, yet in all Likelihood he would have then stood up for the *Doctrine* of Fasting.

If a Man were to be angry at those who neglect or despise the *Service of the Church*, as People who know nothing of Religion, and then tell you that he himself never goes thither, but on *Good-Friday* and the *Thirtieth of January*, you would say that he knew nothing of the Nature of Church-Service.

Now *Justus* shows the same Ignorance of the Nature of Fasting.

For if Prayer and Repentance, and the *Service* of the Church, were not *common Acts* of Devotion, and right and necessary Ways of worshipping God, they would not be necessary upon *Good-Friday*, or any other particular Day.

In like Manner, unless *Fasting* were a *common* and *necessary* Part of Religion, something that was always a proper Means of applying to God, it would neither be *necessary*, nor *acceptable*, on those particular Days.

For it is not the Day that makes the Duty to be *necessary*, but the Day happens to be a *proper* Occasion of exercising a necessary Duty.

Some great *Calamity* happens to you, you do very well to make it an Occasion of exercising great Devotion; but if you stay till some other Calamity happens, before you pray again, or think that Prayer is only *proper* in Times of *Calamity*, you know nothing of Devotion.

It is the same thing in *Fasting;* some great Occasion may justly call you to it, but if you forbear Fasting, till such great Occasions happen again, or think that Fasting is only *proper* for such *public Occasions*, you know nothing of the Nature of Fasting.

If *Justus* were to say that he never *repents* but on those public Days, he might as easily defend himself, as when he says, he only *fasts* at those Times.

For is there any Benefit in Fasting on those particular Days? Does it add anything to your Piety and Devotion? Does it make your Repentance and Sorrow for Sin more real and affecting? Does it calm and abate your Passions, lessen the Power of your Body, and put you in a better State of Devotion, than when you take your usual Meals? If it has not something of this Effect, where is the Use of it at such Times when you would have your Devotions the best performed? And if it has this Effect, how comes it that you will have but one or two such

8

Days in the Year? Why will you not thus affect your Soul, thus assist your Devotions, thus discipline your Body, thus allay your Passions, thus raise your Heart, thus humble yourself till the *Day* comes, on which King *Charles* was Murdered? Is not this like staying till then, before you *repent?*

Our Blessed Saviour saith, *But thou, when thou fastest, anoint thine Head, and wash thy Face, that thou appear not unto Men to fast, but unto thy Father which is in secret, and thy Father which is in secret shall reward thee openly.* *

Here our Saviour's Advice relates wholly to *private Fasting,* to which other People are to be Strangers, to such a Fasting as is a secret Service to God, who will therefore highly reward it. Yet *Justus* tells you that he *fasts* only twice in the Year, and that on *public* Days. Now what is this to be called, is it Weakness, or Perverseness?

If you were to ask me whether *frequent, private* Prayer, be a necessary Duty, I should think it sufficient to read to you the following Passage, *But thou, when thou prayest, enter into thy Closet, and when thou hast shut thy Door, pray to thy Father which is in secret, and thy Father which seeth in secret shall reward thee openly.*

Nothing need be added to this Authority; the Necessity and Advantage of private Prayers is here so expressly taught, that there is no room left to doubt about it.

Justus readily acknowledges all this, how comes it then, *Justus,* that you know nothing of the Necessity and Advantage of *private Fasting?* How comes it that the same Authority and the same Words do not teach you as much in one place as in another? Has not our Saviour expressed himself exactly in the same Manner, and given the same Advice, and proposed the same Reward, to private Fasting, as to private Prayer?

Further, when the Disciples of our Lord, could not cast the evil Spirit out of a Man, who was a *Lunatic,* he not only tells them, that it was through want of Faith, but also gives them a very important Instruction in these Words, *Howbeit this kind goeth not out, but by Prayer and Fasting.*†

Now does this look, as if Fasting were an occasional Thing, only for a Day or two in the Year? Is it ranked with Prayer as having the same *common Nature,* as being equally prevailing with God? And is not this sufficient to teach us, that we must think of Fasting, as we think of Prayer; that it is a proper Way of Devotion, a right Method of applying to God? And if that Prayer is most prevailing, and enters furthest into Heaven, which

---

* Matt. vi. 17. † Matt. xvii. 21.

is attended with Fasting, it is proof enough surely, that Fasting is to be a common ordinary Part of our Devotion.

Is it sufficient and powerful enough to cast out *Devils*, and cure *Lunatics*, and shall we neglect it, when we pray against the evil Tempers and Passions which possess our Hearts ? Shall we not pray to God in the most powerful prevailing Manner that we can ?

If we were to Fast without Praying, would not this be a Way of Worship of our own Invention ? And if we Pray and neglect Fasting, is it not equally choosing a Worship of our own ? For he that has taught us the Use and Advantage of Prayer, has in the same Words taught us the same Things of Fasting, and has also joined them together, as having the same Power with God.

If therefore *Justus* will take his Religion from Scripture, he must own, that Fasting is of the Nature of Prayer, that it has the same Authority from Christ, and that he who only Fasts on a public Day or two in a Year, no more observes the whole Duty of Christian-fasting, than he who only attends some public yearly Days of Prayer, can be said to fulfil the whole Duty of Christian Devotion.

To proceed, we may also observe, that the Reason of Self-denial and Abstinence is constant and perpetual, because we are perpetually united to a Body, that is more or less fit to join with our Souls in Acts of Holiness, according to the State that it is in.

As therefore it is always necessary to take Care what Thoughts and Inclinations we indulge in our Minds, so it is equally necessary, that we be constantly careful, how we alter the State of our Bodies, or indulge them in such Gratifications, as may make them less fit for the Purposes of an holy Life.

For since there are *States* of the Body, which favour Holiness, and these States depend much upon our Manner of Living, it is absolutely necessary, that we avoid every Degree of Indulgence, every Kind of Irregularity and Idleness, or other Course of Life, that may make our Bodies less Active, less *Pure*, and less *conformable* to the Duties of Religion.

And this is to be done, as I said before, not only as a reasonable and advisable Thing, but as of the utmost necessity, it being as essential to Holiness, to purify our Bodies, and practise a strict Temperance, as it is necessary to practise a strict Charity.

Now Christian Temperance is no more that, which may pass for Temperance in the Sight of Men, than Christian Charity, is that which is visible to the World.

A worldly Man may think himself sufficiently Temperate,

8—2

when he only abstains from such Excesses, as may make him fitter to enjoy an healthful *Sensuality*.

But Christian Temperance is of quite another Nature, and for other Ends, it is to put the Body into a State of *Purity*, and *Submission*, and give the Soul a divine and heavenly Taste.

It is therefore to be observed, that Christian Temperance is never enough practised, but when it puts the Body in the fittest State for Devotion and other Acts of Holiness, when our Bodies have all that Good done to them, have all that Purification, and right Tempers which Abstinence and Self-denial can give them, then do we practise Christian Temperance.

There is no other Rule than this to go by, for since Christian Temperance is in order to Holiness, Purity, and heavenly Affection, he can only be said to be *truly* Temperate, whose Temperance is most serviceable to the *highest* Degrees of Holiness.

And to stop short of any known Degrees of Temperance, is like stopping short of any known Degrees of Charity. It is therefore as necessary to practise all the Exercises of Self-denial, and strict Abstinence, as it is necessary to aspire after real Holiness.

For as our Bodies are constant and Home-Enemies, and have a mighty Influence in all our Actions, so far as we preserve them in a State suitable to Holiness, so far we preserve ourselves fit for the Exercise of Religion.

It is out of all question that there is a Purity and Impurity of our Bodies, as well as of our Souls, that is, there are some States and Tempers of our Bodies, that favour and incline to Acts of Virtue, and others that as much incline to all Sorts of Sensuality.

This is as certain, as that *Gluttony* and *Drunkenness* disposes Men to all Sorts of Sins, and give them a Disrelish for all Kinds of Holiness. For as these States of Life have the utmost Contrariety to Religion, so every *Approach* towards them, is in a *certain Degree* partaking of them.

A man who lives in such a State, as not to be called either a *Glutton*, or a *Drunkard*, may yet be so near them, as to Partake of those Tempers and Inclinations, which are the Effects of Gluttony and Drunkenness.

For there are such Degrees in these, as in other Ways of Life. A Man may be vain and uncharitable, yet not so as to be remarkable for his Vanity and Uncharitableness, so he may be also under the Guilt and evil Effects of Eating and Drinking, though not so as to be esteemed either a Glutton or Intemperate.

So that the only Security for a good Christian, is to make it the Care of his Life, to resist all Enjoyments that cherish Vanity and Uncharitableness, not only in such Degrees as are *scandalous* and *visible* in the Eyes of Men, but such as *inwardly* hurt the Humility and Charity of his Mind.

In like manner as to eating and drinking, he is constantly to practise such Abstinence, as may secure him not only from Sensuality in the Sight of the World, but such as may best *Alter, Purify,* and *Humble* his Body, and make it the holy Habitation of a Soul devoted to a spiritual Life.

St. Paul saith, *I therefore so run, not as uncertainly ; so fight I, not as one that beateth the Air.   But I keep under my Body, and bring into subjection, lest that by any Means when I have preached to others, I myself should be a Castaway.*

Let it here be observed, that the Apostle practised this Self-denial and Mortification, not only as a good and advisable Thing, and suitable to Holiness, but as of the last Necessity. It was not, as he was an *Apostle,* and that he might be fitter for the miraculous Gifts of the Holy Ghost, but it was to secure his Salvation, lest when he had preached to others, he should be a *Castaway.*

Let it be considered that this Apostle, who lived in *Infirmities, in Reproaches, in Necessities, in Persecutions, in Distresses for Christ's Sake, who was also full of Signs, and Wonders and mighty Deeds, and who had been caught up into the third Heavens,* yet reckons all his Virtues as insecure, and his Salvation in Danger, without this severity of Self-denial ; he thought all his other Advancements in Piety, without this, to be as vain a Labour, as *beating the Air.*†

So run I, saith he, *not as uncertainly,* by which he plainly teacheth us, that he who does not thus run, who does not thus mortify the Body, runs uncertainly, and fighteth to as little Purpose, as he that beateth the Air.

Can they therefore who live in Ease, and Softness, and bodily Indulgences, who study and seek after every Gratification, be said to be of St. *Paul's* Religion, or to be governed by that Spirit, which governed him ?

An Apostle preaching the Gospel with Signs and Wonders in the midst of Distress and Persecution, thought his own Salvation in Danger, without this Subjection of his own Body, and shall we who are born in the Dregs of Time, who have no Works like his to appeal to, think it safe to feed and indulge in Ease and Plenty ?

---

* 1 Cor. ix. 26.   † 2 Cor. xii.

A Man may indeed practise the outward Part of a Christian, he may be Orthodox in his Faith, and regular in the Forms of Religion, and yet live in Ease and Indulgence. But if he would *put on Christ*, and be clothed with the Humility and Meekness of his true Disciples, if he would *love* his Enemies and be in Christ a *new Creature*, if he would live by *Faith* and have his Conversation in Heaven, if he would be *born again* of God, and *overcome* the World, he must lay the Foundation of all these Graces in the Mortification and Subjection of his Body. For not only Religion, but Reason, can show us, that almost every ill Temper, every Hindrance of Virtue, every Clog in our Way of Piety, and the Strength of every Temptation, chiefly arises from the *State* of our Bodies.

Chapter VIII.

The Subject of Self-denial further continued.

THERE are no Truths of Christianity more plainly delivered in the Scriptures, or more universally acknowledged by all Christians, than these two, viz., the *general Corruption* of human Nature, and the *absolute Necessity* of divine Grace. Now these two Doctrines make the Reason and Necessity of a continual Self-denial, plain and obvious to the meanest Capacity ; and extend it to all those Things or Enjoyments, which either strengthen the Corruption of our Nature, or grieve the Holy Spirit of God, and cause him to leave us.

Let anyone but reflect upon the Nature of these two fundamental Truths, and he will find himself soon convinced, that all those Enjoyments are to be abstained from, which either support our natural Blindness and Corruption, or resist and abate the Inspirations of the Holy Spirit.

He will find also, that this Self-denial must extend itself to every Day of our Lives, unless he can find a Day when he is free from Weakness, or out of the Way of all Temptations, a Day which offers nothing suitable to the Corruption of his Nature, or nothing contrary to the good Motions and Directions of the Holy Ghost. Most People acknowledge this in general, they think it right to avoid Things which strengthen our Corruption, and *grieve* the Spirit of God, but then not conceiving this with any sufficient Exactness, they think that an Abstinence from gross Sins, is a sufficient Security.

But let such People consider, that the Corruption of our Nature is like any other bodily Illness, that never keeps at one Stand, but is either increasing or abating by everything that we do.

A *Dropsy* or a *Gangrene* is not only increased by Drunkenness, or disorderly Indulgences, but receives constant Strength by all little Indulgences that suit with it.

Now the Corruption of our Nature is an inbred Distemper, that possesses us in the Manner of a *Dropsy* or *Gangrene;* if we give into notorious Sins, we become Slaves to this Corruption, and are straightway dead in Sin.

But though we keep clear of such great Offences, yet if we indulge or allow ourselves in such Practices, as suit with the Corruption of our Nature, we as certainly nourish a slow Death, and destroy ourselves by Degrees, as a Man in a *Dropsy*, who abstains from Drunkenness, yet allows himself in such Ways as will not suffer his Distemper to abate.

Now as little Allowances that continually increase a Distemper, will as certainly in Time make it mortal, as if it had been urged on by violent Methods, so little Indulgences which increase the Corruption of our Nature, as certainly tend to a spiritual Death, as other more irregular Methods.

It is therefore absolutely certain, that our *Self-denial* is to be as *universal* as the Means of our Corruption, that it is to last as long as our Disorder, and is to extend itself to every Thing and every Way of Life, that naturally increases it; and this, for as necessary a Reason, as a Man in a *Dropsy*, is not only to abstain from Drunkenness, but from every Indulgence that increases his Distemper.

A State of *Regimen* therefore, that is, a State of holy Discipline, is as necessary to alter the Disorder of our Nature, as it is necessary to remove any distempered Habit of Body.

Let it be considered, that the Corruption of our Nature is but very weakly represented, by comparing it to these Distempers ; that they rather express the Manner of its Cure, and the Necessity of labouring after it, than set forth the Degree of the Disorder.

For a Man in these Distempers, may have only some Part affected with them ; but the Corruption of our Natures is as extensive as our Natures : It is the Corruption of every Faculty and every Power, it is Blindness in our Understandings, it is Vanity in our Wills, Intemperance in our Appetites, it is Self-love, Anger, Lust, Pride, and Revenge, in our Passions, it is

Falseness, Hypocrisy, Hatred, and Malice, in our Hearts.   Now all this, and more than this, makes the miserable Corruption of human Nature.

So that it is as necessary that our Lives be a State of *Regimen*, that we live by such Rules as are contrary to this Variety of Disorders, as it is necessary for a Man under a Complication of habitual Distempers, to enter into a *Course* of Regularity.

I suppose it will be readily granted, that all Tempers are increased by Indulgence, and that the more we yield to any Disposition, the stronger it grows ; it is therefore certain, that *Self-denial* is our only Cure, and that we must practise as many Sorts of Self-denial, as we have ill Tempers to contend with.

Pride, Hypocrisy, Vanity, Hatred, and Detraction, are all disorderly Indulgences, and have their only Cure in Self-denial, as certainly as Drunkenness and Sensuality.

To deny one's self all Indulgences of Pride and Vanity, all Instances of Falseness and Hypocrisy, of Envy, and Spite, requires greater Care and Watchfulness, and a more continual Self-denial, than to avoid the Motives to Intemperance.

And he who thinks to render himself humble, any other Way than by *denying* himself all Instances of Pride, is as absurd as he who intends to be sober, without abstaining from all Degrees of Intemperance.   For *Humility* as truly consists in the Practise of Things that are *humble*, as *Justice* consists in the doing Things that are *just*.

Every Virtue is but a *mere Name*, an empty Sound, till it shows itself by an Abstinence from all Indulgences of the contrary Vice, till it is founded in this Self-denial.

Now this is readily granted to be true in all sensual Vices, that they are only to be cured by a perpetual Self-denial.

But the Practice of the same Self-denial is as absolutely required, to destroy every ill Temper of the Mind, as any sort of Sensuality.

Self-love, Pride, Vanity, Revenge, Hypocrisy, and Malice, are acknowledged to be very gross Sins, and indeed they are of the very Nature of the Devil, and as certainly destroy the Soul, as Murder and Adultery.

But the Misfortune is, that we govern ourselves in these Tempers, not by what is sinful according to the Principles of Religion, but by what is odious in the Eyes of the World.   We don't labour to avoid the *Sin*, but are content to avoid what is *scandalous* in it.

Thus for Instance, People would not be thought proud, but then they are afraid of no Degrees of it, but such as the World condemns ; they don't form their Lives by the Scripture-Rules of Humility, but only endeavour to be decent and fashionable in their Pride.

Others would be very sorry to be remarked for an envious and malicious Spirit, who at the same time make the Faults of their Acquaintance the Pleasure of their Lives, and turn all their Conversation into Evil-speaking and Detraction.

Now all this proceeds from hence, that they govern themselves by the Spirit of the World; the World allows of Evil-speaking and Detraction, and therefore they practise it openly, though it is as contrary to Religion, as Murder and Injustice.

And thus it will be with all these wicked Tempers, till we practise an universal Self-denial, and labour after a religious Perfection in all our Ways of Life.

We are certainly under Habits of Pride, till we are governed by Humility, and we are not governed by Humility till we deny ourselves, and are afraid of every Appearance of Pride, till we are willing to comply with every Thing and every State, that may preserve and secure our Humility.

No Man is governed by a religious Justice, till he is exact in all Degrees of it, till he denies himself all Approaches towards Injustice, till he fears and abhors every Appearance of Fraud, and Crafty Management.

Now it is this Temper and State of Mind that is the Measure of every Virtue.

A common *Liar* may hate some Sorts of Lies, an *unjust* Man may avoid some Sorts of Injustice, so a *proud* Person may dislike some Instances of Pride, but then he has no more Title to Humility, than an unjust Man has a Title to Integrity, because there are some Sorts of Injustice that he avoids.

So that it is not any single Acts, or any particular Restraints, but it is an uniform State and Temper of the Mind, that stands constantly disposed to every Degree of Humility, and averse from every Degree of Pride, that is to denominate a Person to be truly humble.

To measure any virtuous Temper by any other Standard than this, is not to measure ourselves by Religion. How can anyone be said to be religiously *chaste*, unless he abhors and avoids *all* Instances of Lewdness and Impurity ? How could he be said to be *sincerely* pious, unless he was fearful of *every* Occasion of Sin ?

Must it not therefore be the same in Humility and every other Virtue ? Can anyone be reckoned *truly* humble, till he denies himself *all* Instances of Pride ?

Self-denial therefore is so universally necessary, that it is the Foundation of every Virtue ; Humility and Charity requiring more Self-contradiction and Self-denial, than the strictest Temperance.

From these Observations we may be able to pass a true Judgment upon ourselves as to our State of Virtue. If we are denying ourselves, we are so far labouring after Virtue ; but if *Self-love*, if *Idleness* and *Indulgence*, be the State of our Lives, we may be sure that we are as distant from true Religion, as the *Sot* is distant from strict Temperance.

A Life of Idleness, Indulgence, and Self-love, is an entire Resignation of ourselves to every Vice, except such as cannot be committed without Trouble ; and we may assure ourselves, that if we are in this State, we are not only Strangers to Virtue, but ready for every Sin that suits with Ease and Softness.

Persons of this Turn of Mind, lose the very *Form* of Piety, and find it too great a Contradiction to their Idleness, to comply with the very outward Appearance of Religion. They would be oftener at *Church*, but it may be, their *Seat* is crowded, and they can sit with more Ease by their Fire-Side at Home. They would be more exact in kneeling when they are there, if they had always the same Ease in kneeling.

I mention these Particulars, as only small Instances of that general Deadness and Indisposition towards all Parts of Religion, which this Spirit of Idleness and Indulgence creates. For it affects People in the same Manner as to every other part of their Duty, and makes them incapable of attending to it. For a Person that is too idle and self-indulgent to undergo the *constant Trouble* of public Worship, must be at a great Distance from those Virtues, which are to be acquired by *Care* and *Watchfulness*, which are to *crucify* us to the World, and make us alive unto God.

Ambition and worldly *Cares* distract the Mind, and fill it with false Concerns, but even these Tempers are in a nearer State to Religion, and less indispose the Soul to it, than Idleness and Indulgence. For Ambition and worldly Cares, though they employ the Mind wrong, yet as they employ it, they preserve some Degree of Activity in it, which by some Means or other may happen to take a right Turn ; but *Idleness* and *Indulgence* is the Death and Burial of the Soul.

I have been more particular upon this Temper, because it is so common, and even acknowledged without Shame. People who would not be thought *Reprobates*, are yet not afraid to let you know that they hardly do anything but *eat*, and *drink*, and *sleep*, and take such *Diversions* as suit with their Ease ; whereas if such a State of Life be examined by the Rules of Reason and Religion, it will appear as dangerous and frightful, as any other

Reprobate State of Sin. For it is a State that nourishes all the Corruption of our Nature, that exposes us to all the Vanity of the World, and resigns us up to all the Power of the Devil.

Did we design to set ourselves in the fairest Posture for the Devil to hit us, we ought to choose that of Idleness and Indulgence.

Watch and pray, saith our Saviour, *that ye fall not into Temptation.* The Devil's Advice is, be idle and indulge, and then ye will yield to every Temptation. For if Watching and Prayer have any Tendency to prevent our falling into Temptation, it is certain that Idleness and Indulgence must in an equal Degree make us incapable of resisting them.

To return. As certain therefore as our Nature is in a State of Corruption, as certain as this Corruption consists in ill Tempers and Inclinations, so certain is it, that if we would not die in our Sins, we must enter upon such a Course of Life as is a *State of Denial* not only to this or that, but to *all* those corrupt Tempers and Inclinations.

For since Man is only a Compound of corrupt and disorderly Tempers, it is as necessary to deny himself, as to resist Evil; and he is indeed only so far virtuous, as he has put off himself, and is guided and governed by another Spirit.

When we speak of Self-denial, we are apt to confine it to Eating and Drinking; but we ought to consider that though a strict Temperance be necessary in these Things, yet these are the easiest and smallest Instances of Self-denial. Pride, Vanity, Self-love, Covetousness, Envy, and other Inclinations of the like Nature, call for a more constant and watchful Self-denial, than the Appetites of Hunger and Thirst.

Till therefore we make our Self-denial as universal as our Corruption, till we deny ourselves all Degrees of Vanity and Folly, as earnestly as we deny ourselves all Degrees of Drunkenness, till we reject all Sorts of Pride and Envy, as we abhor all Kinds of Gluttony, till we are as exact in all Degrees of Humility, as we are exact in all Rules of Temperance, till we watch and deny all irregular Tempers, as we avoid all Sorts of Sensuality, we can no more be said to practise Self-denial, than he can be said to be Just, who only denies himself the Liberty of stealing.

And till we do enter into this Course of universal Self-denial, we shall make no Progress in true Piety, but our Lives will be a *ridiculous Mixture* of I know not what, *sober* and covetous, proud and *devout, temperate* and vain, *regular* in our Forms of Devotion, and irregular in all our Passions, circumspect in *little Modes* of Behaviour, and careless and negligent of *Tempers* the most essential to Piety.

And thus it will necessarily be with us, till we lay the Axe to the Root of the Tree, till we deny and renounce the whole Corruption of our Nature, and resign ourselves up entirely to the Spirit of God, to think and speak and act by the Wisdom and Purity of Religion.

Let it be supposed that Religion required us to forget a *Language* that we loved, and had been bred in, and constantly to speak in a Language that was *New* and *Difficult*.

Could we possibly forget our former Language that we loved, and was natural to us, any other Way, than by denying ourselves the Liberty of ever speaking it ?

Could we forget it by only forbearing to use it on some particular Occasions ? Would it not be as necessary to abstain from thinking, reading, and writing in it, as to abstain from using it in Conversation ? Could we render our new Language any other Way habitual or natural to us, than by making it the Language of *all* Seasons ?

Now this may teach us the absolute Necessity of an universal Self-denial, for though Religion does not command us to part with an old *Language* that we love, yet it commands us to part with an *old Nature*, and to live and act by a new Heart and a new Spirit.

Now can we think to part with an *old Nature* by fewer Rules of Abstinence, than are necessary to get rid of an old Language ? Must we not deny ourselves the Liberty of ever acting according to it ? Can we get rid of it by only denying it in particular Instances ? Must it not be as necessary to abstain from all its Ways of thinking and wishing, liking and disliking, as to practise any Abstinence at all ? For if the whole is to be changed, if a *new Heart* is to be obtained, we are doing nothing, whilst we only renounce it in part; and can no more be said to live by a new Heart, than they can be said to speak only a new Language, whose general Conversation is in their old natural Tongue.

Indeed a little Attention to the Nature of Man, and the Nature of Christianity, will soon convince us, that *Self-denial* is the very Substance, the beginning and ending of all our Virtues. For,

First, Christianity, is the *Cure* of the Corruption of our natural State. Now what is the Corruption of our natural State ? Why it consists chiefly in *Tempers, and Passions, and Inclinations that fix us to bodily and earthly Enjoyments, as to our proper good.*

Now how is it that Christianity cureth this Corruption of our Nature ? Why it cureth this Corruption of our Nature, by teaching us to live and act by *Principles of Reason and Religion.*

What are these Principles of Reason and Religion?

They are such as these:

First, That God is our *only Good*, that we cannot possibly be happy, but in such Enjoyment of him, as he is pleased to communicate to us.

Secondly, That our Souls, are immortal Spirits, that are here only in a *State of Trial* and *Probation.*

Thirdly, That we must all appear before the Judgment-Seat of God, to receive the Sentence of eternal Life, or eternal Death.

These are the chief Principles of *Reason and Religion*, by which every Christian is to live; judging and thinking, choosing and avoiding, hoping and fearing, loving and hating according to these *Principles*, as becomes a Creature, that is sent hither to prepare himself to live with God in everlasting Happiness.

Now who does not see, that this resolves all our Religion into a State of *Self-denial*, or Contradiction to our natural State?

For first, what can be a greater Self-denial, or more Contradictory to all our habitual Notions, and natural Sentiments, than to live and govern ourselves, by a Happiness that is to be had in *God alone?* A Happiness, which our Senses, our old Guides, neither see, nor feel, nor taste, nor perceive? A Happiness, which gives us neither *Figure* nor *Dignity*, nor *Equipage*, nor *Power*, nor *Glory* amongst one another?

Look at Man in his natural State, acting by the Judgment of his Senses, following the Motions of his Nature, and you will see him acting, as if the World was full of infinite Sorts of Happiness.

He has not only a thousand imaginary Pleasures, but has found out as many Vexations, all which show, that he thinks *Happiness* is everywhere to be found, for no one is vexed at any Thing, but where he thinks he is disappointed of some possible Happiness.

The Happiness therefore of Religion, which is an Happiness in *God alone*, is a great *Contradiction* to all our natural and habitual Tempers and Opinions, not only as it proposes a Good, which our Senses cannot relish, but as it leads us from all those imaginary Enjoyments, upon which our Senses have fixed our Hearts.

To think of Religion in any other Sense, than as a State of *Self-denial*, is knowing nothing at all of it. For its whole Nature is to direct us by a Light, and Knowledge, and Wisdom from God, which is all contrary to the Darkness, Ignorance, and Folly of our Natures.

It is therefore altogether impossible for any Man to enter into the Spirit of Religion, but by *denying himself*, by renouncing all his *natural Tempers* and Judgments, which have been formed by the blind Motions of Flesh and Blood, and strengthened by the Example and Authority of the World. He cannot walk in the *Light* of God, but by rejecting the *Dreams* of his Senses, the *Visions* of his own Thoughts, and the *Darkness* of worldly Wisdom.

We may let our Senses tell us, what we are to *eat* and *drink,* or when we are to *sleep,* we may let them teach us, how near we may draw to a *Fire,* how great a *Burden* we may carry, or into how deep a Water we may go ; in these Things they are our proper Guides.

But if we appeal to them to know the *true Good* of Man, or the proper Happiness of our *rational* Nature, if we ask *them* what *Guilt* there is in Sin, or what *Excellence* there is in Piety, if we consult them as our Guides and Instructors in these Matters, we act as absurdly, as if we were to try to *hear* with our *Eyes,* or to *see* with our *Ears.*

For our Senses are no more fitted to tell us our *true Good,* as we are Christians and rational Creatures, than our *Eyes* are fitted to instruct us in *Sounds,* or our *Ears* in *Sights.*

Religion therefore has just so much Power over us, as it has Power over our *natural Tempers,* and the Judgments of our Senses, so far as it has made us *deny* ourselves, and reject the Opinions and Judgments of Flesh and Blood, so far has it settled its Power within us.

Hence appears the absolute Necessity of our Saviour's Proposal to Mankind, *If any Man will come after me, let him deny himself and follow me.*

For it plainly appears from the Nature of the Thing, that no Man can follow Christ, or walk in the Light that he walked, but by *denying himself,* and walking contrary to the Darkness and Errors of his own Heart and Mind.

All our Ways of thinking and judging of the Nature and Value of Things, are corrupted with the Grossness and Errors of our Senses.

We judge of every Thing in the same Manner, that the *Child* judges of his *Playthings,* that is, it is by our Senses alone that we pass the Judgment, though we think that we act with the *Reason of Men.*

The World is made up of *fine Sights,* Equipage, Sports, Show and Pageantry, which please and captivate the Minds of Men, because Men have yet the Minds of *Children,* and are just the same Slaves to their Senses, that Children are.

As Children and Men see the *same Colours* in Things, so

Children and Men feel the *same sensible* Pleasures, and are affected with external Objects in the same Manner.

But the Misfortune is, that we laugh at the little Pleasures, *poor* Designs and *trifling* Satisfactions of Children, whilst at the same time, the *Wisdom* and *Ambition* and *Greatness* of Men is visibly taken up with the *same Trifles.*

A *Coach and Six* and an *Embroidered Suit* shall make a great *Statesman* as happy, as ever a *Go-cart* and *Feather* made a Child.

When a Man thinks how happy he shall be with a great Estate, he has all the same Thoughts come into his Head, that a Child has, when he thinks what he would do with a great Sum of Money ; he would buy twenty *little Horses,* he would have twenty *fine Coats,* and all *fine Sights,* and the like.

Now promise but a Man a great Estate, and you will raise all these same Thoughts and Designs in his Mind.

Now whence can all this proceed, but from this, that Men act with the *same Vanity* of mind, are under the *same poor* guidance of their Senses, are as ignorant of their *true Happiness,* as great Strangers to their *own Nature,* and as far from a true Sense of their *relation* to God, as when they first set out in Life.

And is not this a plain Argument of the Reasonableness and Necessity of *Self-denial ?* For to indulge ourselves and live according to our *natural Tempers* and Judgments, is to grow old in the Follies of Childhood. And to deny ourselves, is to save ourselves, as it is denying such Tempers and Judgments as are contrary to our eternal Happiness.

To proceed, let us take another view of the weakness and disorder of our Nature, that we may still see a greater Necessity of not walking according to it.

When we see People *drunk* or in a violent Passion, we readily own, that they are, so long as that continues, in a State of *Delusion,* thinking, saying, and doing irregular Things by the mere *Force* of their Blood and Spirits. In these States we all see and acknowledge the Power of our *Bodies* over our Reason, and never suppose a Man capable of judging or acting wisely, so long as he is under the violence of *Passion* or heated with *Drink.*

Now this is more or less the constant State of all Mankind, who are by bodily Impressions, and the Agitations of the Blood and Spirits, in the same kind of *Delusion,* as Men that are *Drunk* or in a *Passion,* though not always in the same Degree.

A Man that is Drunk has heated his Blood to that Degree, that it sends up Spirits to the Brain in too violent a Motion, and in too great a quantity. This violent Motion of the Spirits, raises so many Ideas in the Brain, and in so Disorderly a Manner, that the Man is every Minute different from himself, as fast as different or new Ideas are raised in his Head by the impetuous Course of the Spirits. This is the disorder of a Man that is *Drunk*.

Now this is the State of all People more or less, when they appear to one another as Sober.

For first, Drunkenness is a State of disorder and Delusion, because our Heads are then filled with a Crowd of Ideas, which we have little or no power over, and which for that Reason distract our Judgment.

Now this is in a certain Degree the State of all Men, whilst they are in the Body ; the Constitution of our Bodies, and our Commerce with the World is constantly filling our Heads with Ideas, and Thoughts, that we have little or no Power over, but *intrude* upon our Minds, alter our Opinions, and *affect* our Judgments in the same Manner, as they disorder the Minds of those who are Drunk.

Let anyone but try to *Meditate* upon any the most Important Doctrine of Religion, and he will find the Truth of this Observation, he will find a Thousand Ideas crowd in upon him, in spite of all his Care to avoid them, which will hinder his Meditation, and prevent his seeing Things in that Light in which he would see them, if his Mind was empty of other Thoughts.

Now it is the same Cause that hinders him from Thinking *so well* as he would, that hinders the Drunken man from Thinking *at all ;* that is, an *Involuntary Succession of Ideas*.

So that every Man, so long as he is in the Body, is in some Degree weak and disordered in his Judgment, in the same Manner and for the same Causes, as People who are Drunk.

Secondly, Another Circumstance of *Drunkenness* is this, that Ideas and Thoughts are raised in a disorderly Manner, because the *Blood* is too much heated.

Now this is another constant Circumstance that attends Men in every State of Life.

For first, it is the same Thing whether our Spirits be heated with Liquor, or anything else, if they are heated, all the same Effects are produced.

This is undeniably true, because we daily see, that Passion will heat and disorder People in the same Manner, as they are, who are inflamed with Liquor.

Therefore our own *Thoughts* and *Imaginations* have the same effect upon our Spirits, as *Drink ;* so that it is the same Thing whether a Man be Drunk with Passion, or any violent Set of Thoughts, or heated with Liquor. There is the same Weakness of Mind, the same disordered Imagination, and the same wrong Apprehension of the Nature of Things.

Now though all People are not at all Times Drunk with *Passion*, or some *Violent* Imagination, yet they are always in a Disorder of the same Kind; they have something that affects and hurries their Spirits in the same Manner, that a Man's Spirits are affected in some violent Passion.

And the Reason is, because Men are always in some *Passion* or other, though not to that Degree as to be visible, and give Offence to other People.

We are always in a State either of *Self-love*, Vanity, Pride, Hatred, Spite, Envy, Covetousness or Ambition. Some one or other of these Passions is in some Degree affecting our Spirits in the same Manner, that any violent Passion, or heat of Liquor affects our Spirits, differing only in the Degree.

A silent *Envy*, a secret *Vanity*, which nobody sees, raises Thoughts in our Heads, and disorders our Judgments in the same Manner, as more violent Passions.

But you may increase the *Vanity*, and *Envy* till it ends in Distraction and Madness, as it sometimes happens, but then we may be sure, that it disordered our Understanding in the same Manner, and made us Foolish and Extravagant in some Degree, long before it came to Madness. Whilst therefore we are in the Body, we are constantly in a State of Disorder, like to those who are Drunk or in a violent Passion; we have some Passion or other, either of Self-love, Vanity, Envy or the like, that affects our Spirits, and disorders our Judgment, in the same Manner, though not in the same Degree, as their Spirits are affected, who are in the heat of Drink, or in some violent Passion.

Thirdly, Another Circumstance of Drunkenness is this, that it Forms us to a Taste and Temper peculiar to it, so as to leave a Dulness and Indisposition in the Mind toward any Thing else. An habitual Drunkard has no Pleasure, like that confused Hurry and Heat of Thoughts that arises from inflamed Blood. The repeating of this Pleasure so often has given him a Turn of Mind, that Relishes nothing but what relates to Intemperance.

Now this is the State of all People in some respect or other, there is some way of Life that has got hold of them, and given them a Taste and Relish for it, in the same Manner that Drinking has Formed the Drunkard to a peculiar liking of it. All People are not intemperate, but all are under Habits of Life, that affect the Mind in the same Manner, as Intemperance.

Some People have indulged themselves so long in *Dressing*, others in *Play*, others in *Sports* of the Field, others only in little

9

gossiping Stories, that they are as much Slaves to these Ways of Life, as the intemperate Man is a Slave to Liquor.

Now we readily own that a Man who has enslaved himself to the Pleasures of Drinking and Intemperance, has thereby rendered himself incapable of being a *reasonable Judge* of other Happiness and Pleasure; but then we do not enough consider, that we are hurt in the same Manner, by any other Way of Life, that has taken hold of us, and given us a Temper and Turn of Mind peculiar to it.

It is to as little Purpose to talk of Religion, or the Happiness of Piety, to a Person who is fond of *Dress*, or *Play*, or *Sports*, as to another who is intemperate; for the Pleasures of these particular Ways of Life make him as deaf to all other Proposals of Happiness, and as incapable of judging of other Happiness and Pleasure, as he who is enslaved to Intemperance.

A *Lady* abominates a *Sot*, as a Creature that has only the Shape of a Man; but then she does not consider that drunken as he is, perhaps he can be more content with the Want of *Liquor*, than she can with the Want of *fine Clothes:* And if this be her Case, she only differs from him, as one intemperate Man differs from another.

Thus it appears, that whether we consider the Nature, Circumstances, and Effects of Drunkenness, that all Mankind are more or less in the *same State* of Weakness and Disorder.

I have dwelt the longer upon this Comparison, because it seems so easily to explain the Disorder of our Nature. For as everyone readily sees how the bodily Disorders of Drunkenness, and violent Passion, blind and pervert our Minds, so it seems an easy Step from thence, to imagine how the Body, though in a *cooler State*, does yet disorder the Mind in the same Manner, though not in the same Degree. It is also easy to conceive, that if *violent Passion*, or a heated Imagination, confounds our Judgments, and gives us wrong Apprehensions of Things, that therefore *all Passions*, though more *still* and *secret*, must yet influence our Minds, and make us weak and disordered in our Judgments, in the same Manner, though not in the same Degree, as those are, who are in a violent Passion. So that the meanest Capacity may by this apprehend, that so long as we are in the Body, we are in a State of Weakness and Disorder, that is full of such Blindness and Delusion, as attends a State of Drunkenness and Passion.

It is intended by this Account of human Nature, to convince us of the *absolute Necessity* of renouncing ourselves, of denying all our Tempers and Inclinations, and resigning ourselves wholly to the Light and Wisdom of God. For since by our State of

Corruption and Slavery to the Body, we are always under the Power of its *blind Motions*, since all our Inclinations and Judgments are only the Judgments of heated Blood, drunken Spirits, and disordered Passions, we are under as absolute a Necessity of denying all our natural Tempers and Judgments, as of refraining from Intemperance.

For must a Man who is in a Fit of *violent* Passion, silence that Passion before he can judge of the ordinary Things of Life? Is it a State of such Blindness as makes him blind in the plainest Matters, and unable to judge rightly even of Things which he is acquainted with? And can we think, that our more *still* and *secret* Passions of Self-love, Pride, Vanity, Envy, and the like, make us less blind as to the Things of God, than a heated Passion does as to the Things of this World?

Will an inflamed Passion disorder a Man too much to judge of anything even in his own Business? And will not a Passion of *less Violence* disorder a Man's Judgment in Things of a spiritual Nature, which he never was rightly acquainted with, which he never saw or understood in the Manner that he ought, and which are all contrary to the Impressions of his Senses?

Everyone sees People in the World whom he takes to be incapable of *sober* Judgments, and *wise* Reflections, for this Reason, because he sees that they are full of themselves, blinded with Prejudices, violent in their Passions, wild and extravagant in their Imaginations.

Now as often as we see these People, we should reflect that we see *ourselves ;* for we as certainly see a *true Representation* of ourselves, when we look at such People, as we see a true Picture of our State, when we see a Man in the Sorrows and Agonies of Death.

You are not *dying* as this Man is, you are not in his State of Sickness and Extremity ; but still his State shows you your own *true Picture*, it shows you that your Life is in the *midst of Death*, that you have in you the Seeds of Sickness and Mortality, that you are dying, though not in his *Degree*, and that you are only at a little *uncertain Distance* from those, who are lying upon their last Beds.

When therefore you see Men living in the Disorders of their Passions, blinded with Prejudices, swelling in Pride, full of themselves, vain in their Imaginations, and perverse in their Tempers, you must believe, that you see as true a Representation of your own State, as if you saw a Man in his last Sickness.

You, it may be, are not in the Extravagance of his disordered Tempers, you are at some *uncertain Distance* from his State, but if you fancy that you are not corrupted with *Self-love,* not weakened by Prejudices, not blinded with Pride, not vain in your Imaginations, not ridiculous in your Tempers, because you are not in such Disorders as you find some People, you think as absurdly, as if you were to imagine yourself to be *immortal*, because you are not in that *Extremity* of Death, in which you see some People.

And as the true Way of knowing and being rightly affected with the Weakness and Mortality of our State, is frequently to view the Condition of *dying Men*, as Pictures of ourselves, so the most likely Means to affect us with a just Sense of the Corruption and Disorder of our Hearts, is to consider the Frailties, Corruptions, and Disorders, of other People, as certain Representations of the Frailty and Corruption of our own State.

When therefore you see the Violence of other Men's Passions, the Irregularity of their Tempers, the Strength of their Prejudices, the Folly of their Inclinations, and the Vanity of their Minds, remember that you see so many plain Reasons for *denying* yourself, and resisting your own Nature, which has in it the Seeds of all those evil Tempers, which you see in the most irregular People.

From the foregoing Reflections upon human Nature, we may learn thus much, that Abstinence, as to Eating and Drinking, is but a small part of Christian *Self-denial*.

The Corruption of our Nature has its chief Seat in the Irregularity of our Tempers, the Violence of Passions, the Blindness of our Judgments, and the Vanity of our Minds ; it is as dangerous therefore to indulge these Tempers, as to live in Gluttony and Intemperance.

You think it shameful to be an *Epicure*, you would not be suspected to be fond of *Liquor*, you think these Tempers would too much spoil all your Pretences to Religion ; you are very right in your Judgment, but then proceed a Step farther, and think it as shameful to be fond of *Dress*, or delighted with *yourself*, as to be fond of *Dainties*, and that it is as great a Sin to please any corrupt *Temper* of your Heart, as to please your *Palate ;* remember that Blood heated with *Passion,* is like Blood heated with *Liquor*, and that the Grossness of Gluttony is no greater a Contrariety to Religion, than the Politeness of Pride, and the Vanity of our Minds.

I have been the longer upon this Subject, trying every Way to represent the Weakness and Corruption of our Nature, because so far as we rightly understand it, so far we see into the Reasonableness and Necessity of all religious Duties. If we fancy ourselves to be wise and regular in our Tempers and Judgments, we can see no Reason for denying ourselves ; but if we find that our whole Nature is in Disorder, that our Light is Darkness, our Wisdom Foolishness, that our Tempers and Judgments are as gross and blind as our Appetites, that our Senses govern us as they govern Children, that our Ambition and Greatness is taken up with *Gewgaws* and *Trifles*, that the State of our Bodies is a State of Error and Delusion, like that of Drunkenness and Passion.

If we see ourselves in this true Light, we shall see the whole Reason of Christian *Self-denial*, of Meekness, and Poverty of Spirit, of putting off our old Man, of renouncing our whole Selves, that we may see all Things in God ; of watching and Prayer, and mortifying all our Inclinations, that our Hearts may be moved by a Motion from God, and our Wills and Inclinations be directed by the Light and Wisdom of Religion.

Religion has little or no hold of us, till we have these right Apprehensions of ourselves ; it may serve for a little Decency of outward Behaviour, but it is not the Religion of our Hearts, till we feel the weakness and disorder of our Nature, and embrace Piety and Devotion, as the Means of recovering us to a State of Perfection and Happiness in God.

A Man that thinks himself in *Health*, cannot lament the Sickness of his State.

If we are pleased with the Pride and Vanity of our Minds, if we live in Pleasure and Self-satisfactions, we shall feel no meaning in our Devotions, when we lament the Misery and Corruption of our Nature. We may have Times and Places to mourn for Sins, but we shall feel no more inward Grief, than *hired Mourners* do at a Funeral.

So that as the Corruption of our Nature, is the Foundation and Reason of Self-denial, so a right Sense and Feeling of that Corruption, is necessary to make us rightly affected with the Offices and Devotions of Religion.

I shall now show, that the reasonableness and necessity of Self-denial, is also founded upon another fundamental Doctrine of Religion, namely, the *Necessity* of *Divine Grace*, which I shall leave to be the Subject of the following Chapter.

Chapter IX.

Of the Necessity of Divine Grace, and the several Duties to which it calleth all Christians.

I COME now to another Article of our Religion, namely, the *absolute Necessity of Divine Grace,* which is another universal and constant Reason of *Self-denial.*

The invisible Operation and Assistance of God's Holy Spirit, by which we are disposed towards that which is good, and made able to perform it, is a confessed Doctrine of Christianity.

Our natural Life is preserved by some Union with God, who is the Fountain of Life to all the Creation, to which Union we are altogether Strangers ; we find that we are alive, as we find that we think, but how, or by what Influence from God our Life is supported, is a Secret into which we cannot enter. It is the same Thing with Relation to our spiritual Life, or Life of Grace, it arises from some *invisible Union* with God, or Divine Influence, which in this State of Life we cannot comprehend. Our blessed Saviour saith, *The Wind bloweth where it listeth, and thou hearest the Sound thereof, but cannot tell whence it cometh, and whither it goeth ; so is everyone that is born of God.** This shows us, how ignorant we are of the manner of the Operations of the Holy Spirit ; we may feel its Effects, as we may perceive the Effects of the Wind, but are as much Strangers to its manner of coming upon us, as we are Strangers to that exact Point, from whence the Wind begins to blow, and where it will cease.

The Spirit of God is like the Nature of God, too high for our Conceptions, whilst we are in these dark Houses of Clay. But our blessed Saviour has in some Degree helped our Conceptions in this Matter, by the manner of his giving the Holy Spirit to his Disciples. *And he breathed on them, and said unto them, receive the Holy Ghost.* Now by this Ceremony of breathing, we are taught to conceive of the Communications of the Holy Spirit with some likeness to Breath, or Wind, that its Influences come upon us in some manner most like to a gentle breathing of the Air. Representations of this kind are only

---

* John iii. 8.

made in Compliance with the Weakness of our Apprehensions, which not being able to conceive Things as they are in their own Nature, must be instructed, by comparing them to such Things as our Senses are acquainted with. Thus, the *Wisdom* and *Knowledge* that is revealed from God, is compared to *Light*, not because Light is a true Representation of the Wisdom of God, but because it serves best to represent it to our low Capacities. In like manner, the *Influences* of the Holy Spirit, are set forth by the Ceremony of *breathing* upon us, not because *Breath*, or *Air*, or *Wind*, are true Representations of the Gifts of the Spirit, but because they are the properest Representations, that yet fall within our Knowledge.

But that which is most necessary for us to know, and of which we are sufficiently informed in Scripture, is the *absolute Necessity* of this Divine Assistance.

We are used to consider those only as *inspired* Persons, who are called by God to some extraordinary Designs, and act by immediate Revelation from him. Now as Inspiration implies an *immediate Revelation* from God, in this Sense there has been but few inspired Persons ; but Inspiration, as it signifies an *invisible Operation*, or *Assistance* and *Instruction* of God's Holy Spirit, is the common Gift and Privilege of all Christians ; in this Sense of Inspiration, they are all *inspired Persons. Know ye not*, saith St. *Paul, that your Body is the Temple of the Holy Ghost which is in you.* St. *John* likewise, *Hereby know we that he dwelleth in us by the Spirit, which he has given us. For as many as are led by the Spirit of God, are the Sons of God.* Again, *Now if any Man hath not the Spirit of Christ, he is none of his.**
From these and many other Passages of the like Nature, it is undeniably plain, that the Life which we now live, is a Life in and by the Spirit of God, and that they are only Sons of God, who are led by this Spirit. Now this Doctrine plainly proves the Necessity of a constant Self-denial, for it must be necessary, that we deny ourselves all those Tempers and Ways of Life, which may make God *withhold* his Grace from us ; and likewise all those Enjoyments and Indulgences, which may make us *less able* and *less disposed* to improve and co-operate with those Degrees of Divine Grace, that are communicated to us.

Our blessed Saviour saith, *If any man love me, he will keep my words, and my Father will love him, and we will come unto him, and make our abode with him.*† This teaches us, how we are to *invite* the good Spirit of God to dwell in us : We are to *Prepare* ourselves for the Abode of this Divine Guest, by loving Christ

---

* Rom. viii. 9.   † John xiv. 23.

and keeping his Commandments. Whence we also learn, that the Spirit of God does not *equally Visit* all Persons in all ways of Life, but that we must *Prepare* ourselves for his Presence.

We are also told, that *God resisteth the proud, but giveth grace to the humble.* This also explains to us the Method of Divine Grace, that it is bestowed with regard to the *State* and *Temper* of Persons ; that there are some Dispositions which *separate* us from the Spirit of God, and others that procure to us a larger Share of its Gifts and Graces. We are also here Taught to consider *Pride*, not only as a Sin that has its particular Guilt, but as it has this certain Effect, that it *Extinguishes* the Divine Light, *deprives* us of God's Spirit, and leaves us to sink under the Corruption and Weight of our Nature.

We are to consider *Humility* also, not only as it is a reasonable Duty, and proper to our State, but as it *qualifies* and *prepares* us for larger Degrees of Divine Grace, such as may Purify and Perfect our Souls in all Manner of Holiness. All Instances therefore of Pride are to be avoided, all Sorts of Humility to be practised, not only for their own Sakes, but as necessary Preparatives for Divine Grace, that we may be *fit Temples* for the Holy Ghost to dwell in. Now seeing we are none of Christ's, if the Spirit of Christ be not in us, seeing we are only so far Christians, as we are renewed by the Holy Ghost, nothing can be more necessary to true Piety, than that we Form every Part of our Lives with regard to this Holy Spirit. That we consider all our *Tempers, Pleasures, Cares, Designs* and *Ways* of Life, whether they be such, as *suit* with the Wisdom and Heavenly Guidance of the Holy Spirit. This Doctrine shows us to ourselves in a *new Point* of View, and may serve to teach us several Truths, which we should otherwise not so readily apprehend.

When we are left to consider our Duty with relation to the express Commandments of God ; there are many ways of Life which we think ourselves at Liberty to follow, because they seem to be no plain Breach of any Commandment. But we are to look to a further Rule, and to consider our Pleasures and Cares, our Designs and Endeavours, not only whether they are contrary to the Letter of the Law, but whether they are according to the Spirit of God, for if they are contrary to the Spirit of God, if they suit not with his secret Inspirations, they are as truly to be avoided as if they were contrary to some express Commandment. For we are assured from Scripture, that they only are the Sons of God, *who are led by the Spirit of God,* and none can be said to be led by the Spirit of God, but they whose Lives are according to it, whose Actions, Cares and Pleasures,

Hopes and Fears are such, as may be said to be guided by the Motions of the Holy Ghost.

We are therefore to consider ourselves as *inspired Persons*, that have no Knowledge, or Wisdom but what comes from God, and that this Wisdom will no longer dwell with us, than so long as we act and conduct ourselves Conformably to it. So that we must not vainly deceive ourselves in saying, where is the harm of such *Indulgences*, or such *Vanities* and idle *Amusements*, but must consider, whether they are such as are Conformable to a Life that is to be directed by the Holy Ghost, whether they will *invite* his Assistance, and make him *delight* to dwell with us. In this Manner must we Examine and Try all our Ways of Life, as well our Cares as our Pleasures, and all our Tempers and Inclinations. For unreasonable Cares, as well as unreasonable Pleasures, are equally contrary to the Wisdom of the Holy Spirit, and equally separate us from him. People often think their Designs and Diversions Innocent because they are not *sinful* in their Nature, but they should also consider whether they are not *vain* and *foolish*, and *unsuitable* to the State and Condition of a Christian. For a Life of *Folly*, and *Vanity* and *trifling Designs*, is no more living by the *Spirit of God*, than a Life of *gross Sins*, is keeping the *Commandments*. So that the safest Rule to judge of our Actions by, is to consider them with relation to that Spirit, by which we are to be guided. Is this Design, or this Diversion according to the Wisdom of the Spirit of God? Am I in these Things improving the secret Inspiration of the Holy Ghost? Am I here governed by a Wisdom from above? Are these ways such as I can truly say, that I am led into them by the Spirit of God? Do I allow myself in them, because they serve to set forth the Glory of God, and are agreeable to the Condition of a Disciple of Christ? Are they good Proofs that the Spirit of God dwelleth in me, and that by thus Sowing to the Spirit, I shall of the Spirit Reap everlasting Life. This is the Rule of Perfection, by which Christians are to regulate their Thoughts, Words and Actions, for we are called by God to a State of Purity and Holiness, to act by the Motions of his Holy Spirit, and make no other Use of ourselves, or the World we are in, than such as is conformable to that Dignity of Life, and State of Glory to which we are called. The Spirit of our Religion is to be the Spirit of our Lives, the constant Principle of all our Tempers and Inclinations, which is to render us Reasonable, and Wise and Holy in all our Progress through the World.

The *Renewal* of our Hearts by the Spirit of God consists in *new Thoughts* and *new Desires*, in filling our Minds with great and sublime Truths, and in giving us Desires and Inclinations, Hopes and Fears, Cares and Pleasures suitable to them.

This is being born of the Spirit. Hence appears a plain Reason of an *universal Self-denial*, because the Spirit of the World and the Spirit of our corrupt Hearts, is in a State of Contrariety to this Spirit and Wisdom which is from above. So that it is to be the main Business and Labour of our Lives, to contradict those Motions of our Hearts, and those Tempers of the World, which are *contrary* to this Spirit, which is to be the Principle of our new Life in Christ.

We must therefore deny ourselves all those Ways of Life, all Cares and Enjoyments which too much possess our Minds, and render them insensible of these great Truths. We must Practise all that *Self-denial, Temperance, Abstinence, Care* and *Watchfulness* which can anyway *fit* and *prepare* our Minds to hear and receive, to comprehend and relish the Instructions and Doctrine which come from the Spirit of God. For all these Truths, every Thing that relates to God and Religion have a different Effect upon us, according to the State or Way of Life that we are in. As *Land* must be prepared to receive the best Seed, as *Rocks* can bring forth no Fruit, so unless our Minds are in some *proper State* and Disposition to *Co-operate* with the Holy Spirit, and receive his Instructions, his Gifts and Graces will bring forth no Fruit.

'Tis acknowledged by all, that a Life of *Intemperance* and *Debauchery* makes us dead and senseless of Religion, and incapable of receiving its Truths: But then it is not enough considered, that the *Vanity* of the Mind and Understanding busied in *Trifles*, an *impertinent Course* of Life, will as certainly produce the *same Effect*. If our Understanding is full of foolish Imaginations, devoted to Trifles, Religion can gain no Entrance. A Man may be so earnest in *picking Straws*, as to have no Leisure to think of his Salvation, nor any more Inclination to it, than one that is constantly in *Drink*. *Children* are incapable of Religion, not because they are *intemperate* and *debauched*, but because they have *little Minds*, that are taken up and employed with *little* and *trifling* Entertainments. Now if when we are Men, we have the Minds of Children, and have only changed our *Playthings*, we shall embrace and practise Religion just to as much Purpose as Children do: For a Mind taken up with *Gewgaws*, and *Trifles*, and impertinent Satisfactions, is in the same State, whether it be *four*, or whether it be *fifty Years* old. If it be made silly with *trifling* Concerns, and *false* Satisfactions, it is in a State of as much Disorder, and as contrary to Religion, as a State of *Gluttony* and *Intemperance*.

Thus poor *Amusements*, vain *Arts*, useless *Sciences*, impertinent *Learning*, false *Satisfactions*, a wrong *Turn of Mind*, a State of *Idleness*, or any the vainest *Trifles* of Life, may keep Men at as great a Distance from the true Impressions of Religion, and from living by the Spirit of God, as the *Ignorance* of Childhood, or the *Debaucheries* of Intemperance.

Titius is temperate and regular, but then he is so great a *Mathematician*, that he does not know when *Sunday* comes: He sees People going to *Church*, as he sees others going to Market, he goes on studying, measuring, and calculating, and may as well be called a *Merchant*, as a *Christian*.

All Doctrines of *Religion* are disagreeable to *Philo*, he avoids them as he avoids *Party*; now what's the Reason of it? It is not because he is *debauched* and *intemperate*, but he is a *Virtuoso* devoted to polite *Literature*, his Soul is extended to all the *Curiosities* in the World, and thinks all Time to be lost, that is not spent in the Search of *Shells*, *Urns*, *Inscriptions*, and *broken Pieces* of *Pavements*. This makes the Truths of *Religion*, and the Concerns of *Eternity*, seem small Things in his Eyes, fit only for the Enquiry of narrow, *little* and *unpolite* Souls.

Patronus is fond of a Clergyman who understands *Music*, *Painting*, *Statuary*, and *Architecture*. He is an Enemy to the *Dissenters*, and loves the *Church of England* because of the *Stateliness* and *Beauty* of its Buildings; he never comes to the *Sacrament*, but will go forty Miles to see a *fine Altar-piece*. He goes to Church when there is a *new Tune* to be heard, but never had any more serious Thoughts about *Salvation*, than about *Flying*. If you visit him when he is dying, you will hear his dying Thoughts upon *Architecture*.

Eusebius would read Prayers *twice* every Day in his *Parish*, he would be often with the Poor and Sick, and spend much Time in charitable Visits; he would be wholly taken up in the *Cure* of Souls, but that he is busy in studying the *old Grammarians*, and would fain *reconcile* some Differences amongst them, before he dies.

Lycia has no wicked or irreligious Temper, and she might be pious, but that she is too *easy*, *gay*, and *cheerful*, to admit of Care of any Kind. She can no more *repent*, than she can be *out of Temper*, and must be the same *sparkling cheerful* Creature in the *Church*, as in the *Playhouse*. She might be capable of understanding the Misery of human Nature, and the Necessity of the Comforts of Religion, but that she is so *happy* every time she is *dressed*.

Matrona is old, and has been this *fifty Years*, eating and drinking, sleeping and waking, dressing and undressing, *paying*

and *receiving Visits.*   She has no Profaneness, and if she has no
Piety, it is owing to this, that she never had a *spare half Hour*
in all her Life to think about it.   She envies her Daughters,
because they will *dress* and *visit* when she is dead.

Publius goes to *Church* sometimes, and reads the Scripture,
but he knows not what he reads or prays, his Head is so full of
Politics.   He is so angry at *Kings* and Ministers of *State*, that
he has no Time nor Disposition to call himself to account.   He
has the History of all *Parliaments, Elections, Prosecutions,* and
Impeachments, and dies with little or no Religion, through a constant Fear of *Popery.*

Siccus has neither *Virtues* nor *Vices*, he has been all his life-
long *building* and *pulling down*, making *Canals* and *Ditches*,
raising *Walls* and *Fences.*   People call him a good Man, because
he employs the Poor; *Siccus* might have been a *religious* Man,
but that he thought *building* was the chief Happiness of a
rational Creature.   He is all the Week amongst *Dirt* and
Mortar, and stays at home on *Sundays* to view his Contrivances.
He will die more contentedly, if his Death does not happen
whilst some *Wall* is in building.

Silvius laughs at *preaching* and *praying*, not because he has
any profane Principles, or any Arguments against Religion, but
because he happens to have been used to nothing but *Noise*, and
Hunting, and *Sports.*

I have mentioned these several *Characters*, to show us that it
is not only *Profaneness, Debauchery,* and *open Vices*, that keep
Men from the Impressions of true Religion, but that the mere
Play-things of Life, impertinent *Studies*, vain *Amusements*, false
Satisfactions, idle *Dispositions*, will produce the same Effect.   A
wrong Turn of Mind, *impertinent* Cares, a Succession of the
poorest Trifles, if they take up our Thoughts, leave no more
Room for the Cares and Fears of true Piety, than gross Sensuality.

Our blessed Saviour saith, *Woe unto you Pharisees, for ye love
the uppermost Seats in Synagogues, and Greetings in the Markets.**
The Wisdom of this World would find little to condemn in such
a Behaviour as this, but yet we see that the Wisdom of God
condemns it with a *Woe*, teaching us, that every *wrong Turn* of
Mind, every false Satisfaction, puts the Soul in a State that is
contrary to Religion, and makes Men *unfit* to receive its Doctrines.   This is the Reason why Religion calls us to a State of
Self-denial, Humility, and *Mortification*, because it is a State
that awakens the Soul into right Apprehensions of Things, and

* Luke xi. 43.

qualifies us to see, and hear, and understand the Doctrines of eternal Truth. We must deny ourselves all our Ways of Folly and Vanity, let go every false Satisfaction, that the Soul may be at Liberty with its full Attention, to listen to the Instructions of Religion.

Would we see anything exactly, we must take our Eyes from everything else, so if we would apprehend truly the Things of Religion, we must take our Minds from all other Objects; we must empty ourselves of all false Satisfactions, or we shall never know the Want, nor feel the Excellency of our true Good.

We see even in worldly Matters, that if we propose anything to a Man when he is in the Pursuit of something else, he hardly hears, or understands us, we must stay for a Season of more Leisure and Indifference, till his Thoughts and Passions are at rest.

Now this holds much stronger in Matters of Religion, its Doctrines are neither heard nor understood, because it always finds us in the Pursuit of *something else,* it matters not what this *something else* is, whether it be *loving uppermost Seats in the Synagogues,* a Fondness for *Trifles,* a Joy in *Luxury* and *Idleness,* or a Labour after Riches; the Mind is equally employed wrong, and so not in a Condition to like, or at Leisure to listen to any other Happiness. If you were to propose the same Truths to a Man in another State, when Weariness or Disappointment has made him give up all Designs, or when Sickness or the Approach of Death shows him that he must act no longer in them, they would have quite another Effect upon him; then the great Things of Religion appear great indeed; he *feels* their whole Weight, and is *amazed* that he did not see them always in the same Manner. Now it is the great End and Design of *Self-denial,* to put a Stop to the Follies of Life, and mortify all our Passions, that our Souls may quietly consider, and fully comprehend the Truths which come from God, that our Hearts being at Liberty from a Crowd of foolish Thoughts, may be ready to obey and co-operate with the *Inspirations* of that Spirit, which is to lead and quicken us in all Holiness; that *Death* and *Judgment, Heaven* and *Hell,* may make as deep Impressions upon our Minds in the Middle of our Lives, as at our last Hour; that we may be as wise and prudent as *sick* and *dying* Men, and live with such Apprehensions as most People die with, that we may see the Vanity of the World, the Misery of Sin, the Greatness of Eternity, and the Want of God, as they see it who stand upon the Brink of another World.

This is the great and happy Work of Self-denial, which is to fill us with a Spirit of Wisdom, to awaken us into a true Knowledge of ourselves, and show us who, and where, and what we are. Till this Self-denial has put a Stop to our Follies, and opened our Eyes, our Life is but a *Sleep*, a *Dream*, a mere Succession of *Shadows*, and we act with as little Reason and Judgment, as a Child that is pleased with blowing about a *Feather*. We must therefore not only deny our wicked and sinful Inclinations, but also all our Follies, Impertinences, and vain Satisfactions; for as plain and known Sins harden and corrupt, so Impertinences and false Satisfactions delude and blind our Hearts, and render them insensible of our real Misery, or true Happiness.

We are true Members of the Kingdom of God, when the Kingdom of God is within us, when the Spirit of Religion is the Spirit of our Lives, when seated in our Hearts, it diffuses itself into all our Motions, when we are wise by its Wisdom, sober by its Sobriety, and humble by its Humility ; when it is the Principle of all our Thoughts and Desires, the Spring of all our Hopes and Fears ; when we like and dislike, seek and avoid, mourn and rejoice, as becomes those who are born again of God. Now this is the Work of the Holy Spirit in our Hearts, to give us a *new Understanding*, a *new Judgment*, Temper, Taste, and Relish, new Desires, and new Hopes and Fears. So far therefore as we *prepare* ourselves by Self-denial, for this Change of Heart and Mind, so far we *invite* the Assistance, and *concur* with the Inspirations of the Holy Spirit. And so far as we nourish any foolish Passion, indulge any Vanity of Mind, or Corruption of Heart, so far we *resist the Graces* of God's Holy Spirit, and render ourselves *indisposed* to relish and improve his secret Inspirations. Christians are therefore to consider themselves, not only as Men, that are to act by a Principle of Reason, but as spiritual Beings, who have a higher Principle of Life within them, and are to live by the *Wisdom* and *Instructions* of the Spirit of God.

As reasonable Men would do everything that tended to strengthen and improve their Reason, so wise Christians ought to practise every Way of Life, that can fit them for further Degrees of Grace, that can strengthen and preserve their Union with the Spirit of God. For as a Man without Reason has but the *Figure* of a Man, so a Christian without the Spirit of God, has but the *Form* of a Christian. And as the Perfection of a Man consists in the highest Improvement of his Reason, so the Perfection of a Christian consists in his Growth in Grace, in the *spiritual Turn* and *Temper* of his Heart and Mind. Here therefore must we fix all our Care and Concern, that we may remove all Hindrances of Divine Grace, and preserve this Kingdom of God within us; that we may be truly spiritual in all our Ways and Designs, and indulge no Tempers that may lessen our Union with the Spirit of God.

Some Persons will perhaps refrain from *Grief*, when they find that it hurts their *Eyes;* they will avoid *Passion* and *Anger*, if it ends in Pains of the Head; but they would do well to consider that these Tempers are to be abstained from upon much greater Accounts. *Passion* may disorder our Bodies, waste our Spirits, and leave Pains in our *Heads:* but it leaves greater Marks of Injury in our better Part, as it throws us into a State of Madness, and *banishes* the Holy Spirit of Peace and Gentleness, and *prepares* us for the Suggestions of the Spirit of Darkness. *Grief* may hurt our *Eyes*, but it much more hurts our *Souls*, as it sinks them into a State of Gloom and Darkness, which *expels* and *quenches* the Spirit of God; for Light may as well unite with Darkness, as the Spirit of God dwell with the gloomy Dulness and Horror of stupid Grief. What I have observed of these two Passions, ought to be concluded of every other *Passion* and *Temper;* we are to consider it as it *suits* with, or *resists* that new Spirit by whose holy Motions we are to be preserved in a State of Holiness.

Now seeing this Change of our Hearts, and *Newness* of Spirit is the whole of Religion, we must fear and avoid all *Irregularity* of Spirit, every *unreasonable Temper*, because it affects us in the Seat of Life, because it hurts us in our principal Part, and makes us *less capable* of the Graces, and *less obedient* to the Motions of God's Holy Spirit. We must labour after a State of Peace, Satisfaction and Thankfulness, free from the Folly of vain Hopes, idle Fears, and false Anxieties, that our Souls may be disposed to feel the Joys, to rejoice in the Comforts, and advance in the Graces of the Holy Ghost.

With what *Care* and *Exactness* we are to conduct ourselves, with Regard to the Spirit of God, is fully set forth in the following Words: *Let no corrupt Communication proceed out of your Mouth, but that which is good to the Use of edifying, that it may minister Grace unto the Hearers, and grieve not the Holy Spirit of God, whereby you are sealed unto the Day of Redemption.** That we may not here mistake what is meant by *corrupt Communication*, that we may not fancy it only implies sinful and wicked Discourse, the Apostle adds; *but that which is good to the Use of edifying, that it may minister Grace unto the Hearers.* So that it is a Conversation that does not edify and profit the

---

* Eph. iv. 29.

Hearer, that the Apostle condemns as corrupt, and such as is to be avoided. Let it be observed that the Apostle does not prohibit this kind of Conversation, because it is *useless*, impertinent, and better to be avoided, but for a Reason of the utmost Consequence, that we may *not grieve the Holy Spirit of God*. This shows us, that we Christians are to govern ourselves by no less a Rule, than a *Conformity* to the Spirit of God, that we are not only to deny ourselves vain and foolish Actions, but also idle and unedifying Discourse, and conduct ourselves in all our Behaviour, with such a Spirit of Wisdom and Purity, as may make the Holy Ghost *delight* to dwell in us. This Rule of Perfection is highly conformable to the Nature of our Religion. For as our Religion consists in a *new* Heart and *new* Spirit, it is certain that we are then only arrived to the true State of our Religion, when it governs our Words and Actions, and is the *constant Temper* of our Minds at all Times, and on all Occasions. A *covetous* Man is not only covetous when he is in his *Counting-Room*, he is the same Person, and governed by the same Temper and Way of thinking wherever he is. And the same Thing is equally true of every Way of Life, when it has once entered into our Heart, and become a settled Temper, it is not occasionally exercised in this or that Place, or at set Times, but is always in Being, and constantly disposing us to Thoughts, and Words, and Actions suitable to it.

Some Persons seem to know so little of Religion, that they confine it to Acts of *Devotion*, and *public Occasions* of Divine Service, they don't consider that it consists in a *new* Heart and *new* Spirit, and that Acts of Devotion, Prayer and Preaching, Watchings, Fastings and Sacraments, are only to fill us with this *new Heart and Spirit*, and make it the common constant Spirit of our Lives every Day and in every Place.

A Man may be said to have some regard to Religion, who is *regular* at Places of Divine Worship, but he cannot be reckoned of a *religious Spirit*, till it is his Spirit in every Place, and on every Occasion, till he lives and breathes by it, and thinks and speaks, and acts according to its Motions.

A Man may frequent *Meetings for Mirth*, but yet, if when he is out of them, he gives himself unto Peevishness, Chagrin and Dulness, I presume no one will say, that such a Man is of a *cheerful Spirit*. It is easy to make the Application here, if we are only Attendants at *Places* of Religion, if when we are out of those Places, we are of another Spirit, I don't say Proud or Covetous, but Vain and Foolish, if our Actions are silly, and our Conversation trifling and impertinent, our Tempers vain and worldly, we are no more of a *religious Spirit*, than a dull and peevish Man is of a *cheerful Spirit*, because he is regular at some set Meetings for *Mirth*.

If a Person of *Pride* and *Vanity* in the general Course of his Life, should yet think himself *humble*, because he had his appointed Times of praying for *Humility*, we might justly say of him, that he knew nothing of the Nature of that Virtue: In like manner, if one, whose Conversation, whose Discourse and Carriage, and Temper in *common Life*, are not according to the Spirit of Religion, should yet think himself religious, because he had his appointed Places of Prayer, it might be justly said of him, that he was a Stranger to the Nature of true Religion. For Religion is not ours till we live by it, till it is the Religion of our Thoughts, Words, and Actions, till it goes with us into every Place, sits uppermost on every Occasion, and forms and governs our Hopes and Fears, our Cares and Pleasures. He is the religious Man who watches and guards his Spirit, and endeavours to be always in the Temper of Religion, who worships God in every Place by a Purity of Behaviour, who is as fearful of foolish Thoughts, irregular Tempers, and vain Imaginations, at one Time as at another, who is as Wise and Heavenly at *Home*, or in the *Field*, as in the *House of God*. For when once Religion has got Possession of a Man's Heart, and is become as it ought to be, his ruling Temper, it is as agreeable to such a one in all Places, and at all Times to speak and act according to its Directions, as it is agreeable to the *Ambitious* Man, to act according to the Motions of Ambition. We must therefore take it for granted, that if we are not Religious in our Conversation and common Temper, we are not Religious in our Hearts, we may have a *Formality* of Religion at certain *Times* and *Places*, but we are not of a *religious Spirit*.

We see everybody speaking and conversing according to their *Spirit* and *Temper*, the Covetous, the Ambitious, the Vain and Self-conceited have each of them their proper Language suitable to their Spirit and Temper, they are the *same Persons* in all Places, and always talk like themselves. If therefore we could meet with Persons of a truly Religious Spirit and Temper, we should find them like Men of other Tempers, the same Persons in *all Places*, and always Talking and Acting like themselves. We should find them Living by one Temper, and Conversing with Men with the same Spirit that they converse with God, not one Thing in one Place, and another in another, not formal and grave at a *Funeral*, and mad and frantic at a *Feast*, not listening to Wisdom at *Church*, and delighting in Folly at *Home*, not angry at one foolish Thing, and as much pleased with another, but steady and uniform in the same wise and religious Temper.

Further, as we are not of a *religious Spirit* till it is the Spirit of our Life, and orders our Conversation ; so it is carefully to be observed, that if our Conversation is Vain and Foolish, it keeps us in a State incapable of Religion, by *grieving* the *Holy Spirit.* For as we can do nothing without the Spirit of God, as it is our *Breath,* our *Life,* our *Light* and our *Strength,* so if we live in such a Way as *grieves* and *removes* this Holy Spirit from us, we are as Branches that are broken off from the Tree, and must perish in the Deadness and Corruption of our Nature. Let this therefore teach us to judge Rightly of the Sin and Danger of *Vain, Unedifying* and *Corrupt* Communication ; it is not the Sin of *Idleness* or *Negligence,* it is not the Sin of a *Pardonable Infirmity,* it is not a *little Mistake* in spiritual Wisdom, but it is a Sin that stands between us and the *Tree* of Life, that opposes our whole Happiness, as it *grieves* and *separates* the Holy Spirit from us.   Let this also teach some People the Reason, why they are so *dead* and *senseless* of Religion, and hardly capable of an outward formal Compliance with it ; they are not guilty of gross Sins, they have an aversion to *Cheating* and *Falseness,* but at the same time have no more feeling or relish of Religion, than mere *Reprobates.*   Now the Reason of it is this, they live in such an *Impertinence* of Conversation, their own Communication is so constantly upon *silly* and *vain* Subjects, and they are so fond of those who have the Talent of conversing in the same Manner, that they render themselves *unfit* for the Residence of the Holy Spirit.   Their whole Life is almost nothing else, but a Course of that *Filthiness, foolish Talking and Jesting,* which the Apostle forbids.   Now this kind of Conversation may *grieve* the Holy Spirit, for these two Reasons, first, because it proceeds from too *disordered* a Soul, for the Holy Spirit to delight in ; for such as our Conversation is, such is our *Heart,* for Truth itself has assured us, that *Out of the abundance of the Heart the Mouth speaketh.*   If therefore we are delighted with idle *Raillery, foolish Jestings,* and ridiculous *Stories,* we must not think that we are only Foolish, so far as a *little talk* goes, but we must charge ourselves home, and be assured that it is a foolishness of Heart, a vanity of Soul that we labour under.

Secondly, Another Reason why this Conversation grieves the Holy Spirit, may be this, because it is of so great Consequence, and has so great an Influence in Life.   We don't seem enough to apprehend, either how much *Good* or how much *Evil* there is in Conversation, and I believe it may be affirmed that the greatest Instructions, and the greatest Corruptions proceed from it.   If some People were to give us their true History, they would tell

us that they never had any Religion, since they had such Acquaintance, and others have been insensibly led into a *sincere
Piety*, only by conversing with pious People. For Men's common
Conversation and ordinary Life teach much more effectually, than
anything they say or do at set Times and Occasions.

When a Clergyman Preaches, he is for the most part considered as doing his Duty, as Acting according to his Profession,
and doing that which all Clergymen do, whether *good* or *bad*.
But if he is the same wise and virtuous Man in his Communication, that he is in the *Pulpit*, if his Speech be *seasoned with Salt*,
that it may minister Grace unto the Hearers, if the *common* and
ordinary Actions of his Life be visibly governed by a Spirit of
Piety. Such a one will make Converts to Holiness ; he will be
heard with Reverence on the *Sunday*, not so much for the
Weight of what he says, as for what he says and does all the
Week. And on the contrary, if a *Clergyman* when he comes out
of the *Pulpit*, is but like other Men, as *Irregular* in his Tempers,
as *Trifling* in his Conversation, as *Eager* in Diversions, and as
Ridiculous in his Pleasures, as *Vain* in his Designs, as other
People, he will mightily lessen his Power over the Hearts of his
Hearers. A *Father* now and then gives his Son virtuous Advice,
and the Son perhaps would be much the better for it, but that
he never hears him talking Virtuously, but when he is giving him
Advice, this makes him think, that he is then only Acting the
Part of a *Father*, as when he is buying him *Clothes*, or putting
him out to an *Employment.* Whereas if he saw his Father's
ordinary Life and Conversation to be under the Rules of Religion,
and his everyday Temper, a Temper of Piety, 'tis very likely,
that he would be won into an Imitation of it.

A *Mother*, orders her Daughter to be taught the *Catechism*, and
desires that she may have Books of *Devotion*. The Daughter
would have imagined that she was to have formed herself by
these Books, she would have read them when she was alone, but
that she finds her Mother sits up at Night to read *Romances*, and
if she is ill, must be read to Sleep with a *Play*. She might have
had some Notion of religious *Modesty* and *Humility*, but that she
sees her Mother eager after *all Diversions*, Impatient till she
knows *all Intrigues*, fond of the Wit and Flattery of *Rakes*,
pleased with the Gentility of *Fops*, and the Gracefulness of
Players.

Now a Daughter educated with a Mother of this Temper and
Conversation, is rendered almost incapable of Religion.

This therefore may be one Reason, why a vain unedifying
Conversation *grieves* the Holy Spirit, *viz.*, because it not only
proceeds from a Corruption of Heart, a disordered State of the

10—2

Soul, but because it is so powerful in its Influences, and does so much harm to those whom we converse with. For it is our Communication, our *ordinary Temper*, and manner of *common Life* that affects other People, that either hardens them in Sin, or awakens them to a Sense of Piety. Let therefore all *Clergymen*, and *Masters* and *Mistresses* of Families, look carefully to themselves, let them consider, that if their *ordinary Life*, their Communication be *vain, impertinent*, and *unedifying*, that they are not only in a corrupt State of Heart, but are guilty of corrupting and perverting the Hearts of those who belong to them. Let them not think, that they have sufficiently discharged their Duty, by seeing that those who relate to them, have their proper Instructions, for it is next to impossible for such Instructions to have their proper Effect, against the Temper and Example of those we converse with. If a *Clergyman Plays*, and *Drinks* and *Sports* with his Flock in the Week-Days, let him not wonder, if he preaches them asleep on *Sundays*. If a *Father* is *intemperate*, if he *Swears*, and converses *foolishly* with his Friends, let him not wonder, that his Children cannot be made virtuous. For there is nothing that teaches to any Purpose, but our ordinary Temper, our common Life and Conversation; and almost all People will be such as those, amongst whom they were born and bred. It is therefore the necessary Duty of all Christians in all States of Life, to look carefully to their *ordinary Behaviour*, that it be not the Means of poisoning and corrupting the Hearts of those whom they converse with. They must consider, that all the Follies, and Impertinences of their ordinary Life and Conversation, have the Guilt of destroying Souls, and that the Blood of those, whom their Follies have destroyed, will be required at their Hands.

It is sometimes said of a *foolish, irregular* and *vain* Person, that he is only his *own Enemy ;* but this is as absurd as to say, that a Person of *exemplary* and *eminent* Piety, is only his *own Friend ;* for as his lively Piety will certainly communicate itself to those about him, so the Folly and impertinent Spirit of an irregular Man, will naturally infect those who are obliged to be near him.

A *Mistress* whose daily Conversation is a daily Proof to her *Maids*, that she is governed by a Spirit of true Piety in all that she says and does, whose regular Life is a continual visible Labour to *work out her Salvation with Fear and Trembling*, is a Blessing to all who stand about her; she communicates Happiness even to those who are born of her Servants; they will be educated in Piety, because their Parents learnt what Piety was, in waiting on such a *Mistress*.

A *good-natured, drinking, sleeping, playing, swearing Master*, is a Curse to those who attend upon him; they are led into all Irregularities, by following his Steps, and are sent into the World hardened in Follies, and insensible of Religion, by having lived with such a *Master.* This therefore ought carefully to be considered by all Christians, as a mighty Encouragement to an exact Strictness and Regularity of Behaviour; that as a *holy Conversation* entitles us to a Reward for other People's Virtues, so an *evil Communication* and the Folly of our Lives, makes us liable to a Punishment for other Men's Sins. For we can neither live well nor ill to ourselves alone, but must of Necessity do either Good or Harm to others, by our Manner of Conversation. This is one great Reason why a vain corrupt Communication does so *grieve* the Holy Spirit, because it is so infecting an Evil, and does so corrupt the Manners of those whom we converse with. This Doctrine of abstaining from corrupt Communication, that we may not *grieve* the Spirit of God, teaches us a high Aim and exalted Degree of Perfection, which is peculiar to Christianity. As Christianity lays the Design of uniting us to God, and raising us to a more intimate Participation of the Divine Nature, so we are to make the *Spirit* of our Religion, and the *Greatness* of its Designs, the *Rule* of our Perfection.

We must not only conduct ourselves by Rules of Morality, but pursue such Degrees of Purity, as can only be expressed by an *Imitation* of God, and aspire after such Wisdom, as is suggested to us, by considering that we are *Temples* of the Holy Ghost, and must live like Beings *consecrated* by the Spirit of Wisdom. If we were frequently to consider the Holy Presence of this God within us, and to ask ourselves, Does this Discourse, this Behaviour, become one who is to act according to the *Inspirations* of the Divine Spirit? we should find, that the very Thought of this Dignity of our State, would determine several Points where no express Law condemns us; we should find such a contrariety in many of our allowed Ways, to our Christian Greatness, to this Holy Spirit that is given unto us, as would sufficiently check our Behaviour, only by showing us that we acted below ourselves.

It is common in Life to hear a Man say, this does not become a *Gentleman,* that does not become a Man of *Quality:* Now I would have us find out something like this in Religion; for certainly if any State of Life has its Dignity, which can excite Men to a suitable Greatness of Action, surely the State of a Christian, which is a State of such relation to God, which unites us to his Holy Spirit, ought to raise in us a Desire of acting suitably to so exalted a Condition. For who can so justly be afraid of acting *below himself,* as he who is made one with Christ? Who can so reasonably think that he is never wise, or holy, or pure enough, as he who is to walk with God in the Light of his Holy Spirit, whose Soul and Body is made a *sacred Temple* for the Divine Presence?

The *Heathen Philosophers* exhorted Man to reverence his *Reason*, as a *Ray* of the Deity; but we can go much higher, we can exhort him to reverence the Deity that dwelleth in him, and to act with such Purity, as becomes Persons who are *inspired* by the Holy Ghost.

This is the Improvement that we are to make of this Doctrine of Divine Grace; it must make us exact and careful of our Behaviour, that we may walk worthy of that Holy Spirit that dwelleth in us.

Chapter X.

The Necessity of Divine Grace, obligeth all Christians to a constant Purity, and Holiness of Conversation; wherein is shown, the great Danger, and great Impiety, of reading vain and impertinent Books.

I HAVE shown in the foregoing Chapter, that the *Necessity of Divine Grace* is a mighty Argument for an universal Care and Exactness of Life and Conversation. I come now to speak of one remarkable Branch of it; *Let no corrupt Communication proceed out of your Mouth, but that which is good to the Use of edifying, that it may minister Grace to the Hearers, and grieve not the Holy Spirit of God, whereby ye are sealed to the Day of Redemption.* Now if we are to let no corrupt Communication proceed out of our Mouth, that we may not *grieve the Holy Spirit*, and separate him from us, then it follows, that we are also to deny ourselves the Entertainment of all *corrupt, impertinent,* and *unedifying* Books. For if vain and idle Words are not to proceed out of our Mouths, we must be under the same Necessity of not letting them enter into our Hearts.

If we would know what Books are to be avoided, as corrupt and grievous to the Holy Spirit, we must look back to the Rule of our Communication; for as that Communication is there said

to be *corrupt,* that does not *edify* and minister Grace to the
Hearers, so must we look upon all those Books as corrupt,
which do not improve and confirm our Hearts in Virtue, or, in
the Apostle's Words, such as do not *edify and minister Grace* to
the Readers. Now this Book-entertainment is as certainly forbidden by the Apostle, as *Cheating* is forbidden by the *Eighth*
Commandment : For if I am not to say foolish and impertinent
Things myself, because such a Communication *grieves* and removes the Holy Spirit of God, I am as certainly forbid the
reading the corrupt and impertinent Sayings of other People.
The Books which mostly corrupt our Hearts, and fill us with a
Spirit of Folly, are such, as almost all the World allow themselves to read, I mean, Books of *Wit* and *Humour, Romances,
Plays,* and other Productions of the *Poets.* Thus a *grave orthodox* old Gentleman, if he hears that his *Niece* is very good, and
delights in Reading, will fill her Closet with Volumes of *Plays,*
and Poems on *several Occasions,* on purpose to encourage her
to spend her Time well. There is not perhaps a more surprising
Infatuation in the Conduct of Christians, than with regard to
these Books.

A *Father* would be very much troubled to see his Daughter
in Conversation pleased with the *lewd* Remarks of a *Rake ;* he
would be afraid that she had lost the Virtue of her Mind, if she
could relish such a Turn of Conversation. Yet this same Father
shall help his Daughter to a Volume of *Occasional Poems,* for her
Closet-Entertainment, full of such *gross Immodesties,* as hardly
any *Rake* would venture to express in any Conversation. It is
perhaps a Collection of the *Poet's* finest, strongest, and most
finished Thoughts in Lewdness and Immodesty. Every Wantonness of Imagination, every Transport of Passion, every Extravagance of Thought, which ever seized him in his Life, is there
preserved for the Meditation of the Christian Reader ; as if
Profaneness, Blasphemy, the grossest Descriptions of Lust, and
the wildest Sallies of impure Passions, were made good and
useful for a Christian, by being put into *Rhyme* and *Measure.*
And what shows this *Infatuation* in a yet higher Degree, is this,
that it is still a prevailing Opinion in the World, that the reading virtuous Books is a great Means of improving in Virtue;
whereas one would suppose, that the Books I have mentioned
could only be allowed upon a Belief, that there was neither
Good nor Harm to be got by Reading.

But, however, let us remember that though the Way of the
World which is thus inconsistent, may allow this *polite* kind of
Entertainment, yet this is no Rule or Security for our Conduct,
since we are no more to make the Spirit of the World our Guide,

than we are to make the Riches of the World our Happiness. The Doctrines of the Scriptures are the only Rule by which we are now to live, and the Rule by which we shall hereafter be judged. Now if we will allow ourselves in the reading *profane, impure,* and *impertinent* Books, which have everything in them that can *pervert* our Understandings, and *corrupt* our Hearts, though the Scripture forbids all *unedifying Discourse,* as a Thing that grieves the Holy Spirit, it must be said, that we act as contrary to Scripture, as if we indulged and pleased ourselves in *Malice* and *Revenge.*

You read a *Play,* I tell you that you read *Ribaldry* and *Profaneness,* that you fill your Mind with extravagant Thoughts, lewd Intrigues, vain Fictions, wanton Ideas, and impure Descriptions. If you ask me where is the Sin of this, you may as well ask me where is the Sin of *Swearing* and *Lying :* For it is a Sin not only against this or that *particular* Text, but it is a Sin against the *whole Nature* and Spirit of our Religion ; it is a Contradiction to all Holiness and to all the Methods of arriving at it. For if evil unedifying Communication be forbidden in Scripture, and for this Reason, because it grieves the Spirit of God, then the Entertainment of such Books is certainly forbidden. For certainly the wild Rant, the profane Speeches, filthy Jests, and impure Passions, which there abound, are an evil Communication in the highest Degree, and must therefore highly grieve and separate the Holy Spirit from us. Can therefore any Practice be forbid upon a more dreadful Penalty than this ? For without the Spirit of God, we are but Figures of Christians, and must die in our Sins. If therefore we can prove it to be a small Matter to grieve the Spirit of God, then we may allow that it is but a small Offence, to please ourselves in reading those corrupt Books. Our Blessed Saviour saith, *Out of the Heart proceed evil Thoughts,* and that *these are the Things that defile a Man ;* must it not therefore be a great Defilement to take evil Thoughts into our Hearts? Need we any other Motive than this, to watch and guard the Purity of our Minds? He that, notwithstanding this Doctrine of our Saviour's, dares to set apart Times for the reading the evil and impure Thoughts that are in these Books, does as plainly despise the Doctrine of Christ, as he that murders, despises the Doctrine of the Sixth Commandment.

You will say, perhaps, that you only read these Books now and then, for *Amusement,* and only to *divert* your Spirits, and that most of the Time which you devote to Reading, is spent in reading Books that may improve your Piety. If this be your Case, you can say that for yourself which very few can ; for the

Generality of Readers make other Books their chief and most constant Entertainment. But to speak now to your Excuse, you only read such Books now and then, for your Amusement, and to divert your Spirits; that is, you entertain your Mind with *evil* Thoughts, you read, relish, and digest, the *Lewdness, Profaneness,* and *Impurity,* of these Books, not with a serious Design of making yourself lewd, profane, and impure, but only as it were in jest, and to have a little Pleasure from them. Now this is the plain Meaning of this Excuse, which is as absurd as anything can well be supposed. It is as if a Man, who allows himself now and then to get *drunk,* and *swear,* and *rant,* should say in his Excuse, that he is for the most part very sober, and that when he takes these Liberties, it is not through any Desire or Liking of the Sin of Drunkenness, but only as it were in jest, and through the mere Gaiety of his Spirits. You will ask, perhaps, if the Sin of reading *Plays* be like the Sin of *Drunkenness.* I answer, very like it, and perhaps equally grievous to the Spirit of God. For is not evil Thoughts, Vanity of Mind, and Impurity of Heart, the most dreadful State that we can be in? Can you therefore imagine that the *feeding* and *entertaining* your Mind with evil Thoughts, and impure Discourses, is a less Sin than *drinking* too much? What Rule of Reason or Scripture have you to go by in such a Judgment? You may fancy that there is something much more gross and shameful in Drunkenness, than in this Practice; but if you would judge not by Fancy, but by the Light of Religion, you would find, that it is a Drunkenness and Intemperance of the Mind, as *gross* and *shameful,* as abominable in the Sight of God, and as contrary to Piety, as that stupid intemperance which consists in drinking too much.

One great Shame of Drunkenness, is this, that it fits us for *Ribaldry,* and all the *Folly* of Discourse; that it makes us say silly Things ourselves, and be pleased with the most *foolish* Rant and *extravagant* Nonsense of other People. Are not you therefore doing that which is most *shameful* in Drunkenness? And is it not a Sign of greater Impurity, and greater Want of Piety, for you *coolly* and *soberly* to seek and relish such *Rant* and *Folly* of Discourse, such profane Jests and Wantonness of Wit, as Men are most pleased with, when Drink has made them *half mad.* Now the liking of such Discourse as this, makes up great Part of the Guilt of Drunkenness, must it not therefore imply a greater Guilt in you, who like such foolish Discourse when you are sober? *Drunken* Men like ill Discourse, because Reason and Religion have then no Power over them; if therefore you have as false a Judgment, and relish a Discourse that is equally foolish and mad, must it not be owing to the same Thing, because *Reason* and *Religion* have then no Power over you? *Drunken* Men like any sort of Madness; they are not nice in their Taste ; if a Discourse be but wild or lewd, they delight in it, but you like only a Madness that is put into *Verse,* you only delight in the impure Descriptions and Ravings of Lust, when they are adorned with *beautiful* Expressions and made *Musical* to the Ear. So that the Difference betwixt you and a *drunken* Man does not consist in this, that you have a more *religious Taste,* or *Purity* of Mind than he ; but in this, that he likes *all Sorts* of Rant, and Wantonness of Discourse, but you do not like it, unless it be in *Rhyme,* and divided into *Acts* and *Scenes.* He likes a Song because it is a *Song,* but you do not like it, unless its Impurity and Profaneness be made more Charming by soft and dying Sounds. If therefore a young Lady will go to Bed with her *Play,* she must not reckon herself better Employed, than her Brother who is at the same time *half Mad* over his *Bottle.* For it is impossible to show, that the entertaining ourselves with such *evil* Thoughts and *filthy* Communications is a less Sin, than to be Ranting over a *Bottle.* He that can do this, may also prove, that it is a less Sin to tell a Lie when you are *Sober,* than when you are *Drunk.*

Again, you say in your Excuse, that you only read these Books now and then, to divert your Spirits, and that you mostly read good Books. Now this Excuse carries its own Conviction, for it acknowledges all that is necessary to condemn it. For it owns that these Books are *Vain* and *Corrupting,* that they are of a contrary Nature to good Books, and naturally produce contrary Effects : And you reckon yourself only secure from being hurt by them, for this Reason, because your Mind is so well Seasoned and Strengthened by the Use of good Books. But pray consider the absurdity of all this. For this is saying, I venture into Temptations, not because I cannot avoid them, or am ignorant that they are Temptations, but because I know myself to be *Strong.* I read *impure* Imaginations, *filthy* Jests, and *Profane* Harangues, not because they are an harmless, innocent Diversion, but because the Purity and Piety of my Mind is too great to receive the least Injury from them.

Now nothing can be conceived more Absurd and Irreligious than such an Excuse as this. Yet what Christian who reads *Plays* can possibly make a better. For to say that our *Plays* are not full of *profane Rant, filthy Jests* and *gross* Descriptions of Impurity, is the same Thing as to say that we have no *Plays* in English.

Further, there is a proper Time for every Thing that is lawful to be done : Now can you tell me when it is proper for a Christian to Meditate upon these Books. Is it to be left to your Temper to entertain yourself as it suits with you, or can your Reason point out the convenient Seasons for it ? If you are blindly to follow your Temper, then you are in no better State, than other People who are blindly following other Tempers. If your Reason can appoint any Time for such Entertainment, it must be because there is some Time that is proper for it. Now the different Times or States of our Mind may perhaps be all comprehended under some one of these.

There is a Time when our Hearts are more than ordinarily raised towards God, when we feel the Joys and Comforts of Religion, and enjoy a Peace that passes all Understanding. Now I suppose Reason will not allot this Time for the Diversion of such Books.

There is a Time, when either through the Neglect of Duty, Remorse of Mind, worldly Vexations, bodily Tempers, or the Absence of God's Spirit, that we sink into Dejection and Dulness, grow burdensome to ourselves, and can hardly think of anything with Satisfaction. Now if Reason is to judge, this is of all Times the most improper for such Entertainment. For if there is any Time that is more proper than another to think upon God, it is when we are *in Heaviness.*

When we are *Sick,* it is time to apply to the *Physician,* when we are *Weary* it is a proper Time to *Rest ;* now there is the same natural Fitness in having recourse to God and Religion, when we are under any dejection of Mind. For it is not more the sole Property of Light to dispel Darkness, than it is the sole Property of Religion to relieve all Uneasiness. *Is anyone Afflicted,* says the Apostle, *let him pray.* Now this we are to look upon, not only as wise Advice of something that is very good to be done in Affliction, but as a strict Command, that leaves us no Choice of doing anything in the stead of it.

It is as absolute a Command, as if he said, *Hath anyone Sinned, let him Repent.* For an Application to God, is as much the one thing to be done in the Hour of Trouble, as Repentance is the one thing to be done in Time of Sin. Our Blessed Saviour saith, *Be of good comfort, I have overcome the World.* He therefore who in the want of Comfort, seeks for it in anything else, but in the Redemption of Christ, in his Conquest over the World, is no more a true Christian, than he who does not believe in Christ.

You seem to make Times of Dulness, the Occasion of your Reading those Books, by saying that you only read them to *divert* your Spirits. So that, that which you take to be a Reason for reading them, is a strong Objection against it. For it is never so improper to read those Books, as when you want to have your Spirits raised, or your Mind made easy to itself. For it is the highest Abuse you can put upon yourself, to look for Ease and Quiet in anything, but in right Apprehensions of God's Providence. And it is a Sin against the *whole Nature* of Religion, not to make it the whole Measure and Reason of all your Peace and Enjoyment in every Occurrence of Life.

If you must amuse yourself with a Volume of *Plays*, because you are laid up with a *Broken leg*, or have *lost a Friend*, you are as far from Wisdom, as a *Child* who is to be made quiet with a *Rattle*, and not much more Religious than those, who worship *Idols ;* for to seek to such things for Relief and Refreshment, is like applying to the Devil in *Distress.* A Man who drinks *Drams* every time he is dull or uneasy, is a *wise, prudent,* and *sober* Man, if compared to the Christian who in Seasons of Dejection, has recourse to *wanton* Wit and *profane* Rant to divert his Spirits: He destroys the Religion and Purity of his Mind, much more effectually, than the other destroys the Constitution and Health of his Body.

Some People think that in *great Distresses*, it is proper to seek Comfort in God and religious Reflections, but that in the *little Troubles* and Vexations of Life, anything that can divert the Mind from them, is as well. But this is very absurd, for surely if God is our proper and sufficient Comfort in great Distresses, he must also be our *best Relief* in those that are smaller. Unless it can be said, that the Truths of Religion are able to make us bear *Persecution* and *Martyrdom* with content, but not great enough to make us easy in *little Trials.*

Secondly, To seek for Relief in foolish Diversions, is not only applying to a false Remedy, but is also destroying the chief Power of Religion. For as Religion has no Power over us, but . as it is our Happiness, so far as we neglect, or refuse to make Use of its Comforts, so far we lessen and destroy its Power over us. For it cannot otherwise be the ordinary daily Care of our Lives, than by being our ordinary Happiness and Consolation in all the Changes and Chances of Life. A Christian therefore is to make his Christianity his Comfort, not only in Times of *great Trial* and Sufferings, but in all the *lesser Vexations* of Life, that by this Means every little Occasion of Grief or Disquiet, may be an Occasion of his being more affected with Religion, and made more sensible of its true Comforts.

Thirdly, Those who are for driving away the ordinary Cares, and *little Vexations*, of human Life, by *Diversions*, don't enough consider the Nature of human Life. For the little ordinary

Troubles of Life, make up the *whole Trouble* of Life, and the Reason why so many People are full of Trouble and Uneasiness, is, because they are unable to bear little ordinary Troubles ; and they are unable to bear them, because they don't use the proper Means. For since every Disquiet is at something or other that concerns our State and Condition, there is no Way of relieving us from this Disquiet, but by getting right Notions of our Condition. If *Children* were capable of knowing themselves, or could be taught the Nature of Things, we should not use such Methods of pleasing them as we do ; but as they cannot think and reflect, we never endeavour to reason them into Content ; but if they have lost one *Plaything*, we only promise them another. The Application is here very easy : For if *Men* will make themselves happy, as Children are made happy, not by considering the Nature of Things, but by a *Change of Amusements*, they must also expect to have the Vexations and Torments of Children, and be, like them, laughing and crying at they know not what, all the Days of their Life. For Children are only easily vexed, because they are easily pleased ; and it is certain, that they who can be pleased with Things without knowing their Worth and Value, must in the same Degree be liable to be displeased at Things, without knowing their Weight and Importance. And as this is the true State of Childhood, so whosoever is in this State, whatever his *Age* may be, his *Office* or his *Dignity* in Life, is yet as truly in the State and Folly of Childhood, as he that is but four Years old. Take an Instance or two.

A *Child* whose Heart is half broken at some Misfortune, may perhaps be made easy with a Picture of a *Huntsman* and a *Pack of Hounds ;* but if you would comfort the *Father* who grieves for his eldest Son, the *Hounds* must be all *alive*, they must *cry* and *run*, and follow a *Hare*, and this will make the Father as easy, as the *Picture* made the Child ; such Happiness will make him bear the Loss of his Son.

A *Mother* comforts her little Girl with a *Pack of Cards* that are finely *painted :* By-and-by she wants to be comforted herself, some *great Calamity* has happened to her. Now you must not think to comfort her with *painted Cards*, or building Houses with them, her Grief is too great, and she has been too long a *Mother*, to be pleased with such Things ; it is only *serious Ombre* that can dry her Eyes, and remove Sorrow from her Heart.

I might easily multiply Instances of this kind, but these are sufficient to show us, that Persons of *Age* and *Authority* often differ only from Children, as one Child may differ from another. This is the true Reason why human Life is so full of Complaint, why it is such a *Mixture* of ridiculous Pleasures, and vain Dis-

quiets ; namely, because we live in an entire Ignorance of the
Nature of Things, never considering why we are pleased with
this, or displeased with that, nor any more appeal to Religion to
correct our Judgments, than Children appeal to Reason to
form their Tempers.   For if we will only *play*, or lull ourselves
into Repose, as Children are *rocked* to Sleep, it is not to be
wondered at, if, like them, we *cry* as soon as we are *awake*.   For
every false Relief that is not founded in Reason, is only adding
to the Weakness and Disorder of our Nature, and making us
more liable to further Vexations.   For it is absolutely certain,
that a Person who is made easy by vain and false Satisfactions,
is in the same Degree capable of being made uneasy by vain
and ridiculous Vexations.   They therefore who don't think it
necessary to apply to Religion in all the *common* and *ordinary*
Disquiets of Life, mistake the Nature of human Life, not considering that it is our applying false Relief to these, that is the
Occasion of all our Troubles, and that we are *weak* and *impatient, fretful* and *dissatisfied*, for no other Reason, but because
we never made use of the right Remedy against the *ordinary
Accidents* of Life ; for had we but learnt to bear *little Troubles*
and Disappointments upon right Reasons, because we are
Christians, and Children of God, we should find but few
Troubles that would have any great Trial in them.   And the
Reason why People *seemingly* religious, are subject to the same
Dulness and *Peevishness*, to the same *Vexations*, and Variety of
Griefs, that other People are, is this, because they make no more
Use of their Religion on these Occasions, than other People :
They don't so much as intend to keep themselves *easy, thankful,*
and *cheerful*, by making Religion the *Measure* and *Standard* of
all their Thoughts and Judgments, in all the common Chances
of Life, any more than those do, who have no Thoughts about
Religion.   And this is the Reason why you see them as ridiculous in common Life, as vainly pleased, and as foolishly vexed,
as other People.

For Religion makes no further Difference betwixt People,
than so far as it is applied.   If one Man is constant at *Church*,
and another is mostly absent, the Difference betwixt them may
yet be only the Difference of frequenting and not frequenting
the Service of the Church.   For a Religion only carried thus
far, makes no further Difference betwixt People.   You must not
therefore expect that they must be different Persons in the
ordinary Behaviour of their common Life, for they may, notwithstanding this Difference, be equally *vain* and *unreasonable*
in their Ways, and equally Slaves to the Folly and Humour of
their *particular Temper*.   And all this for this plain Reason,

because Religion, like anything else, can have no Effect but where it is applied.

Suppose a Person had *lame* Feet, and *bad* Eyes, and that he had an *Oil* that was an infallible Cure for them both, when applied to both; if you saw him only using it for his *Eyes*, you would not wonder that it had not cured his *Feet ;* you would know that his anointing his *Eyes*, could only cure his *Eyes*, and that there was no Ground to expect, that his *Feet* should be any better, till he anointed his *Feet*. And all this for this plain Reason, because Things, however good in themselves, can have no further Effect than as they are applied. Now it is just thus in Religion. If it consists only in Devotions and *public Worship*, it has made this Alteration in a Man, that it has taught him to attend to Devotion and public Worship; it has operated so far as he has applied it. But why must you wonder that he is not of a *wise, virtuous*, and *religious* Temper, in all the Actions of his ordinary Life? Is not this wondering why the *Oil* has not cured a Man's *Feet*, when he has never applied it to them, but has only anointed his *Eyes ?*

When the regular Churchman as plainly makes Religion the *Measure* of his ordinary Life, as he makes it the *Rule* of his going to *Church*, when he as directly uses it to this Purpose, as a Man anoints his Eyes, who would be cured by anointing them ; then you will see him as different in his *ordinary Life* from other People, as different in his Pleasures and Griefs, in his Cares and Concerns, as he is different from them in *Forms and Regularity* of Worship. But till Men do this, till they apply the Principles of Religion to all the Actions of *ordinary Life*, till they make it the *Measure* of all their daily Tempers, their Joys and Fears, till they think there is as much Piety in being *wise* and *holy* in their common Tempers, as in being *devout* at Church, as much Sin in being vainly pleased and foolishly vexed, as in neglecting the Divine Service; till they thus directly apply Religion to common Life, as a Man applies a Remedy to the Part that he would have cured, it is no more to be expected, that a Religion of *Forms of Worship* and Devotion, should make a Man religious in the common Judgments and Actions of his ordinary Life, than it is to be expected that an *Oil* which is only applied to our *Eyes*, should cure our *Feet*. So that it is the Manner of our *ordinary Life*, which carries on a Course of Fears and Cares, Pleasures and Amusements, Loves and Hatreds, suitable to our *Tempers* and *Condition* of Life; it is this Manner of our ordinary Life, which we think is thus left to ourselves, that makes Religion so insignificant in the World ; it lies by, like a *Remedy* that is *unapplied*, it has no Effect, because it is used only as a *formal Thing*, that has its Devotions and Duties at *set Times* and Occasions; whereas it should be used and considered as the *Rule and Reason* of all our Judgments and Actions, as the *Measure* of all our Cares and Pleasures, as the *Life* of our Life, the Spirit of our Spirit, and the very Form and Essence of all our Tempers. It is to be in us, like a *new Reason* and Judgment of our Minds, that is, to reason and judge of everything that we do, and to preside over, and govern, all the Motions of our Hearts. *Is anyone merry*, saith the Apostle, *let him sing Psalms; is anyone afflicted, let him pray.* This is Religion in the Apostle's Account; it is not only an Attendance at the public Worship, but it is the *ruling Habit* of our Minds, something that constantly devotes us wholly to God, that allows of no Mirth in our common Life, but a Mirth proper for the Brethren of Christ, a Mirth that can express itself by a rejoicing in God; that allows of no other Cure for Grief or Vexation, than what is to be had from Recourse to God. And indeed, what can be more senseless and absurd, than to see a Christian ever acting in any other Consideration than as a Christian? He is senseless to a Degree of Madness, when he indulges a Thought, or a Motion of his Heart, when he either takes a Pleasure, or relieves a Grief, where he cannot say, I do this as a Christian, as suitable to that State in which Christianity has placed me.

We reckon a Man sufficiently *Mad* that fancies himself a *King*, and governing his Subjects, at the same Time that he is tied to a Bed of *Straw*. So that Madness consists in mistaking our Condition, in having a Set of Thoughts not suitable to it. Now a *Christian* repeats every Day, *I believe in the Forgiveness of Sin, the Resurrection of the Body, and the Life Everlasting*, he thanks God for the *Redemption of Jesus Christ, for the Means of Grace, and for the Hope of Glory.* Yet at the same Time, in this State of *Greatness*, he fancies himself in a *thousand Wants and Miseries.* He cries and labours and toils for a Happiness, that has no Existence but in his *own Imagination;* he fancies himself a *Being*, that is to be made happy with *Sauces*, and *Ragouts*, with *painted Clothes*, and shining *Diamonds;* he seeks the Pleasures of *Rakes* and *Libertines*, is grieved and fretted like a Child at the loss of a *Feather;* and must be diverted as they are, with *Shows* and *Plays*, and imaginary Scenes of Rant and Nonsense.

Now is not such a one *Mad?* Does he not know as little of his *State*, as the Man in *Straw*, who fancies himself a *King*. But for a Christian in Times of Dulness or Vexation, to seek Relief in foolish Amusements, in the loose, wild Discourses of *Plays*, when he should *acquaint himself with God, and be at Peace*, is a

Degree of Madness that exceeds all others; it is acting as contrary to the Nature of Things, as if a Man who had lost the Use of his *Limbs,* should choose to comfort his Lameness with *painted Shoes,* when he might have the Use of his Feet restored. For the Consolations of Religion relieve Uneasiness and Trouble, as a *lame* Man is relieved, when his *Limbs* are restored; they conquer Grief, not by cheating and deluding the Weakness of our Minds, but as the *Resurrection* conquers Death, by restoring us to a new and glorious Life. If you need any further Conviction, that Times of Grief and Uneasiness are highly improper for these *Diversions,* let me desire you to suppose that you knew a Christian, who in his last Hours sent for *Buffoons* and *Jugglers* to divert his Mind from the Apprehensions of *Death.* I daresay you have religious Arguments enough, to prove such a Practice to be stupid and profane in the highest Degree. But perhaps you are not aware, that every Argument against such a Practice as this, concludes as strongly against the same Practice at any other Time of our Life. Try therefore with yourself, if every good Argument against such Folly when we are dying, will not be the same Argument against the same Folly in any other Part of our Life. For every Argument that shows the Impiety and Folly of applying to *foolish Diversions,* when we are under the Troubles of *Death,* will show the same Impiety and Folly of applying to such Relief in any Troubles of Life. For to imagine, that we may be ridiculous and vain, and foolish in the *Troubles* of Life, but serious, holy, and religious in the *Troubles* of Death, is the same Folly and Absurdity, as to suppose, that we must be devout and penitent on our Death-Beds, but need not be devout and penitent in the other Parts of our Life. For as there is no Religion or Repentance on our Death-Bed, but what ought to be the Religion of our Lives; so is there no Wisdom, or Seriousness, or Application to God in the *Sorrows of Death,* but what is equally necessary and proper in all the *Sorrows of Life.* For we are obliged to live unto God in the same manner that we are to die unto God. For why must I think rightly of Death? Why must I then apply to God? Why must I reason and judge rightly at that Time? Why may I not then divert my Mind with *loose* and *impertinent* Entertainments? Now give but the true Reason of this, and you will give the Reason why I am always to live in the same manner. For as the Reasons of Wisdom and Holiness are not founded in Death, so do they receive no Alteration by the Approach of Death; there is no Wisdom and Holiness but what is equally necessary, whether I am twenty *Years* or twenty *Days* from Death. Death may bring me into a greater Fear of Folly, but it does not bring me into a greater

11

Necessity of avoiding it, than I was in before; because *all the Reasons* of Piety, Wisdom, and Devotion to God, have been *equally Reasons* all my Life; for the Holiness and Wisdom of Persons in Health, is as necessary, and as much the Terms of Acceptance with God, as the Holiness and Wisdom of dying Persons. And he who dares to be Foolish and Vain, and seek impertinent Entertainments, because he is *Strong and in Health*, is governed by the same Spirit, and sins against the same Reasons of Piety, as he who dares to be *vain, foolish*, and impertinent at the Approach of *Death*. When therefore you think fit to amuse yourself with foolish Diversions, and drive away, what you may call, dull Hours, with the impertinent and wild Imaginations of *Plays, &c.*, you must remember, that you are under the same Condemnation as they are, who apply to the same Relief to ease them of the Thoughts of Death. For as we always stand in the same Relation to God, as he is as much the true Happiness of *living*, as of *dying* Men, so Wisdom and Holiness, and right Dispositions of our Minds, are always Duties of the *same Necessity*.

If it were ever lawful to forget our Happiness in God, and seek for a ridiculous Happiness in vain and extravagant Diversions, if it were ever proper to *live* in this Temper, it would be equally proper to *die* in the same Temper. For we are not upon any *new Terms* with God at our Death, nor under any other Obligations, but such as are equally necessary to make us live in his Favour.

We often wonder at the Worldly-mindedness, the Hardness, Impenitence and Insensibility of *dying Men*. But we should do well to remember, that Worldly-mindedness, Folly, Impenitence, Vanity, and Insensibility, are as much to be wondered at in *living, healthful Men;* and that they are the same odious Sins, and as contrary to all Sense and Reason, and make us as unlike to God, at one Time as at another. Either therefore you must say, that *Plays* and such like *Books* are proper Meditations for dying Men, that they keep up a *right Turn* of Mind, and do not render the Soul unacceptable to God, or else you must own that they are also improper at *all other Times*. For any Thing that indulges a State of Mind that is not according to the *Wisdom* and *Holiness* of Religion, is equally unlawful at *all Times*. *Again,* do but consider your own Notions that you have of *Plays*, and you will find, that if you were consistent with yourself, you would never read them. Not only you, but the Generality of Readers, would think it very improper, and contrary to Piety, to read *Plays* on the *Sunday*. Now I would have you ask yourself why it would be so irreligious, to read these Books on the *Sunday?* Is it because there is such a *Contrariety* betwixt the Subjects of such Books, and the Design of the *Sunday?* Is it because they are contrary to such Meditations, as we should make on that Day? Is it because they are vain and loose, and profane, full of impure Thoughts and wanton Descriptions? There can be no possible Reason given, why we may not read these Books on the *Sunday*, but because they are thus *contrary* to Piety. Need a Christian therefore have any other Argument to persuade him to refrain from these Books? Is it not a sufficient Proof, that they are never to be read, because they are not to be read when his Mind ought to have a religious Turn? Can these Books be more thoroughly condemned, than by being thought too bad to be opened on the *Sunday.* Or need we only stay till *Monday*, to be *vain* and *foolish*, to put on a *new Temper*, and take delight in such Thoughts and Reflections, as we durst not touch the Day before? If therefore we would be consistent with ourselves, we must either prove that *Plays* and such like *Books* are proper Meditations for pious Christians, fit for the Piety and Devotion of the *Sunday*, or else acknowledge that they are equally unfit for their Entertainment at any other Time: For it is manifestly certain, that we are to indulge *no Temper* of Mind on any Day, that we may not *improve* and *delight* in on the *Sunday.*

For to suppose, that we are to have a *new Heart*, and mind on the *Sunday*, different from that *Taste* and *Temper* which we may indulge all the Week, is the same Folly as to suppose, that we need only be *Christians* on the *Sunday.* The Difference betwixt *Sundays* and other Days, does not consist in any Difference in the *inward State* of our Minds, but in the outward Circumstances of the Day, as a general Rest from our lawful Callings, and a public Celebration of Divine Worship. This is the particular Holiness of the Sunday, which requires a particular Rest from Labour, and Attendance at divine Worship, but requires no particular *inward Holiness* of the Mind, but such as is the necessary Holiness of every Day. So that whatever is *contrary* to that Holiness, Purity, and Wisdom of Mind, which is to be our *Temper* on the Sunday, is as much to be abhorred and avoided all the Week as on the Sunday, because though Sunday differs from other Days in *outward Marks* of Holiness, yet Christians are to be every Day alike as to the *inward State* and Temper of their Minds.

Therefore, though the *Labours* of our ordinary Employment and other Actions are to be forborne on the Sunday, and yet are very Lawful on other Days; yet the Case is very different as to these *Books*, they are *unfit* to be read at any time, for the *same*

Reason that they are not fit to be read on Sundays. And the Reason is this, because though we may do things on the Week-Days, that we ought not to do on the Sunday, yet we must indulge *no Temper*, nor support any *Turn of Mind*, that is contrary to that Purity of Heart and Mind, which we are to aspire after on the Sunday. We may *Labour* on the Week-Days, because Labour is an *external Action*, that is not contrary to any Purity or Holiness of Mind, but we must no more be *covetous* on the Week-Days, than on Sundays, because Covetousness is a *Temper of the Mind*, a wrong *Disposition* of the Heart, that is equally contrary to Religion on *all Days*.

Now reading is not the Labour of our *Hands*, or our *Feet*, but is the Entertainment and Exercise of the *Heart* and *Mind*; a Delight in either good or bad Books, is as truly a *Temper* and *Disposition* of the Heart, as *Covetousness* and *Pride* is a Disposition of the Heart. For the same Reason therefore that *Pride* and *Covetousness* are constantly to be avoided on every Day of our Lives, because they are *wrong Tempers* of the Mind, and *contrary* to essential Holiness : For the same Reason is the *Pleasure* of Reading *ill* and *corrupt* Books, always to be avoided at all times, because it is a *Temper* and *Disposition* of our Hearts, that is contrary to that State of Holiness which is essential to Christianity.

If you were to hear a Christian say, that on Sundays he abstained from *evil Speaking*, and *corrupt* Communication, but not on the Week-Days, you would think him either very Ignorant of the Nature of Religion, or very Profane. Yet this is as Wise and Religious, as to forbear reading *ill Books* and *wanton Poems* only on Sundays, and to take the Liberty of Reading them at other times. For that Vanity of Mind, that Foolishness of Heart, that depraved Taste, which can relish the wild Fictions, the lewd Speeches, the profane Language of mad Heroes, disappointed Lovers, raving in all the furious Expressions of Lust and Passion, and Madness, is as *corrupt a Temper*, as contrary to Holiness, and as odious on its own Account, as *evil Speaking* and *Malice*.

When therefore you see a Person reading a *Play*, as soon as he comes from the Sunday's Solemnity of public Service, you abhor his Profaneness, but pray be so just to yourself, so consistent with common Sense, as to think everyone liable to the *same Accusation*, who delights in the same Book on any other Time of the Week; and that the Difference of reading *Plays* on Week-Days and not on Sundays, is only the Difference of *Speaking evil* on Week-Days, and not on Sundays.

From these Reflections, I hope, it sufficiently appears, that the reading vain and impertinent Books, is no Matter of Indifference, but that it is justly to be reckoned amongst our *greatest Corruptions*, that it is as unlawful, as *Malice* and *evil Speaking*, and is no more to be allowed in any Part of our Life, than *Pride* or *Covetousness*.

Reading, when it is an Exercise of the Mind upon wise and pious Subjects, is, next to *Prayer*, the best Improvement of our Hearts. It enlightens our Minds, collects our Thoughts, calms and allays our Passions, and begets in us wise and pious Resolutions. It is a Labour that has so many Benefits, that does so much Good to our Minds, that it ought never to be employed amiss: It enters so far into our Souls, that it cannot have a little Effect upon us. We commonly say, that a Man is known by his *Companions;* but it is certain, that a Man is much more known by the Books that he converses with. These *Closet-companions* with whom we choose to be alone and in private, are never-failing Proofs of the State and Disposition of our Hearts.

When we are abroad, we must take such as the World gives us, we must be with such People, and hear such Discourse, as the common State of our Life exposes us to. This is what we must bear with, because not altogether to be avoided. And as it is not altogether Matter of Choice, so it is no Proof of what Temper we are of. But if we make our *Closet* an Entertainment of greater Vanity and Impertinence, than any Conversation we can meet with abroad, if *rakish, libertine* Writers are welcome to us in secret, if *Histories* of Scandal and *romantic* Intrigues are to be with us in our private Retirements, this is a plain Discovery of our *Inside,* and is a manifest Proof, that we are as vain, and foolish, and vicious, as the *Authors* that we choose to read. If a *wanton Poem* pleases you, you may fairly reckon yourself in the same State and Condition with him who made it. In like manner, if Histories of *Nonsense* and *Folly,* if Compositions of *Intrigue* and *Scandal* suit your Temper, such Books do as truly represent your Nature, as they represent the Nature of their Authors.

Julia has buried her Husband, and married her Daughters, since that she spends her time in reading. She is always reading *foolish* and *unedifying* Books: She tells you every time she sees you, that she is almost at the End of the silliest Book, that ever she read in her Life; that the best of it is, it is very long, and serves to dispose of a good deal of her time. She tells you that all *Romances* are sad Stuff, yet is very impatient till she can get all that she can hear of. Histories of *Intrigue* and *Scandal,* are the Books that *Julia* thinks are always too short. If *Julia* were to drink *Drams* in private, and had no Enjoyment of herself without them, she would not tell you this, because she knows it

would be plainly telling you that she was a *poor disordered Sot.*
See here therefore the Weakness of *Julia;* she would not be
thought to be a *Reprobate,* yet she lets you know that she lives
upon *Folly,* and *Scandal,* and *Impertinence,* in her *Closet,* that she
cannot be in *private* without them, that they are the only Support
of her dull Hours, and yet she does not perceive, that this is as
plainly telling you that she is in a *miserable, disordered, reprobate* State of Mind.

To return. It is reckoned very dangerous not to guard our
Eyes; but it is much more dangerous not to guard our *Medita-
tions;* because whatever enters that way, enters deeper into our
Souls, than anything that only affects our Sight. Reading and
Meditation is that to our Souls, which Food and Nourishment
is to our Bodies, and becomes a part of us in the same Manner;
so that we cannot do ourselves either a *little* Good, or *little*
Harm, by the Books that we read.

You perhaps think, that it is a *dull Task* to read only religious
and moral Books, but when you have the Spirit of Religion,
when you can think of God, as your only Happiness, when you
are not afraid of the Joys of Eternity, you will think it a dull
Task to read any other Books. Don't fancy therefore that your
Heart is right, and that you are well enough affected with
Religion, though you had rather read Books upon other
Subjects; for it is there that you are to charge your *Dulness;*
Religion has no hold of you, the Things of Eternity are not the
Concerns of your Mind, it is *dull* and *tiresome* to you to be *wise*
and *pious,* and that makes it a dull Task to read Books that
treat only upon such Subjects. When it is the Care of your
Soul to be humble, holy, pious, and heavenly-minded, when you
know anything of the Guilt and Misery of Sin, or feel a real
Desire of Salvation, you will find religious Books to be the
greatest Feast and Joy of your Mind.

If you think it dull and tedious to be in wise, prudent, and
sober *Company,* it is because you are neither *wise* nor *sober* yourself: So if it is dull and tiresome to you to be often upon
Subjects of Piety and Religion, it is as sure a Proof that you
are neither *pious* nor *religious.* If therefore you can suppose,
that a wise and sober Man may be most delighted with the
Noise and *Revellings* of Drunkenness, then you may suppose,
that it is possible for you to be truly religious, and yet be most
pleased with the *Folly* and *Impertinence* of corrupt and unedifying
Books. You perhaps will say, that you have so much spare
Time for reading, that you think you need not employ it all in
reading good Books. It may be so, you may have also more
Time than you need devote to Acts and Offices of *Charity;* but

will you thence conclude, that you may at those Times do Things *contrary* to Charity, and indulge yourself in *Spite* and *Mischief?*

If you have every Day more Time than you can employ in Reading, Meditation, and Prayer; if this Time hangs upon your Hands, and cannot be turned to any Advantage, let me desire you to go to *sleep,* or *pick Straws :* For it is much better to do this, than to have recourse to corrupt and impertinent Books. Time lost in *Sleep,* or *picking Straws,* is better lost than in such Exercises of the Mind. Consider further, that *idle* and *spare Time,* is a dangerous State, and calls for great Care and Watchfulness ; to have recourse then to evil and impertinent Books, is like inviting the Devil because you are alone. If you could read ill Books when you were in Haste, or in a Hurry of other Matters, it would do you much less Harm, than to read them, because your Time hangs upon your Hands. So that that Season which you take to be an Excuse for such *Reading,* is a stronger Argument against it ; because evil Thoughts and vain Subjects have twice the Effect, and make double Impressions, when they are admitted at Times of Leisure and Idleness. Consider again, to what a miserable unchristian State you are reduced, when you are forced to have recourse to foolish Books, to get rid of your Time. Your Fortune perhaps has removed you from the Necessity of labouring for your *Bread,* you have been politely educated in Softness, you have no Trade or Employment to take up your Time, and so are left to be devoured by corrupt Passions and Pleasures. Whilst poor People are at hard Labour, whilst your Servants are drudging in the meanest Offices of Life, you, oppressed with *Idleness* and *Indulgence,* are relieving yourself with *foolish* and *impertinent* Books, feeding and delighting a disordered Mind with *romantic* Nonsense, and *poetic* Follies. If this be the Effect of *Riches* and *Fortune,* only to expose People to the Power of disordered Passions, and give them time to corrupt their Hearts with Madness and Folly, well might our Blessed Lord say, *Woe unto you that are rich !*

When you see a *poor Creature* drudging in the meanest Offices of Life, and glad of the dirtiest Work to get his *Bread,* you are apt to look upon him as a *miserable Wretch :* it raises a *Mixture* of Pity and Contempt in you, and you hardly know, whether you *pity* or *disregard* him most. But remember, that every time you see such a Person, you see a more reasonable Creature than yourself, and one who is much more *nobly employed* than you are. He is acting *conformably* to the State of human Life, and bearing a hard Part with Patience ; he is doing a Work, which, mean as it is, will be looked upon as done unto the Lord ; whilst you, idling in *Softness* and *Pleasures,* are unable to bear your

Time, unless it be stolen away from you by *foolish*, *corrupt*, and *unedifying* Books.

Fancy that you saw a *patient Christian*, old, broken, and crooked, with carrying Burdens all his Life ; fancy that you saw another Christian lolling in *State* and *Softness*, and making every Day a Day of *Vanity* and *Impertinence*, of *foolish Readings*, and vain Imaginations ; which of them do you think is most likely to die into the Hands of good *Angels*, and be carried into *Abraham's Bosom?*

But after all, what a vain Imagination it is, to think that you have any such thing as *spare Time?* Is there any Time for which you are not accountable to God? Is there any Time which God has so left to your own Disposal, that you may sacrifice it to the Indulgence of vain Tempers, and the Corruption of your Heart? You can no more show this, than you can show that all your Time is your own. To talk therefore of *spare Time*, is to talk of *something* that never did nor ever will belong to any Christian. You may have a *spare Time* from this or that *Labour* or *Necessity*, you may abate, or change any *particular Exercise*, you may leave off this or that Way, you may take this or that Refreshment, you have all these *spare Times* from particular Actions, but you have no *spare Time* that releases you from the Laws of Christianity, or that leaves you at Liberty, not to act by the Principles of Religion and Piety.

You have a *spare Time* to recreate and refresh yourself, but this Time is to be governed by the same Principles of religious Wisdom, as the Time that is spent in Cares and Labours. For your Recreations and Pleasures are only lawful, so far as they are directed by such Wisdom and Piety, as is to direct your Cares and Labours. If therefore the Providence of God has placed you above the Necessity of labouring for your Livelihood, you must not think that you have so much *spare Time* to spend, as you please, but that you are as certainly called to some *other Labour*, as others are called to labour for their *Bread*. Great part of the World is doomed to Labour and Slavery, they have it not in their Power to choose any other Way of Life, and their Labour is therefore an acceptable Service to God, because it is such as their State requires. Happy you, therefore, if you knew your Happiness, who have it in your Power to be always doing the *best Things*, who, free from Labour and Hardships, are at Liberty to choose the *best Ways* of Life, to study all the Arts of *Self-improvement*, to practise all the Ways of doing Good, and to spend your Time in all the noblest Instances of Piety, Humility, Charity, and Devotion! Bless God therefore, not because you have *spare Time*, for that you have none, but that you have *spare Time* to employ in the best Ways that you can find, that whilst others are oppressed with Burdens, and worn out in Slavery, you have Time, and Leisure, and Retirement, to think and meditate upon the greatest and best of things, to enlighten your Mind, to correct the Disorders of your Hearts, to study the Laws of God, to contemplate the Wonders of his Providence, to convince yourself of the Vanity and Folly of the World, and to comfort and delight your Soul with those great and glorious Things, which God has prepared for those that love him. This is the Happiness of being free from Labour, and Want ; not to have *spare Time* to squander away in *Vanity* and *Impertinence,* but to have *spare Time* to spend in the Study of Wisdom, in the Exercise of Devotion, in the Practice of Piety, in all the Ways and Means of doing Good, and exalting our Souls to a State of *Christian Perfection.*

It is a Doctrine of Scripture, and highly agreeable to Reason, *That unto whomsoever much is given, of him shall much be required.* Consider therefore, that a Life of Leisure, and Freedom from Want and Hardships, is *as much* as can well be given you in this World, as it is giving you an Opportunity of living wholly unto God, and making all the Parts of your Life useful to the best Purposes. As sure therefore as it is a State, that has so many Advantages, that furnishes you with so many Means of being eminent in Piety, so sure is it that it is a State from which God expects Fruits that are worthy of it. Had it been your *Lot* to labour in a *Mine,* or serve under some cruel Master, you must have served as unto God, and in so doing, you had finished the Work which God had given you. But as you are free from all these States of Life, you must look upon yourself as God's *Servant,* as called to choose that Way of labouring and spending your Time, which may most promote that which God desires to be most promoted. God has given you Liberty to choose, but it is only that you may have the Blessedness of choosing the *best Ways* of spending your Time. Though therefore you are at Liberty from servile and mean Labour, yet you are under a Necessity of labouring in all good Works, and making all your Time, and Fortune, and Abilities, serviceable to the best Ends of Life. You have no more Time that is your own, than he has who is to live by constant Labour ; the only Difference betwixt you and him, is this, that he is to be diligent in a poor slavish Labour, that oppresses the Body, and dulls and dejects the Mind ; but you in a *Service that is perfect Freedom,* that renders your Body a *fit Temple* for the Holy Ghost, and fills your Soul with such Light, and Peace, and Joy, as is not to be found in any other Way of Life.

Do you think that a *poor Slave* would displease God by refusing to act in that painful Drudgery that is fallen to his Share? And do you think that God will not be more displeased with you, if you refuse to act your *full part* in the best of Labours, or neglect that happy joyful Business of doing Good, which your State of Life has called you to? Is it expected that *poor People* should make a right Use of their Condition, and turn all their Labour into a Service unto God? And can you think that you are not obliged to make the proper Improvement of your Condition, and turn all your *Rest*, and *Ease*, and *Freedom* from Labour, into a Service unto God? Tell me therefore no more, that you indulge yourself in idle Amusements, in vain, corrupt, and unedifying Books, because you have *spare Time ;* for it is absolutely false to say that you have any such thing ; it is also saying, that because God has given you *spare Time* from servile Labour, that you may choose the best Ways of Life, devote yourself to the most Divine Exercises, and become eminent and exemplary in all the Instances of a holy and heavenly Life ; therefore you presume to throw it away in Idleness and Impertinence.

Chapter XI.

A further Consideration of that Purity and Holiness of Conversation, to which the Necessity of Divine Grace calleth all Christians ; wherein is shown, that the Entertainment of the Stage, is a corrupt and sinful Entertainment, contrary to the whole Nature of Christian Piety, and constantly to be avoided by all sincere Christians.

I HAVE shown in the foregoing Chapter, that the reading of *Plays*, or any other Books of that kind, is a dangerous and sinful Entertainment, that corrupts our Hearts, and separates the Holy Spirit from us. You will now perhaps ask me, if it is unlawful for a Christian to go to the *Playhouse*. I answer, that it is absolutely unlawful. As un-

lawful, as for a Christian to be a *Drunkard* or a *Glutton,* or to
Curse and *Swear.* This I think, after what has been above observed, will be easily proved.

For let us resume the Doctrine of the Apostle, we are absolutely forbid all *corrupt Communication,* and for this important
Reason, because it *grieves* and *separates* the Holy Spirit from
us. Is it unlawful therefore to have any *corrupt Communication*
of our own ? And can we think it *lawful* to go *to Places set
apart* for that Purpose? To give our Money, and *hire* Persons
to corrupt our Hearts with ill Discourses, and inflame all the
disorderly Passions of our Nature ? We have the Authority of
Scripture to affirm, That *evil Communication corrupts good
Manners ;* and that *unedifying Discourses grieve the Holy
Spirit.* Now the *third* Commandment is not more plain and
express against *Swearing,* than this Doctrine is plain and
positive against going to the *Playhouse.* If you should see a
Person, who acknowledges the *third* Commandment to be a
Divine Prohibition against Swearing, yet going to a *House,* and
giving his *Money* to Persons, who were there met, to *Curse* and
Swear in fine Language, and invent *musical Oaths* and *Impreca-
tions,* would you not think him Mad in the highest Degree ?
Now consider, whether there be a less Degree of Madness in
going to the Playhouse. You own, that God has called you to
a great Purity of Conversation, that you are forbid all *foolish
Discourse,* and *filthy Jestings,* as expressly as you are forbid
Swearing ; that you are to let no *corrupt Communication* proceed out of your Mouth, but *such as is good for the Use of edifying ;* and yet you go to the *House set apart* for corrupt Communications, you hire Persons to entertain you with all manner
of *Ribaldry, Profaneness, Rant,* and *Impurity* of Discourse ;
who are to present you with *vile* Thoughts, and *lewd* Imaginations in *fine Language,* and to make *wicked, vain,* and *impure*
Discourse, more lively and effecting, than you could possibly
have it in any ill Company. Now, is not this sinning with as
high a Hand, and as grossly offending against the plain Doctrines of Scripture, as if you were to give your *Money* to be
entertained with *musical Oaths* and *Curses ?* You might
reasonably think that *Woman* very ridiculous in her *Piety,* who
durst not Swear herself, but should nevertheless frequent *Places*
to hear *Oaths.* But you may as justly think her very ridiculous
in her *Modesty,* who, though she dares not to say, or look, or do
an immodest Thing herself, shall yet give her *Money,* to see
Women forget the *Modesty* of their Sex, and talk *impudently* in
a public *Playhouse.* If the *Playhouse* were filled with *Rakes* and
ill *Women,* there would be nothing to be wondered at in such an

Assembly ; for *such Persons* to be delighted with such Entertainments, is as natural, as for any *Animal* to delight in its proper *Element*.   But for Persons who profess Purity and Holiness, who would not be suspected of *Immodesty* or *corrupt Communication*, for them to come under the Roof of a *House devoted* to such ill Purposes, and be pleased Spectators of such Actions and Discourses, as are the Pleasure of the most abandoned Persons, for them to give their Money to be thus entertained, is such a Contradiction to all Piety and common Sense, as cannot be sufficiently exposed.

Again, when you see the *Players* acting with Life and Spirit, Men and Women *equally bold* in all Instances of *Profaneness*, *Passion*, and *Immodesty*, I dare say, you never suspect any of them to be Persons of *Christian Piety*.   You can't even in your Imagination join Piety to such Manners, and such a Way of Life.   Your Mind will no more allow you to join Piety with the Behaviour of the *Stage*, than it will allow you to think *two* and *two* to be *ten*. And perhaps you had rather see your Son chained to a *Galley*, or your Daughter driving *Plough*, than getting their Bread on the *Stage*, by administering in so scandalous a Manner to the Vices and corrupt Pleasures of the World.   Let this therefore be another Argument to prove the *absolute Unlawfulness* of going to a *Play*.   For consider with yourself : is the Business of *Players* so contrary to Piety, so inconsistent with the Spirit and Temper of a true Christian, that it is next to a Contradiction to suppose them united ?   How then can you take yourself to be *Innocent*, who *delight* in their Sins, and *hire* them to commit them ?   You may make yourself a Partaker of other Men's Sins, by Negligence, and for want of reproving them ; but certainly, if you stand by, and assist Men in their evil Actions, if you make their Vices your Pleasure and Entertainment, and pay your Money to be so entertained, you make yourself a Partaker of their Sins in a very high Degree.   And consequently it must be as unlawful to go to a *Play*, as it is unlawful to approve, encourage, assist, and reward a Man for *renouncing* a Christian Life.   Let therefore every *Man* or *Woman* who goes to a *Play*, ask themselves this Question, Whether it suits with their Religion to act the *Parts* that are there acted ?   Perhaps they would think this as inconsistent with that Degree of Piety that they profess, as to do the vilest Things.   But let them consider, that it must be a wicked and unlawful Pleasure, to delight in any Thing that they dare not do themselves.   Let them also consider, that they are really *acting* those Indecencies and Impieties themselves, which they think is the particular Guilt of the *Players*.   For a Person may very justly be said to do that *himself,* which he *pays* for the doing, and which is done for his Pleasure. You must, therefore, if you would be consistent with yourself, as much abhor the Thoughts of being at a *Play,* as of being a *Player* yourself, for to think that you must forbear the one and not the other, is as absurd, as to suppose, that you must be temperate yourself, but may assist, encourage, and reward other People for their Intemperance. The Business of a *Player,* is profane, wicked, lewd, and immodest, to be any way therefore approving, assisting, or encouraging him in such a Way of Life, is as evidently sinful, as it is sinful to assist and encourage a Man in *stealing,* or any other Wickedness.

To proceed. When I consider *Churches,* and the Matter of *Divine Service,* that it consists of holy Readings, Prayers, and Exhortations to Piety, there is Reason to think, that the House of God, is a natural Means of Promoting Piety, and Religion, and rendering Men devout and sensible of their Duty to God. The very Nature of divine Assemblies thus carried on, has this direct Tendency. I ask you whether this is not very plain, that *Churches* thus employed should have this Effect.

Consider therefore the *Playhouse,* and the Matter of the Entertainment there, as it consists of *Love-intrigues, blasphemous Passions, profane Discourses, lewd Descriptions, filthy Jests,* and all the most extravagant Rant of wanton, vile, profligate Persons of both Sexes, heating and inflaming one another with all the *Wantonness* of Address, the *Immodesty* of Motion, and *Lewdness* of Thought, that Wit can invent ; consider, I say, whether it be not plain, that a House so employed, is as certainly serving the Cause of *Immorality* and *Vice,* as the House of God is serving the Cause of *Piety?* For what is there in our *Church-Service,* that shows it to be *useful* to Piety and Holiness, what is there in divine Worship to correct and amend the Heart, but what is directly *contrary* to all that is doing in the *Playhouse?* So that one may with the same Assurance affirm, that the *Playhouse,* not only when some very profane Play is on the *Stage,* but in its *daily, common* Entertainment, is as certainly the *House of the Devil,* as the Church is the *House of God.* For though the Devil be not professedly Worshipped by Hymns directed to him, yet most that is there Sung, is to his Service, he is there *obeyed* and *pleased* in as certain a Manner, as God is Worshipped and Honoured in the Church.

You must easily see, that this Charge against the *Playhouse,* is not the Effect of any *particular Temper,* or *Weakness* of Mind, that it is not an *uncertain Conjecture,* or *religious Whimsy,* but is a Judgment founded as plainly in the *Nature* and *Reason* of

Things, as when it is affirmed that the House of God, is of Service to Religion. And he who absolutely condemns the *Playhouse*, as wicked and corrupting, proceeds upon as much Truth and Certainty, as he who absolutely commends the *House of God*, as Holy, and tending to promote Piety.

When therefore anyone pretends to vindicate the *Stage* to you, as a proper Entertainment for holy and religious Persons, you ought to reject the Attempt with as much Abhorrence, as if he should offer to show you, that our *Church-Service* was rightly formed for those Persons to join in, who are *devoted to the Devil*. For to talk of the *Lawfulness* and *Usefulness* of the *Stage*, is fully as absurd, as contrary to the plain Nature of Things, as to talk of the *Unlawfulness* and *Mischief* of the Service of the Church. He therefore who tells you, that you may safely go to the *Playhouse*, as an innocent, useful Entertainment of your Mind, commits the same Offence, against common Sense, as if he should tell you, that it was dangerous to attend at Divine Service, and that its *Prayers* and *Hymns* were great *Pollutions* of the Mind.

For the Matter and Manner of *Stage-entertainments*, is as undeniable a Proof, and as obvious to common Sense, that the House belongs to the Devil, and is the Place of his Honour, as the Matter and Manner of *Church-Service* proves that the Place is appropriated to God.

Observe therefore, that as you do not want the Assistance of anyone, to show you the *Usefulness* and *Advantage* of Divine Service, because the thing is plain, and speaks for itself. So neither, on the other hand, need you anyone to show you the *Unlawfulness* and *Mischief* of the Stage, because there the thing is equally plain, and speaks for itself. So that you are to consider yourself, as having the same Assurance that the *Stage* is wicked, and to be abhorred and avoided by all Christians, as you have that the Service of the Church is Holy, and to be sought after by all Lovers of Holiness. Consider therefore, that your Conduct, with relation to the *Stage*, is not a Matter of *Nicety* or *scrupulous Exactness*, but that you are as certain that you do wrong in as notorious a Manner, when you go to the *Playhouse*, as you are certain that you do right, when you go to Church.

Now it is of mighty Use to conceive things in a right Manner, and to see them as they are in their own Nature. While you consider the Playhouse, as only a *Place of Diversion*, it may perhaps give no Offence to your Mind: There is nothing *shocking* in the Thought of it ; but if you would lay aside this Name of it for awhile, and consider it in its *own Nature*, as it really is, you would find that you are as much deceived, if you consider the *Playhouse,* as only a *Place of Diversion,* as you would be, if you considered the House of God only as a *Place of Labour.*

When therefore you are tempted to go to a *Play,* either from your own Inclination, or the Desire of a Friend, fancy that you were asked in plain Terms to go to the Place of the *Devil's Abode,* where he holds his *filthy Court* of evil Spirits ; that you were asked to join in an Entertainment, where he was at the *Head* of it, where the whole of it was in order to his Glory, that Men's Hearts and Minds might be separated from God, and plunged into all the Pollutions of Sin and Brutality. Fancy that you were going to a Place that as certainly belongs to the Devil, as the *Heathen Temples* of old, where *Brutes* were Worshipped, where *wanton Hymns* were Sung to *Venus,* and *drunken Songs* to the God of *Wine.* Fancy that you were as certainly going to the Devil's Triumph, as if you were going to those *old Sports,* where People committed Murder, and offered Christians to be devoured by wild Beasts, for the Diversion of Spectators. Now whilst you consider the *Playhouse* in this View, I suppose that you can no more go to a *Play,* than you can expressly renounce your Christianity.

Consider therefore now, that you have not been frightening yourself with *groundless Imaginations,* but that what you have here fancied of the *Playhouse* is as strictly true, as if you had been fancying, that when you go to Church, you go into the House of God, where the heavenly Host attend upon his Service, and that when you there read the Scriptures, and Sing holy Hymns, you join with the Choirs above, and do God's Will on Earth as it is done in Heaven. For observe, I pray you, how justly that Opinion of the *Playhouse* is founded. For, was it a Joy and Delight to the Devil to see *Idols worshipped,* to see Hymns and Adorations offered up to impure and filthy Deities ? Were Places and Festivals appointed for such Ends, justly esteemed Places and Festivals devoted to the Devil ? Now give the Reason why all this was justly reckoned a Service to the Devil, and you will give as good a Reason, why the *Playhouse* is to be esteemed his *Temple.* For, what though Hymns and Adorations are not offered to impure and filthy Deities, yet if *Impurity* and *Filthiness* is there the *Entertainment,* if immodest Songs, profane Rant, if Lust and Passion entertain the Audience, the Business is the same, and the Assembly does the *same Honour* to the Devil, though they are not gathered together in the Name of some *Heathen God.*

For Impurity and Profaneness in the Worshippers of the true

God, is as acceptable a Service to the Devil, as Impurity and Profaneness in any Idolaters, and perhaps a *lewd Song* in an Assembly of Christians gives him greater Delight, than if it had been sung in a Congregation of *Heathens*.

If therefore we may justly say, that a *House* or *Festival* was the Devil's, because he was *delighted* with it, because what was there done, was an *acceptable Service* to him, we may be assured that the *Playhouse*, is as really the House of the Devil, as any other House ever was. Nay, it is reasonable to think that the *Playhouses* in this Kingdom, are a greater Pleasure to him than any *Temple* he ever had in the *Heathen World*. For as it is a greater Conquest to make the Disciples of Christ delight in *Lewdness* and *Profaneness*, than ignorant Heathens, so a *House*, that in the Midst of *Christian Churches*, trains up Christians in *Lewdness* and *Profaneness*, that makes the Worshippers of Christ flock together in Crowds to rejoice in an Entertainment, that is as contrary to the Spirit of Christ, as *Hell* is contrary to *Heaven*, a House so employed, may justly be reckoned a more delightful Habitation of the Devil, than any Temple in the Heathen World. When therefore you go to the *Playhouse*, you have as much Assurance, that you go to the Devil's peculiar Habitation, that you submit to his Designs, and rejoice in his Diversions (which are his best Devices against Christianity), you have as much Assurance of this, as that they who worshipped filthy Deities, were in reality Worshippers of the Devil.

Again, Consider those *old Sports* and *Diversions*, where Christians were sometimes thrown to wild Beasts, consider why such Sports might well be looked upon as the *Devil's Triumph*. I suppose you are at no stand with yourself, whether you should impute such Entertainments to the Devil. Consider, therefore, why you should not as readily allow the *Stage* to be his Entertainment.

For were it a Delight to the Devil to see Heathens sporting with the bodily Death of Christians? And must it not be a greater Delight to him to see Christians sporting themselves in the Death of their Souls?

The Heathens could only kill the Body, and separate it from the Soul, but these Christian-Diversions murder the Soul, and separate it from God. I daresay, no Arguments could convince you, that it was *lawful* to rejoice at those Sports, which were thus defiled with human Blood ; but then pray remember, that if the Death of the Soul be as great a Cruelty, as the Death of the Body, if it be as dreadful for a Soul to be separated from God, as to be separated from the Body, you ought to think it as entirely unlawful to enter that House where so many eternal

Lives are sacrificed, or ever to partake of those Diversions which separate such Numbers of Souls from God.

Hence it appears, that if instead of considering the *Playhouse*, as only a Place of Diversion, you will but examine what Materials it is made of, if you will but consider the Nature of the Entertainment, and what is there doing, you will find it as wicked a Place, as sinful a Diversion, and as truly the peculiar Pleasure and Triumph of the Devil, as any wicked Place, or sinful Diversion, in the Heathen World. When therefore you are asked to go to a *Play*, don't think that you are asked only to go to a *Diversion*, but be assured that you are asked to *yield* to the Devil, to go over to his *Party*, and to make one of his Congregation; that if you do go, you have not only the Guilt of *buying* so much vain and corrupt Communication, but are also as certainly guilty of going to the Devil's House, and doing him the same Honour, as if you were to partake of some *Heathen Festival*.

You must consider, that all the Laughter there, is not only vain and foolish, but that it is a Laughter amongst Devils, that you are upon *profane Ground*, and hearing Music in the very Porch of Hell.

Thus it is in the Reason of the Thing, and if we should now consider the State of our *Playhouse* as it is in Fact, we should find it answering all these Characters, and producing Effects suitable to its Nature : But I shall forbear this Consideration, it being as unnecessary to tell the Reader that our *Playhouse* is in Fact the *Sink of Corruption and Debauchery*, that it is the general Rendezvous of the most profligate Persons of both Sexes, that it corrupts the Air, and turns the adjacent Places into public Nuisances; this is as unnecessary, as to tell him, that the *Exchange* is a Place of *Merchandise*.

Now it is to be observed, that this is not the State of the *Playhouse*, through any accidental Abuse, as any innocent or good Thing may be abused; but that Corruption and Debauchery are the truly natural and genuine Effects of the *Stage-Entertainment*. Let not therefore anyone say, that he is not answerable for those Vices and Debaucheries, which are occasioned by the *Playhouse*, for so far as he partakes of the Pleasure of the *Stage*, and is an Encourager of it, so far he is chargeable with those Disorders which necessarily are occasioned by it. If Evil arises from our doing our Duty, or our Attendance at any *good Design*, we are not to be frightened at it; but if Evil arises from any-thing as its *natural* and *genuine* Effect, in all such Cases, so far as we contribute to the Cause, so far we make ourselves guilty of the Effects. So that all who any way assist the *Play-*

12

house, or ever encourage it by their Presence, make themselves chargeable in some Degree, with all the Evils and Vices which follow from it. Since therefore it cannot be doubted by any-one, whether the *Playhouse* be a Nursery of Vice and Debauchery, since the evil Effects it has upon People's Manners, is as visible as the Sun at Noon, one would imagine, that all People of Virtue and Modesty, should not only avoid it, but avoid it with the utmost Abhorrence; that they should be so far from entering into it, that they should detest the very Sight of it. For what a Contradiction is it to common Sense, to hear a Woman lamenting the miserable Lewdness and Debauchery of the Age, the vicious Taste, and irregular Pleasures of the World, and at the same time dressing herself to meet the lewdest Part of the World, at the Fountain-Head of all Lewdness, and making herself one of that Crowd, where every abandoned Wretch is glad to be present? She may fancy that she hates and abominates their Vices, but she may depend upon it, that till she hates and abominates the Place of vicious Pleasures, till she dare not come near an Enter-tainment which is the Cause of so great Debauchery, and the Pleasure of the most debauched People, till she is thus disposed, she wants the truest Sign of a real and religious Abhorrence of the Vices of the Age.

For to waive all other Considerations, I would only ask her a Question or two on the single Article of *Modesty*. What is Modesty? Is it a little *mechanical outside* Behaviour, that goes no further than a few *Forms and Modes* at particular Times and Places? Or is it a *real Temper*, a rational Disposition of the Heart, that is founded in *Religion?* Now if Modesty is only a mechanical Observance of a little outside Behaviour, then I can easily perceive how a modest Woman may frequent *Plays;* there is no Inconsistency for such a one to be one Thing in one Place, and another in another Place, to disdain an immodest Conversation, and yet at the same time, relish and delight in immodest and impudent Speeches in a public *Playhouse.* But if Modesty is a *real Temper* and Disposition of the Heart, that is founded in the Principles of Religion, then I confess, I cannot comprehend how a Person of such Modesty, should ever come twice into a *Playhouse.* For it is Reason and Religion that has inspired her with a modest Heart, that makes her careful of her Behaviour, that makes her hate and abhor every Word, or Look, or Hint, in Conversation, that has the Ap-pearance of Lewdness, that makes her shun the Company of such as talk with too much Freedom; if she is thus modest in *common Life*, from a Principle of Religion, a Temper of Heart, is it possible for such a one (I don't say to seek) but to bear with the Immodesty and Impudence of the *Stage?* For must not Immodesty and Impudence, must not loose and wanton Discourse be the same *hateful Things,* and give the same Offence to a modest Mind, in one Place, as in another? And must not that Place, which is the Seat of Immodesty, where Men and Women are trained up in Lewdness, where almost every Day in the Year, is a Day devoted to the foolish Representations of *Rant, Lust,* and *Passion;* must not such a Place, of all others, be the most odious, to a Mind that is *truly modest* upon Principles of *Reason and Religion?* One would suppose, that such a Person should as much abominate the Place, as any other filthy Sight, and be as much offended with an Invitation to it, as if she were invited to see an immodest Picture. For the Representations of the *Stage,* the inflamed Passions of Lovers there described, are as gross an Offence to the Ear, as any Representation that can offend the Eye.

It ought not to be concluded, that because I affirm the *Playhouse* to be an Entertainment *contrary* to Modesty, that therefore I accuse all People as void of Modesty, who ever go to it. I might affirm, that *Transubstantiation* is contrary to all *Sense and Reason;* but then it would be a wrong Conclusion to say, that I affirmed that all who believe it are void of all Sense and Reason. Now as *Prejudices,* the Force of *Education,* the Authority of *Numbers,* the Way of the *World,* the Example of *great Names,* may make People *believe,* so the same Causes may make People *act* against *all Sense and Reason,* and be guilty of Practices which no more suit with the *Purity* of their Religion, than *Transubstantiation* agrees with *common Sense.*

To proceed. I once heard a young Lady thus excusing herself for going to the *Playhouse,* that she went but seldom, and then in Company of her *Mother* and her *Aunt,* that they always knew their *Play* beforehand, and never went on the *Sacrament Week.* And what Harm, pray, says she, can there be in this? It breaks in upon no Rules of my Life, I neglect no part of my Duty, I go to *Church,* and perform the same Devotions at Home, as on other Days. It ought to be observed, that this Excuse can only be allowed where the *Diversion* itself is *innocent;* it must therefore be first considered, what the Entertainment is in itself, whether it be suitable to the Spirit and Temper of Religion ; for if it is right and proper in itself, it needs no Excuse ; but if it be *wrong,* and *dangerous* to Religion, we are not to use it *cautiously,* but to avoid it *constantly.*

Secondly, It is no Proof of the Innocency of a Thing, that it does not interfere with our *Hours of Duty,* nor break the Regularity of our Lives, for very wicked Ways of spending Time,

12—2

may yet be consistent with a regular Distribution of our Hours. She must therefore consider, not only whether such a Diversion hinders the Regularity of her Life, or breaks in upon her Devotions, public or private, but whether it hinders or any way affects that *Spirit and Temper*, which all her Devotions aspire after. Is it conformable to that Heavenly Affection, that Love of God, that Purity of Heart, that Wisdom of Mind, that Perfection of Holiness, that Contempt of the World, that Watchfulness and Self-denial, that Humility and Fear of Sin? Is it conformable to these Graces, which are to be the *daily Subject* of all her Prayers? This is the only way for her to know the *Innocency* of going to a *Play*. If what she there hears and sees, has no *Contrariety* to any *Graces* or *Virtues* which she prays for, if all that there passes be fit for the *Purity* and *Piety* of one who is led by the Spirit of Christ, and is working out her Salvation *with Fear and Trembling*, if the *Stage* be an Entertainment, that may be thought according to the Will of God, then she disposes of an Hour very innocently, though her *Mother* or her *Aunt* were not with her. But if the contrary to all this be true, if most of what she there hears and sees, be as *contrary* to the *Piety* and *Purity* of Christianity, as *Feasting* is contrary to *Fasting;* if the House which she supports by her Money, and encourages by her Presence, be a notorious Means of Corruption, visibly carrying on the Cause of Vice and Debauchery, she must not then think herself excused for being with her *Mother*.

Thirdly, The same Person would perhaps think it strange to hear one of her virtuous Acquaintance, giving the like excuse for going now and then to a *Masquerade*.

Now this Diversion is new in our Country, and therefore People judge of it in the manner that they should, because they are not blinded by *Use and Custom;* but let anyone give but the true Reasons why a Person of Virtue and Piety should not give into such Entertainments, and the same Reasons will show, that a Person of strict Piety, should keep at as great a Distance from the *Playhouse*. For the Entertainment of the *Stage* is as directly opposite to the *Purity* of Religion, and is as much the *natural Means* of Corruption, and serves all bad Ends in as high a Manner as *Masquerades*, they only differ, as bad Things of the same kind may differ from one another. So that if the evil Use, the ill Consequences of *Masquerades*, be a sufficient Reason to deter People of Piety, from partaking of them, the same evil Use and ill Consequences of the *Stage*, ought to keep all People of Virtue from it. If People will consult their *Temper* only, they may take the Entertainment of one, and condemn the other, as following the same Guide, they may abhor *Intemperance,* and indulge *Malice,* but if they will consult Religion, and make that the Ground of their Opinions, they would find as strong Reasons for a constant Abhorrence of the *Stage,* as of *Masquerades.*

Further, she that is for going only to the *Playhouse* now and then, with this Care and Discretion, does not seem to have enough considered the Matter, or to act by Reason, for if the *Stage* be an innocent and proper Entertainment, if in its own Nature it be as harmless and useful, as *walking, riding, taking the Air,* or *conversing* with virtuous People, if this be the Nature of it, then there is no need of this Care and Abstinence, a virtuous Lady need not excuse herself, that she goes but very seldom. But if it be the very Reverse of all this, if it be that Fountain of Corruption and Debauchery, which has been observed, then to go to it at any Time admits of no excuse, but is as absurd, as contrary to Reason and Religion, as to do any other ill Thing with the same Care and Discretion. If you should hear a Person excusing her Use of *Paint* in this manner, that truly she painted but *very seldom,* that she always said her Prayers first, that she never used it on *Sundays,* or the Week before the *Communion,* would you not pity such a *Mixture* of Religion and Weakness ? Would you not desire her to use her Reason, and either allow *painting* to be an innocent Ornament, suitable to the *Sobriety* and *Humility* of a Christian, or else to think it as unlawful at one time as at another? Would you not think it strange that she should condemn *painting* as odious and sinful, and yet think, that the Regularity of her Life, the Exactness of her Devotions, and her Observance of Religion, might make it lawful for her to *paint now and then ?* I don't doubt, but you plainly see the Weakness and Folly of such a Pretence for *painting* under such Rules at certain Times. And if you would but as impartially consider your Pretences for going sometimes to the *Playhouse,* you would certainly find them equally Weak and Unreasonable. For *Painting* may with more Reason be reckoned an *innocent Ornament,* than the *Playhouse* an innocent Diversion ; and it supposes a greater Vanity of Mind, a more perverted Judgment, and a deeper Corruption of Heart, to seek the Diversion of the *Stage,* than to take the Pleasure of a *borrowed Colour.*

I know you are offended at this *Comparison,* because you judge by your *Temper* and *Prejudices,* and don't consider the Things, as they are in themselves, by the pure Light of Reason and Religion. *Painting* has not been the Way of your *Family,* it is supposed to be the Practice but of *very few,* and those who use it, endeavour to *conceal* it, this makes you readily condemn it ;

On the contrary, your *Mother* and your *Aunt* carry you to a *Play*, you see *virtuous* People there, and the same Persons that fill our *Churches*, so that your *Temper* is as much engaged to think it lawful to go sometimes to a *Play*, as it is engaged to think the Use of *Paint* odious and sinful.   Lay aside therefore these Prejudices for a while, fancy that you had been trained up in some Corner of the World, in the Principles of Christianity, and had never heard either of the *Playhouse* or *Painting*.   Imagine now that you were to examine the Lawfulness of them by the Doctrines of Scripture.   You would first desire to be told the Nature of these Things, and what they meant.   They would tell you that *painting* was the borrowing of *Colours* from Art, to make the Face look more beautiful.   Now though you found no express Text of Scripture against *painting*, you would find, that it was expressly against *Tempers* required in Scripture; you would therefore condemn it, as proceeding from a *Vanity* of Mind, a *Fondness* of Beauty; you would see that the Harm of *painting* consisted in this, that it proceeded from a *Temper* of Mind, contrary to the *Sobriety* and *Humility* of a Christian, which indeed is harm enough, because this Humility and Sobriety of Mind is as *essential* to Religion, as Charity and Devotion.   So that in judging according to Scripture, you would hold it as unreasonable to *paint sometimes*, as to be sometimes *malicious, indevout, proud,* or *false*.

You are now to consider the *Stage*, you are to keep close to Scripture, and fancy that you yet know nothing of *Plays*.   You ask therefore first what the *Stage* or *Playhouse* is.   You are told that it is a *Place* where all Sorts of People meet to be entertained with *Discourses, Actions,* and *Representations*, which are recommended to the Heart, by beautiful Scenes, the Splendour of Lights, and the Harmony of Music.   You are told, that these Discourses are the Inventions of Men of Wit and Imagination, which describe imaginary *Intrigues* and *Scenes of Love*, and introduce *Men* and *Women* discoursing, raving, and acting in all the wild, indecent Transports of *Lust* and *Passion*. You are told that the Diversion partly consists of *lewd* and *Profane* Songs, sung to fine Music, and partly of extravagant Dialogues between *immodest Persons*, talking in a Style of *Love* and *Madness*, that is nowhere else to be found, and entertaining the *Christian Audience*, with all the Violence of Passion, Corruption of Heart, Wantonness of Mind, Immodesty of Thought, and profane Jests, that the Wit of the *Poet* is able to invent. You are told, that the *Players*, Men and Women, are trained up to act and represent all the Descriptions of Lust and Passion in the *liveliest Manner*, to add a Lewdness of Action to lewd

Speeches ; that they get their Livelihood, by *Cursing, Swearing,* and *Ranting,* for three Hours together to an Assembly of *Christians.*

Now though you find no particular Text of Scripture condemning the *Stage,* or *Tragedy,* or *Comedy,* in express Words, yet, what is much more, you find that such Entertainments are a gross Contradiction to the *whole Nature* of Religion. They are not contrary to this or that particular Temper, but are contrary to that *whole Turn* of Heart and Mind which Religion requires. *Painting* is contrary to *Humility,* and therefore is always to be avoided as sinful. But the Entertainment of the *Stage,* as it consists of *blasphemous* Expressions, *wicked* Speeches, *Swearing, Cursing,* and *Profaning* the Name of God, as it abounds with *impious* Rant, *filthy* Jests, *distracted* Passions, gross Descriptions of *Lust,* and *wanton Songs,* is a *contradiction to every Doctrine* that our Saviour and his Apostles have taught us. So that to abhor *Painting* at all Times, because it supposes a Vanity of Mind, and is contrary to Humility, and yet think there is a lawful Time to go to the *Playhouse,* is as contrary to common Sense, as if a Man should hold that it was lawful sometimes to offend against *all the Doctrines* of Religion, and yet always unlawful to offend against *any one* Doctrine of Religion.

If therefore you were to come (as I supposed) from some Corner of the World, where you had been used to live and judge by the Rules of Religion, and upon your arrival here, had been told what *Painting,* and the *Stage* was ; as you would not expect to see Persons of *religious Humility* carrying their Daughters to *Paint-shops,* or inviting their *pious Friends* to go along with them, so much less would you expect to hear, that *devout, pious* and *modest* Women carried their Daughters, and invited their virtuous Friends to meet them at the *Play.* Least of all could you imagine, that there were any People *too pious* and *devout* to indulge the Vanity of *Painting,* and yet not devout or pious enough to *abhor* the Immodesty, Profaneness, Ribaldry, Immorality, and Blasphemy of the *Stage.*

To proceed. A *polite Writer** of a late Paper thought he had sufficiently ridiculed a certain Lady's Pretension to *Piety,* when speaking of her *Closet,* he says :

> *Together lie her Prayer-book and Paint,*
> *At once t' improve the Sinner and the Saint.*

Now whence comes it that this *Writer* judges so rightly, and speaks the Truth so plainly in the Matter of *Painting?* Whence

---

* *Spectator,* No, 79.

comes it that the generality of his Readers, think his Observation just, and join with him in it ? It is because *Painting* is not yet an *acknowledged Practice*, but is for the most Part reckoned a *shameful Instance* of Vanity. Now as we are not prejudiced in Favour of this Practice, and have no Excuses to make for our *own Share* in it, so we judge of it impartially, and immediately perceive its Contrariety to a religious Temper and State of Mind. This *Writer* saw this in so strong a Light, that he does not scruple to suppose, that *Paint* is as natural and proper a Means to improve the *Sinner*, as the Prayer-book is to improve the *Saint.*

I should therefore hope, that it need not be imputed to any *Sourness* of Temper, religious *Weakness* or *Dulness* of Spirits, if a *Clergyman* should imagine, that the Profaneness, Debauchery, Lewdness, and Blasphemy of the *Stage*, is as natural a Means to improve the *Sinner*, as a *Bottle of Paint ;* or if he should venture to show, that the *Church* and the *Playhouse* are as ridiculous a Contradiction, and do no more suit with the *same* Person, than the *Prayer-book* and *Paint.*

Again, Suppose you were told that the *holy Angels* delight in the Repentance and Devotion of Christians, that they attend at God's *Altar*, and rejoice in the Prayers and Praises, which are there offered unto God ; I imagine you could easily believe it, you could think it very agreeable to the Nature of such good Beings, to see *fallen Spirits* returning unto God. Suppose you were told also, that these same heavenly Beings delighted to be with Men in their *Drunkenness, Revellings,* and *Debaucheries,* and were as much pleased with their Vices and Corruptions, as with their Devotions, you would know, that both these Accounts could not possibly be true ; you could no more doubt in your Mind, whether *good Angels* that delight in the Conversion and Devotion of Christians, do also delight in their Vices and Follies, than you can doubt, whether the same Person can be *alive* and *dead* at the same time. You would be sure, that in Proportion as they delighted in the *Piety* and *Holiness* of Men, they must necessarily in the same Degree abhor and dislike their *Vices* and *Corruptions.* So that, supposing the Matter of our *Church-Service*, the Excellency of its Devotions, its heavenly Petitions, its lofty Hymns, its solemn Praises of the most High God, be such a glorious Service as invites and procures the Attendance of that *blessed* Choir, if this be true, I suppose you are as certain as you can be of the plainest Truth, that the *Filthiness*, the *Rant, Ribaldry, Profaneness,* and *Impiety* of the *Stage*, must be the Hatred and Aversion of those *good Spirits.* You are sure, that it is as impossible for them to behold the *Stage* with Pleasure, as to look upon the *Holy Altar* with Abhorrence.

Consider a while on this Matter, and think how it can be lawful for you to go to a *Place*, where if a *good Angel* was to look with Pleasure, it would cease to be good? For as that which makes Angels good, is the same *right Temper* which makes you good, so the same Tempers which would render Angels evil, must also render you evil. You may perhaps tell me, that you are not an *Angel*. I grant it, neither are you Jesus Christ, neither are you God, yet you are called to be *Holy* as Jesus Christ was *Holy*, and *to be Perfect as your Father which is in Heaven is Perfect.* Though you are not an *Angel*, yet it is Part of your glorious Hope, that you shall be *as the Angels of God*, so that as you are capable of their Happiness, you must think yourself obliged to be as like them in your Temper, as the Infirmity of your present State will permit. If *Angels* are to rejoice in singing the Praises of God, though their Joy may exceed yours, yet you are as much obliged to your Degree of Joy in this Duty, as they are. Angels by the Light and Strength of their Nature, may abhor all manner of Sin with stronger Aversion, a higher Degree of Abhorrence, yet you are as much obliged to abhor all manner of Sin, as they are. So that it is no more lawful for you to delight in impure, profane Diversions, which *good Angels* abhor, than it is lawful for you to hate those *Praises* and *Adorations* which are their Delight.

You are to consider also, that these *contradictory Tempers* are no more possible in the *same Men*, than in the *same Angels ;* 'tis no more possible for your Heart truly to delight in the Service of the Church, to be in earnest in all its Devotions, and at the same time delight in the Entertainment of the *Stage*, than it is possible for an *Angel* to delight in them both.

You may fancy that you relish these Entertainments, and at the same time relish and delight in the Service of God, and are very hearty in your Devotions ; you may fancy this, as *cruel* Men may fancy themselves to be *merciful,* the *covetous* and *proud* may fancy themselves to be *humble* and *heavenly-minded ;* but then take Notice, that it is all but mere Fancy : For it is as impossible to be really devout with your Reason and Understanding, and at the same time delight in the Entertainment of the *Stage*, as 'tis impossible to be really *charitable,* and delighting in *Malice* at the same time. There is indeed a *Falseness* in our Hearts, a *Mechanism* in our Constitution, which will deceive those, who do not constantly *suspect* themselves. There are *Forms of Devotion*, little Rules of Religion, which are fixed in us by *Education*, which we can no more part with, than we can part with any other Customs, which we have long used. Now this makes many People think themselves mighty pious, because they find it is not in their Nature to forbear or neglect such and such *Forms of Piety ;* they fancy that Religion must have its Seat in their Heart, because their Heart is so unalterable in *certain Rules* of Religion. Thus a Person who is exact in his Times of Prayer, will perhaps think himself much injured, if you were to tell him that it is his *want of Piety*, that makes him relish the Diversion of the *Stage :* His Heart immediately justifies him against such an Accusation, and tells him how constant he is in his Devotions ; whereas it is very possible, that he may have but little more Piety, than what consists in some *Rules* and *Forms*, and that his Constancy to such Rules, may be owing to the same Cause, which makes others constantly *sleepy* at such an Hour, that is, the mere *Mechanism* of his Constitution, and the Force of *Custom*. This is the State of Numbers of People, otherwise it would not be so common, to see the same People constant and unalterable in *some Rules* of Religion, and as constant and unalterable in *Pride, Passion,* and *Vanity*.

Again, there are many other Instances of a false Piety : Some People feel themselves capable of *religious Fervours*, they have their Passions frequently affected with *religious Subjects*, who from thence imagine, that their Hearts are in a true State of Religion. But such a Conclusion is very deceitful. For the mere *Mechanism* and natural Temper of our Bodies, and our present Condition, may be the chief Foundation of all this. Thus a *Lady* may find herself, as she thinks, *warm* in her Devotions, and praise God at *Church* with a Sense of Joy ; she thinks she is very good because she finds herself thus *affected* and *pleased* with the Service of the *Church ;* whereas it may be, the very Reason why she is more than ordinarily devout, and thinks it a Pleasure to praise God, is, because she is going to a *Ball*, or a *Play*, as soon as Divine Service is over. This agreeable Expectation has so put her Spirits in Order, that she can be very *thankful* to God all the time she is at *Church*.

Another has been pleased with the Compliments paid to her Person, she finds herself very *finely dressed*, she is full of Joy under *such Thoughts*, and so can easily break out into *Fervours of Devotion*, and rejoice in God at a Time, when she can rejoice in *anything*. These frequent Starts of Devotion, make her think herself to be far advanced in Piety, and she does not perceive that the *Height* of her Devotion, is owing to the *Height* of her Vanity. Let her but be *less pleased* with herself, let her be *unregarded, undressed*, without such *pleasing Reflections*, and she will find herself sunk into a strange *Dulness* towards Devotion.

The same Temper is very frequent in *common Life ;* you meet a Person who is very fond of you, full of Affection, and pleased

with everything you say or do ; you must not imagine that he
has more *Friendship* for you, than when he saw you last, and
hardly took any Notice of you : The Matter is only this, the
Man is in a *State of Joy* at something or other, he is pleased
with *himself*, and so is easily pleased with you, stay but till this
flow of Spirits is gone off, and he will show you no more Affection, than he used to do. This is the Religion of *Numbers* of
People ; they are devout by *Fits* and *Starts,* in the same Manner
as they are pleased by *Fits* and *Starts*, and their Devotion at
those very Times is no more a Sign of true *Piety*, than the
Civility and Compliments of a Person *overjoyed*, are Signs of
true *Friendship*. But still these little Flashes of Devotion make
People think themselves in a State of Religion.

Take another instance of a false Piety of another kind :
Junius has been orthodox in his Faith, a Lover of Churchmen,
a Hater of Heretics, these several Years ; he is the first who is
sorry for a *dangerous Book* that is come out, he is amazed what
People would be at by such Writings, but thanks God there is
Learning enough in the World to confute them. He reads all
the Confutations of *Atheists, Deists*, and *Heretics,* there is only
one sort of Books, for which *Junius* has no Taste, and that is,
Books of *Devotion*. He freely owns that they are not for his
Taste, he does not *understand their Flights*.

If another Person were to say so much, it would be imputed to
his want of Piety : but because *Junius* is known to be an Enemy
to Irreligion, because he is constantly at Church, you suppose
him to be a pious Man, though he thus confesses that he wants
the *Spirit of Piety*. It is in the same Manner that *Junius* de-
ceives himself, his Heart permits him to neglect Books of Devotion, because his Heart is constantly showing him his *Zeal* for
Religion, and *Honour* for the Church ; this makes him no more
suspect himself to want any Degrees of Piety, than he suspects
himself to be a Favourer of *Heresy*. If he never thinks any ill
of himself, if he never suspects any Falseness in his own Heart,
if he is prejudiced in favour of all his own Ways, it is because
he is prejudiced in favour of all *orthodox Men*. *Junius* reads
much Controversy, yet he does not take it ill, that you pretend
to inform him in Matters of *Controversy ;* on the contrary, he
never reads Books of Devotion, yet is angry if you pretend to
correct him in Matters of that kind. You may suppose him
mistaken in something that he is always studying, and he will
be thankful to you for setting him right ; but if you suppose
him mistaken in Things that he never applies himself to, if you
suppose that any Body knows what *Humility, Heavenly-mindedness, Devotion, Self-denial, Mortification, Repentance, Charity*, or

the *Love* of God is, better than he, you provoke his Temper, and he won't suffer himself to be informed by you. *Great Numbers* of People are like *Junius* in this Respect, they think they are very religious by listening to Instruction upon *certain Points*, by reading *certain Books*, and being ready to receive further Light, who yet can't bear to be instructed in Matters where they are most likely to be deceived, and where the Deceit is of the utmost Danger. They will be thankful for your telling them the particular Times in which the *Gospels* were written, for explaining the Word *Euroclydon*, or *Anathema Maranatha*, they will be glad of such useful Instruction, but if you touch upon such Subjects as really concern them in a high Degree, such as try the *State* and *Way* of their Lives, these religious People, who are so fond of religious Truths, cannot bear to be thus instructed.

What is the Reason that when we consult *Lawyers*, it is not to hear Harangues upon the *Law*, or its several *Courts ;* it is not to hear the Variety of Cases that concern other People, but it is to be instructed and assisted in our *own Case?* Why do we thank them for dealing impartially with us, for searching and examining into the true State of our *Case*, and informing us of every Thing that concerns us? What is the Reason that we apply to *Physicians*, not to hear the Rise and Progress of *Physic*, or the History of Disputes amongst them, not to hear of other People's Distempers, but to tell them our own *particular State*, and learn the *Cure* of our own Distempers? Why do we thank them for being *nicely exact* in searching us out, for examining into every Part of our Lives, our Ways of *eating*, *drinking*, and *sleeping*, and not suffering us to deceive ourselves with wrong Opinions and Practices? What is the Reason why we act thus consistently, and in the same Manner, in both these Instances? Now the only Reason is this, because in both these Instances we are *really in earnest*. When you are in earnest in your Religion, you will act as consistently and in the same Manner there. When you desire *solid Piety*, as you desire *sound Health*, your chief Concern will be about your *own Disorders ;* you will thank *Divines* and *Casuists* for making you their chief Care, you will be glad to have them examine and search into your Ways of Life, to be rightly informed of the Follies, Vanities, and Dangers, of your State. You will be glad to read those Books, and consult those *Casuists*, which are most *exact* and *faithful* in discovering your Faults, who question and examine all your Ways, who discover to you your *secret* Corruptions, and *unsuspected* Follies, and who are best able to give you the surest Rules of arriving at Christian Perfection ; when you are in earnest in your Religion, you will as certainly act in this Manner, as you act in the same Manner with the *Lawyer* or *Physician.* Take this also for an undeniable Truth, that till you do act in this Manner, you are not in earnest in your Religion. This therefore is a good Rule to examine yourself by. Do you find that you act in Religion as you do in other Cases, where you are in earnest? Are you as suspicious of yourself, as fearful of Mistake, as watchful of Danger, as glad of Assistance, as desirous of Success, as in other Matters where your Life or Fortune are at stake, or where your Heart is engaged? Never imagine that your Religion is founded in a true Fear of God, and a hearty Desire of Salvation, till you find yourself acting as you do in other Matters, where your Fears are great, and your Desires hearty. If you had rather read Books that *entertain* the Mind, than *correct* the Heart, if you had rather hear a *Casuist* examine other People's Lives, than your's, if you had rather hear him talk of the Excellency and Wisdom of Religion, than be exact in trying the Excellency and Wisdom of your way of Life, you must take it for granted, that you are not in earnest in the Reformation of your Life, and that there are *some Tempers* in you more strong and powerful, that more rule and govern you, than the Fear of God, and a Desire of Salvation. To return now to my Subject.

I had observed that People who are religious upon a true Principle, who are devout with their *Reason* and *Understanding*, cannot possibly either *relish* or *allow* the Entertainment of the *Stage.* I observed that these contradictory Tempers, a Delight in the Offices and Divine Services of the *Church*, and a Delight in the Entertainments of the *Stage*, are no more possible to be in the same *good Men*, than in the same *good Angels.* This made it necessary for me to step a little aside from my Subject, to consider some *false Appearances* of Religion, which are chiefly founded in *natural Temper, Custom, Education*, and the *Way* of the World; which yet so far deceive People, as to make them fancy themselves in a good State of Religion, while they live and act by another Spirit and Temper.

Now I readily own, a Man may come up to these Appearances of Religion, he may carry on a Course of such Piety as this, and yet *relish* the Diversion of the *Stage.* It is no Contradiction for a Man to like to say his Prayers, to be often delighted with the Service of the *Church*, to hear *Sermons*, to read *Divinity*, to detest *Heretics*, and yet find a constant *Pleasure* in the vain Entertainments of the *Stage.* The World abounds with Instances of People who *swear, drink*, and *debauch*, with all these *Appearances* of Religion. Now as we are sure that where we see these

Vices, those Persons have only an *Appearance* of Religion, which is founded in something else than a true Fear of God; so wherever we see sober and regular People, Lovers of the Church, and Friends to Religion, taking the Pleasure of the *Stage*, we may be as sure that their Religion is *defective*, and founded in something that is *weak*, and *false*, and *blind*, that permits them to act so inconsistently. For the reasoning is full as strong in one Case as in the other. Now although I would not have People to be solely guided by what they feel, or think they feel, in their own Minds, yet this we may depend upon, as certain in our Tempers, that we never *love* or *affect* anything *truly*, but we *hate* and *avoid* all that is *contrary* to it in an equal Degree. So that we may be assured, that all that Love, or Zeal, or Affection, that we pretend for anything, is but mere Pretence, and a *blind Motion*, unless it appears by a zealous, lively Abhorrence of everything that is *contrary* to it. Upon this Ground I again affirm, that it is impossible for truly religious People to *bear* the Entertainments of the *Stage*. For consider only the Matter in this short View. A truly religious Person is to love and fear, and adore God, with *all his Heart, and with all his Soul, and with all his Strength ;* now I ask you, who is it that has this true Love of God? Is it he that delights in Profaneness at *all Times*? Or is it he that can bear with Profaneness *sometimes*? Or is it he that abhors and avoids it at *all Times* and in *all Places*? Which of these three hath a Right to be esteemed a true Lover of God? Now he that goes to a *Play* at any time, though he may say that he does not delight in *Profaneness*, yet he must own, that he can sometimes, and in some Places, bear with Profaneness. For Profaneness of some kind or other, is in most of our *Plays*, almost as common, as the Name of God in Scripture. But I will suppose it were only now and then, and that no Profaneness either of Thought or Expression happened above *twice* or *thrice* in an Entertainment, yet this is *Profaneness*, and he that can bear with *so much*, that can seek the Entertainment as a Pleasure, must acknowledge, that though he does not delight in Profaneness as such, yet he can *bear* with Profaneness for the Sake of *other Delight*. Now ask yourself, has not he a truer Love of God, whose Piety will not suffer him to bear with Profaneness at any Time, or in any Place, or for any Pleasure? Am I not therefore supported by plain Reason and common Sense, when I affirm, that it is for want of true Piety, that any People are able to bear the Entertainment of the *Stage?*

You see also that no higher Degree of Piety, is required to fill one with a constant Abhorrence of the *Stage*, than such a

Piety, as implies an Abhorrence of Profaneness at *all* Times, and in *all* Places.

When you are thus pious, when you thus love God, you will have a Piety, a Love of God that will not suffer you to be at an Entertainment that has any *Mixture* of Profaneness. Now as there must be this manifest Defect in true Piety, before you can bear with the Profaneness of the *Stage ;* so if you consider every other Part of the Character of a truly religious Man, you will find, that there must be the same Defect run through the whole of it, before he can be fit for such Diversion.

You tell me that you love the *Church,* and rejoice at the Returns of Divine Service, though you now and then go to a *Play.* Now consider what it is which these Words mean, *If you love and delight in the Service of the Church,* then you love to be in a *State* of Devotion, you love to *draw near* to God, you love to be made sensible of the *Misery, Guilt,* and *Weight* of Sin, you love to *abhor* and *deplore* your Iniquities, and to lament the *Misery* and *Vanity* of human Life ; you love to hear the Instructions of *Divine Wisdom,* to *raise* your Soul unto God, and *sing* his Praises ; you love to be on your Knees *praying* against all the *Vanities* and *Follies* of Life, and for all the *Gifts* and *Graces* of God's Holy Spirit.

Now all this is implied in the true Love of *Church-Service ;* for unless you love it *for what it is,* and because you feel its Excellency, your Love is only a *blind, mechanical* Motion ; but if you love it in Truth and Reality, if you are thus affected with it, because all its Parts so highly suit the Condition of human Nature, whilst you are thus disposed, you can no more relish the *wicked Spirit* and *foolish Temper* of Stage Entertainments, than *sincere, dying* Penitents can delight in the *Guilt* of their Sins.

Never imagine therefore, that you are sincerely affected with the *Confessions* of the Church, or that you are truly *glad* for the Return of those Hours, which humble you in the Sight of God, never imagine that you truly feel the Misery and Weight of Sin, or sincerely lament the Corruption of your Nature, whilst you dare go to the Fountain-head of Corruption, the Place where Sin reigns and exercises its highest Power.

Never imagine that you have the Spirit of Devotion, that your Heart is renewed with the Holy Ghost, that it truly rejoices in the Means of Grace, and the Hope of Glory ; never imagine that it is your Joy and Delight to worship God in the Beauty of Holiness, to send up your Soul to him in Prayers and Praises, so long as the Way of the *Stage,* its *impious* Nonsense, *vile* Jests, *profane* Passions, and *lewd* Speeches, are not your utter Abhorrence. For it is not more absurd to believe, that a *corrupt* Tree may bring forth *good Fruit*, than to believe, that a pious Mind, truly devoted to God, should taste and relish the Entertainment of the *Stage*. For the *Taste* and *Relish* of the Mind, is a more certain Sign of the State and Nature of the Mind, than the Quality of *Fruit* is a Sign of the State and Nature of *Trees*.

Had the *impure Spirits* which asked our Blessed Saviour, to suffer them to enter into the *Herd of Swine*, said at the same time, that it was their only *Delight* and *Joy* to dwell in the Light and Splendour of God, no one could have believed them, any more than he could believe Light and Darkness to be the same Thing.

When you have the Spirit of Christ, when you are devoted to God, when Purity, Holiness, and Perfection is your real Care, when you desire to live in the Light of God's Holy Spirit, to act by his Motions, to rise from Grace to Grace, till you are finished in Glory, it will be as impossible for you, whilst you continue so disposed, either to *seek* or *bear* the Entertainment of the *Stage*, as it is impossible for *pure* and *holy Spirits* to ask to enter into a *Herd of Swine*. If you want the Delight of so corrupt an Entertainment, so contrary to the *Spirit* and *Purity* of Religion, you ought no more to believe yourself, when you pretend to true Piety and Devotion, than you ought to have believed those *impure Spirits*, if they had pretended to have been *Angels of Light*. For this is absolutely certain, and what you ought carefully to consider, that nothing ever gives us any Pleasure, but what is *suitable* to the *State* and *Temper* of Mind that we are then in. So that if the *Corruption*, the *Immorality*, the *profane* Spirit and *wanton* Temper of the *Stage-Entertainment* can give you any Pleasure, you are as sure that there is *something* like *all these Vices* in your Heart, as you can be of anything that relates to a human Mind.

Lastly, Ask yourself, when you think that you have a true Love for Divine Service, whether he is not a truer Lover of it, whose Soul is so *fashioned* to it, so *deeply affected* with it, that he can delight in nothing that is *contrary* to it; who can bear with *no* Entertainment that is made up of *Speeches*, *Passions*, *Harangues*, and Songs so *opposite* to the Wisdom, the Discourses, Instructions, and Hymns, of Divine Service. This I believe, you cannot deny, and if this cannot be denied, then it must be owned as a certain Truth, that he who can bear with the *Stage-Entertainment*, has this further Defect, that he wants the *true Love* of Divine Service.

Again, it is Part of a truly religious Man, to *love* the Scriptures, and *delight* in reading them; you say this is your Temper, though you go to *Plays.* I answer, that it is for want of a true Love and Delight in the Scriptures, that you are able to relish *Plays.* You may perhaps so love the Scriptures, that you may think it your Duty to read them ; and desire to understand them. But when you once so love the Scriptures, as to *love* to be *like* them, to desire that the Spirit and Temper of Scripture, may be the *one Spirit and Temper* of your Life : When, for Instance, you love this Doctrine, *strive to enter in at the strait Gate. If thy right Eye offend thee, pluck it out and cast it from thee.* When you are of the same Mind with this Scripture, *be sober, be vigilant, because your Adversary the Devil,* as a roaring Lion, *walketh about seeking whom he may devour.**

When you are intent upon this Truth, *for we must all appear before the Judgment-Seat of Christ, that everyone may receive the things done in his Body.*† When this Text has taken Possession of your Heart, *Seeing then that all these things must be dissolved, what Manner of Persons ought ye to be in all holy Conversation and Godliness ?*‡

When you resign up your whole Soul to this Exhortation, *Take my Yoke upon you, and learn of me ; for I am meek and lowly in Heart.*§ When your Heart can truly bear you witness to this Doctrine, that you *put on the whole Armour of Christ, that you may be able to stand, that you live by Faith and not by Sight, pressing after the Prize of your high Calling.* When you thus love and delight in the Scriptures, when you thus enter into its Spirit and Temper, when its Purity is your Purity, its Fears, and Hopes, and Joys are your Fears, and Hopes, and Joys, you will find yourself one of those, who constantly and at *all Times* abominate the Folly, Impertinence and Profaneness of the *Stage.*

Let me desire you, when you are dressed for a *Play,* to read over our Saviour's Divine Sermon on the *Mount* before you go ; try whether your Soul is full of the Spirit that is there taught, examine whether you then feel in your Heart such a Love of the Scripture, as to love *those Conditions* of Blessedness that are there described, *Blessed are the Poor in Spirit, blessed are they that Mourn, blessed are they that Hunger and Thirst after Righteousness.* Do you find yourself in these heights of *Holiness?* Is your Soul reformed, purified and exalted according to *these Doctrines?* Or can you imagine, that you are *conforming* yourself to those Doctrines, that you *depart* from none of them, when you are preparing yourself for a Pleasure, which is the proper Pleasure of the most corrupt and debauched Minds ? *Blessed are the pure in Heart, for they shall see God.* Can you

---

* 1 Pet. v. 8. † 2 Cor. v. 10. ‡ 2 Pet. iii. 11. § Matt. xi. 29.

13

think that you are rightly affected with this Doctrine, that you are labouring after this Purity, that you are preparing to see God, when you are going to an Entertainment, to which they ought only to go, who have no Thoughts of seeing God, nor any Desires after that Purity which prepares us for it?

Lastly, Another Virtue essential to Christian Holiness is *Chastity,* our Blessed Saviour has given us the Measure of this Virtue in these Words: *But I say unto you, that whosoever looketh on a Woman to lust after her, hath committed Adultery with her already in his Heart.* We are sure therefore that this Virtue is not preserved, unless we keep ourselves clear from all immodest Thoughts and impure Imaginations; we are sure also that the Guilt of these, is like the Guilt of Adultery. This is the Doctrine of Christ. Look now into the *Playhouse,* and think whether any Thing can be imagined more contrary to this Doctrine?

For, not to consider the monstrous Lewdness and Immodesty of the *Stage,* take it in its *best State,* when some admired *Tragedy* is upon it. Are the extravagant Passions of *distracted Lovers,* the impure Ravings of *inflamed Heroes,* the tender Complaints, the Joys and Torments of Love, and *gross Descriptions* of Lust; are the *indecent* Actions, the amorous Transports, the *wanton Address* of the Actors, which make so great a Part of the *most sober and modest* Tragedies, are these Things an Entertainment consistent with this Christian Doctrine? You may as well imagine, that Murder and Rapine are consistent with Charity and Meekness. I hope it will not now be said, that I have spent too much Time upon a Subject, that seems not necessary in a Treatise upon *Christian Perfection.* For though these Things are generally looked upon as *little* because they are called *Pleasures* and *Diversions,* yet they may as justly be called *Vices* and *Debaucheries;* they affect Religion, as *Lies* and *Falsehood* affect it, in the very Heart and Essence, and render People as incapable of true Piety, as any of the grossest Indulgences of Sensuality and Intemperance. And perhaps it may be true, that more People are kept Strangers to the true Spirit of Religion, by what are called *Pleasures, Diversions,* and *Amusements,* than by *confessed Vices,* or the Cares and Business of Life. I have now only one Thing to beg of the *Reader,* that he would not think it a sufficient Answer to all this, to say in general, that it is a Doctrine too *strict* and *rigid,* but that he would consider every Argument as it is in itself, not whether it be strict and rigid, but whether it be false Reasoning, or more strict and rigid than the Doctrine of Scripture: If it prescribes a Purity and Holiness which is not according to the Spirit and Temper of the Scriptures, let it be rejected, not as too strict and rigid, but as a

Species of false Worship, as vain and ridiculous as *Idolatry:* But if what is here asserted, be highly conformable to the most plain Doctrines of Scripture, the saying that it is too strict and rigid, is of no more Weight against it, than if it were said, that it was *too true.* It is not my Intention to trouble the World with any particular Notions of my own; or to impose any unnecessary Rules, or fancied Degrees of Perfection upon any People. But in declaring against the *Stage*, as I have done, I have no more followed any particular Spirit or private Temper, or any more exceeded the plain Doctrine of Scripture, than if I had declared against *Drunkenness* and *Debauchery.* Let a Man but be so much a *Christian*, as not to think it too *high a Degree* of Perfection, or too *strict* and *rigid* to be in earnest in these two Petitions, *Lead us not into Temptation, but deliver us from Evil;* and he has Christianity enough to persuade him, that it is neither too high a Perfection, nor too *strict* and *rigid*, constantly to declare against, and always to avoid the Entertainment of the *Stage.*

Chapter XII.

Christians are called to a constant State of Prayer and Devotion.

IT is one principal Article of our Religion, to believe, that our Blessed Saviour is now at the Right Hand of God, there making *perpetual Intercession* for us, till the Redemption of Mankind is finished. Prayer therefore is undoubtedly a proper Means of drawing near to God, a necessary Method of restoring Sinners to his Favour, since he who has conquered Sin and Death, who is constituted Lord of all, is yet, as the *great Advocate* for Sinners, obliged to make *perpetual* Intercession for them.

Whenever, therefore, we are in the Spirit of Prayer, when our Hearts are lifted up to God, breathing out Holy Petitions to the Throne of Grace, we have this Encouragement to be *constant* and *fervent* in it, that we are then joining with an Intercession at the Right Hand of God, and doing that for ourselves on Earth, which our Blessed Saviour is perpetually doing for us in Heaven. This Reason of Prayer is perhaps not much considered, yet it certainly contains a most powerful Motive to it. For who, that considers his Redemption, as now carrying on by an *Intercession* in Heaven, can think himself so agreeable to God, so like his Saviour, as when the Constancy of his own Prayers bears some Resemblance

13—2

to that never-ceasing Intercession which is made above? This shows us also, that we are most of all to desire those Prayers, which are offered up at the *Altar*, where the Body and Blood of Christ are joined with them. For as our Prayers are only acceptable to God through the Merits of Jesus Christ, so we may be sure, that we are praying to God in the most prevailing Way, when we thus pray in the Name of *Christ*, and plead his Merits in the *highest Manner* that we can.

Devotion may be considered, either as an Exercise of public or private Prayers at set Times and Occasions, or as a Temper of the Mind, a State and Disposition of the Heart, which is rightly affected with such Exercises. Now external Acts of Devotion, are like other external Actions, very liable to Falseness, and are only so far good and valuable, as they proceed from a right Disposition of Heart and Mind. Zealous Professions of *Friendship* are but the more abominable Hypocrisy, for being often repeated, unless there be an equal Zeal in the Heart; so solemn Prayers, rapturous Devotions, are but repeated Hypocrisies, unless the Heart and Mind be *conformable* to them. Since therefore it is the Heart only, that is devout, since the Regularity and Fervency of the Heart, is the Regularity and Fervency of Devotion; I shall consider Devotion chiefly in this Respect, as it is a *State* and *Temper* of the Heart. For it is in this Sense only, that Christians are called to a *constant State of* Devotion, they are not to be always on their Knees in Acts of Prayer, but they are to be always in the State and Temper of Devotion.

Friendship does not require us to be always waiting upon our Friends in external Services, these Offices have their Times and Seasons of Intermission, it is only the Service of the Heart, the Friendship of the Mind, that is never to intermit; it is not to begin and end, as external Services do, but is to persevere in a Constancy like the Motion of our Heart, or the Beating of our Pulse. It is just so in Devotion, *Prayers* have their *Hours*, their Beginning and Ending, but that turn of Mind, that Disposition of the Heart towards God, which is the Life and Spirit of Prayer, is to be as constant and lasting as our own Life and Spirit.

The repeating of a *Creed* at certain Times, is an Act of Faith, but that Faith which *overcometh* the World, stays neither for Times nor Seasons, but is a living Principle of the Soul, that is always believing, trusting, and depending upon God. In the same manner, verbal Prayers are Acts of Devotion, but that Prayer which saveth, which openeth the Gates of Heaven, stops not at *Forms* and *Manuals* of Devotion, but is a Language of the Soul, a Judgment of the Heart, which worships, adores, and delights in God, at all Times and Seasons.

The *Necessity* and *Reason* of Prayer, is like all other Duties of Piety, founded in the Nature of God, and the Nature of Man. It is founded in the Nature of God, as he is the sole Fountain and Cause of all Happiness ; it is founded in the Nature of Man, as he is weak and helpless, and full of Wants. So that Prayer is an *earnest Application or Ascent of the Heart to God, as to the sole Cause of all Happiness.* He therefore that most truly feels the Misery, Corruption, and Weakness of his own Nature, who is most fully convinced that a Relief from all these Disorders, and a true Happiness, is to be found in God alone, he who is most fully convinced of these two Truths, is most fully possessed of the Spirit of Prayer. There is but one Way therefore to arrive at a true State of Devotion, and that is, to get right Notions of ourselves, and of the Divine Nature, that having a full View of the Relation we bear to God, our Souls may as constantly aspire to him, as they as constantly aspire after Happiness. This also shows us the absolute Necessity of all those forementioned Doctrines of *Humility, Self-denial,* and *Renunciation of the World.* For if Devotion is founded in a Sense of the Poverty, Misery, and Weakness of our Nature, then nothing can more effectually destroy the Spirit of Devotion, than *Pride, Vanity,* and *Indulgence,* of any kind. These Things stop the Breath of Prayer, and as necessarily extinguish the Flame of Devotion, as Water extinguishes common Fire.

If Prayer is also founded in right Notions of God, in believing him to be the sole Fountain and Cause of all our Happiness, then everything that takes this Truth out of our Minds, that makes us *less sensible* of it, makes us so far *less capable* of Devotion ; so that worldly Cares, vain Pleasures, false Satisfactions, are all to be renounced, that we may be able to pray. For the Spirit of Prayer has no further hold of us, than so far as we see our Wants, Imperfections, and Weakness, and likewise the infinite Fulness and All-sufficiency of God ; when we thoroughly feel these two great Truths, then are we in the true Spirit of Prayer. Would you therefore be in the State and Temper of Devotion, you must practise all those Ways of Life, that may humble you in your own Sight ; you must forbear all those Indulgences and Vanities which blind your Heart, and give you false Notions of yourself ; you must seek that Way of Life, accustom yourself to such Practices as may best convince you of the Vanity of the World, and the Littleness of everything but God. This is the only Foundation of Prayer. When you don't enough see either your own Littleness, or the Greatness of God, when you either seek for Pleasure in yourself, or think that it is anywhere to be found, except in God, you put yourself out of a State of Devotion. For you can desire nothing, but what you think you want, and you can desire it only in such a degree, as you feel the Want of it. It is certain therefore, that whatever lessens or abates the Feeling of your own Wants, whatever takes you from looking to God, as the only possible Relief of them, so far lessens and abates the Spirit and Fervour of your Devotion.

We sometimes exhort People to Fervour in Devotion, but this can only mean as to the outward Acts of it; for to exhort People to be Fervent in Devotion, as that implies a Temper of the Heart, is to as little Purpose, as to exhort People to be *Merry*, or to be *Sorry*. For these Tempers always follow the Judgments and Opinions of our Minds, when we perceive Things to be, as we like them, then we are *Merry;* when we find Things in a contrary State, then we are *Sorry*. It comes to pass after the same manner in *Devotion*, bid a Man be fervent in Devotion, tell him it is an excellent Temper, he knows no more how to go about it, than how to be merry, because he is bid to be so. Stay till *old Age*, till *Sickness, Misfortunes*, or the Approach of *Death*, has convinced him that he has nothing good in himself, that there is nothing valuable in the World, that all that is good, or great, or glorious is in God alone, and then he will find himself as disposed to Devotion, and zealous Desires after God, as the Man is disposed to Cheerfulness, who sees Things in that State in which he would have them to be. So that the one and only way to be devout, is to see and feel our own Weakness, the Vanity of the World, and the Greatness of God, as dying Men see and feel them. It is as impossible to be *devout* without seeing Things in *this View*, as it is impossible to be *cheerful* without perceiving something in our Condition, that is according to *our Mind*. Hence therefore we may learn to admire the Wisdom and Divinity of the Christian Religion, which calls all its Members to *Humility, Self-denial,* and a Renunciation of *worldly Tempers*, as a necessary Foundation of Piety and Devotion. It was in these Practices that our Saviour first instituted his Religion; it was on these Conditions that the Apostles embraced it, and taught it to others; it was in these Doctrines that the primitive Christians became such worthy Followers of our Saviour and his Apostles. These Doctrines are still in the Gospel, and till they are to be found in our Lives, we shall never find ourselves in a State of Devotion. For I must again repeat, what my Reader cannot too much reflect upon; that since Devotion is an earnest Application of the Soul to God, as the only Cause and Fountain of Happiness, that it is impossible for the Soul to have this Desire, without having such Reasons to produce and support it, as are necessary to produce and support other Tempers of the Mind.

Now it is impossible for a Man to *grieve* when he finds his Condition answering his Desires ; or to be *overjoyed* when he finds his State to be full of Misery, yet this is as possible, as consistent with our Nature, as for a Man to *aspire* after, and *delight* in God as his only Happiness, whilst he is *delighting* in himself and the Vanity of the World. So that to pretend to Devotion without great *Humility,* and an entire Renunciation of all *worldly Tempers,* is to pretend to Impossibilities ; it is as if a Man should pretend to be *cheerful,* whilst he is in Vexation and Impatience ; he must first bring himself to a State of Satisfaction and Contentment, and then Cheerfulness will flow from it ; so he that would be devout, must first be humble, have a full View of his own Miseries and Wants, and the Vanity of the World, and then his Soul will be full of Desires after God. A *proud,* or *vain,* or *worldly-minded* Man, may use a *Manual* of Prayers, but he cannot be *devout,* because Devotion is the Application of an *humble* Heart to God, as its only Happiness.

Hence we may also perceive, why People of *Learning* and great Application to *Books,* who seem to have retired from the Corruptions of the World, to spend their time in their Studies, are yet often not Devout. The Reason is, because Devotion is founded in great Humility, and a full Sense of the Vanity and Littleness of *every Thing* but God. Whereas it is often the *same Vanity* that wears out some Scholars in their *Studies,* that wears out other People at *Court,* in the *Camp,* or at *Sea.* They do not want to be *Merchants,* or *Colonels,* or *Secretaries* of State, but they want to be *Critics, Grammarians,* and *Historians.* They, it may be, disregard Riches and Equipage, despise the Sports and Diversions of the *present Age,* avoid the Folly of Conversation, but then it is to contemplate the *Riches* and *Equipage,* the *Sports* and *Diversions* of the ancient *Romans.*

The Vanity of some *Ladies* and *Gentlemen* would be touched, if you should tell them, that they did not understand *Dress :* Some great *Scholars* would be more dejected, if you should suppose them Ignorant of a *Fold* in the *Roman Garments.*

The *Bulk* of Mankind are so dull and tasteless, so illiterate, as to set their Hearts upon *current Coin,* large *Fields,* and Flocks and Herds of *Cattle.* Great Learning has raised some Men above this grossness of Taste, their Hearts only beat at the Sight of a *Medal* and *ancient Coins,* they are only afraid of dying before they have outdone the World, in their Collections of *Shells, Skins, Stones, Animals, Flies, and Insects.*

You would not expect that a *Merchant* should be devout because he traded in all Parts of *Europe*, or that a *Lady* should be pious, because she understands all Sorts of *fine Work* and *Embroidery*. Now if you were to look into the Business of many profound Scholars, if you were to consider the Nature of such Learning as makes the greatest Figure in the World, you will find no more Tendency in it to Piety and Devotion, than there is in *Merchandise* or *Embroidery*.

When Men retire into their Studies to *change* their Nature, to *correct* and *reform* their Passions, to find out the Folly, the Falseness, the Corruption and Weakness of their Hearts, to *penetrate* into the Vanity and Emptiness of all worldly Attainments, when they read and meditate to fill their Souls with religious Wisdom and heavenly Affections, and to raise their Hearts unto God, when this is *Learning* (and what else deserves the Name), then Learning will lead Men unto God, learned Men will be very Devout, and great *Scholars* will be great *Saints*.

Hence we also learn, why so many People seemingly Religious, are yet Strangers to the Spirit of Devotion. *Crito* buys *Manuals* of Devotion, he finds nothing in them but what is according to the Doctrines of Religion, yet he is not able to keep pace with them, he feels nothing of what he reads, and throws them by, as something that does not *suit* his Taste : He does not consider that the *fault* is in himself, and that these *very same* Books will suit him when he is *dying*. He does not consider, that whilst he is so well pleased with himself, so fond of the World, so delighted with a Variety of Schemes that he has on foot, it is as impossible for him to be Devout, as for a *Stone* to hang by itself in the Air, or a Building to stand without anything to stand upon. If *Crito* was to begin his Devotion to God, with *Humility*, *Self-denial*, and a Renunciation of all *worldly Tempers*, he would show that he used common Sense in his Religion, that he was as wise as that Builder, who begins his House by laying a Foundation. But to think of adding Devotion to a Life that does not naturally lead to it, that is not so ordered, as to be so many Steps towards it, is as absurd, as if a Man should think of getting to the End of his Journey, without going through any of the Way that leads to it. For as it is a Temper of the Mind, it must arise from the State of our Mind, and must have its proper Causes to produce it, as all other Tempers have.

Suppose you were to call a Man from some joyful Feast, from the Pleasures of *Songs*, *Music*, and *Dancing*, and tell him to go into the next Room to *grieve* for half an Hour, and then return to his Mirth ; suppose you were to tell him that he must mourn that half Hour from the Bottom of his Heart, that it was a very excellent Thing, and highly becoming a rational Creature. It is possible he might obey you so far, as to go into the *Room* appointed for Mourning, he may be able to sit still, look grave, sigh and hang down his Head, and stay out his *half Hour*, but you are sure that he cannot *really grieve*, and for this Reason, because he is in a State of festival Joy, and is returning to his Feast. Now this is the State of *Crito*, and great Numbers of Christians, they are always at a *Feast ;* their Life is nothing else but a Succession of such Pleasures, Satisfactions, and Amusements, as affect and hurry their Minds, like the festival Joys of *Drinking*, *Music*, and *Dancing*. So that when they go to Devotion, they are just as capable of it, as a Man that is rejoicing at a Feast, is capable of mourning at the same time. Let not the Reader imagine, that this is the Case only of such great People, as live in such a constant Scene of Pleasure, as their Fortunes can procure, for it is a Case that equally concerns almost all States of Life. For as a Man rejoicing at an ordinary Feast, is as indisposed for Grief, as one that is merry at a more splendid Entertainment ; so that Course of Pleasures and worldly Delights, which falls in with lower States of Life, may render such People as *Incapable* of Devotion, as they are, who have other Entertainments provided for them. Now no one wonders that he cannot *put on* Grief, when he is rejoicing at a *Feast* of any kind, because he knows there is sufficient Reason for it, because his Mind is then otherwise engaged. But if *Crito* would but deal thus faithfully with himself, he would as readily own, that he cannot *relish* Strains of Devotion, that his Heart does not enter into them, for this Reason, because it is *otherwise* engaged. For People certainly *relish* everything that *suits* with the State of Life that they live, and can have no Taste or Relish, but such as arises from the Way and Manner of Life that they are in. Whoever therefore finds himself unable to relish Strains of Devotion, dull and unaffected with them, may take it for certain, that it is owing to the *Way* and *State* of Life that he is in : He may also be further assured, that his Life is wanting in the Virtues of *Humility*, *Self-denial*, and a *Renunciation of worldly Goods*, since these Virtues as naturally *prepare* and *dispose* the Soul to aspire to God, as a Sense of *Sickness* disposes People to wish for *Health*.

Let us now put these Things together ; it is certain, that Devotion, as a Temper of the Mind, must have something to produce it, as all other Tempers have, that it cannot be taken up at Times and Occasions, but must arise from the State of the Soul, as all other Tempers and Desires do. It is also equally certain, that Humility, Self-denial, and a Renunciation of the World, are the only Foundation of Devotion, that it can only proceed from these, as from its proper Causes. Here therefore we must fix our Rule to take the just Measure of ourselves. We must not consider how many Books of Devotion we have, how often we go to Church, or how often we have felt a Warmth and Fervour in our Prayers, these are uncertain Signs; but we must look to the Foundation, and assure ourselves, that our Devotion neither is, nor can be, greater than our Humility, Self-denial, and Renunciation of the World. For as it must proceed only from these Causes, so it can rise no higher than they carry it, and must be in the same State of Strength or Weakness that they are. If our Humility is false, our Self-denial hypocritical and trifling, and our worldly Tempers not half mortified, our Devotion will be just in the same State of Falseness, Hypocrisy, and Imperfection. The Care therefore of our Devotion, seems wholly to consist in the Care of these Duties; so far as we proceed in them, so far we advance in Devotion. We must alter our Lives, in order to alter our Hearts, for it is impossible to *live* one way, and *pray* another.

This may teach us to account for the several false Kinds of Devotion which appear in the World, they cannot be otherwise than they are, because they have no Bottom to support them. Devotion is like *Friendship*, you hear of it everywhere, but find it nowhere; in like manner, Devotion is everywhere to be seen in *Modes* of Worship, in *Forms* of Speech, in outward Adorations, but is in *reality* scarcely to be found. Hence also it is, that you see as much difference in the Devotion, as in the Faces of Christians, for wanting its true Foundation, being like an affected Friendship, it has as many *Shapes*, as there are *Tempers* of Men. Many people are thus far sincere in their Devotions, that they would be glad to pray Devoutly, they strive to be Fervent, but never attain to it, because they never took the only possible Way. They never thought of altering their Lives, or of living different from the rest of the World, but hope to be Devout, merely by reading over Books of Devotion. Which is as odd a Fancy, as if a Man should expect to be Happy, by reading Discourses upon Happiness. When these People dare take Christianity as it is offered to them in the Gospel, when they deny themselves, and renounce the World, as our Saviour exhorted his Followers, they will then have begun Devotion.

Trebonius, asks how often he shall pray : He thinks the nicety of the Question shows the *Piety* and *Exactness* of his Heart; but *Trebonius* is deceived, for the Question proves that he is a stranger to Devotion. *Trebonius* has a Friend, he is constantly

Visiting him, he is never well out of his Company; if he is absent Letters are sent at all Opportunities. Now what is the Reason that he never asks how often he shall Visit, how often he shall delight in, how often he shall write to his Friend? It is because his Friend has his Heart, and his Heart is his faithful and sufficient Instructor. When *Trebonius* has given his Heart to God, when he takes God to be as great a Good, as substantial a Happiness, as his Friend, he will have done asking how often he shall pray.

Julius goes to Prayers, he confessés himself to be a miserable Sinner, he accuses himself to God with all the Aggravations that can be, as having *no health* in him, yet *Julius* cannot bear to be informed of any Imperfection, or suspected to be wanting in any Degree of Virtue. Now can there be a stronger Proof, that *Julius* is wanting in the Sincerity of his Devotions? Is not this a plain Sign, that his Confessions to God are only Words of *Course*, an humble *Civility* of Speech to his Maker, in which his Heart has no Share?

If a Man were to confess that his *Eyes* were bad, his *Hands* weak, his *Feet* feeble, and his *Body* helpless, he would not be angry with those who supposed he was not in perfect Strength, or that he might stand in need of some Assistance. Yet *Julius* confesses himself to be in great Weakness, Corruption, Disorder, and Infirmity, and yet is angry at anyone, that does but suppose him defective in any Virtue. Is it not the same thing as if he had said, *You must not imagine that I am in earnest in my Devotions?*

It would be endless to produce Instances of false Devotion; I shall therefore proceed no further in it, but rather endeavour to explain and illustrate that which is true. Devotion, we see, *is an earnest Application of the Soul to God as its only Happiness.* This is Devotion considered as a *State* and *Temper* of the Mind. All those Texts of Scripture which call us to God, as our true and only Good, which exhort us to a Fulness of Faith, of Hope, of Joy, and Trust in God, are to be considered as so many Exhortations to Devotion. Because Devotion is only another Name for the Exercise of all these Virtues. That Soul is devoted to God, which constantly rises and tends towards God in Habits of Love, Desire, Faith, Hope, Joy, and Trust. The End and Design of Religion, as it proposes to raise Man to a Life of Glory with Christ at the Right Hand of God, carries a stronger Reason for Devotion, than any particular Exhortation to Prayer. Beloved, saith St. *John, It doth not yet appear what we shall be, but we know that when he shall appear, we shall be like him, for we shall see him as he is.* St. *Paul* also saith, *As we have borne* *the Image of the Earthly, we shall also bear the Image of the Heavenly.**

Now these and such like Texts seem to me to carry the most powerful Motives, to awaken the Soul into a State of Devotion. For as the Apostle saith, *He that hath this Hope, purifieth himself, even as he is Pure.* So he that hath this Hope of being taken into so glorious an Enjoyment of the Divine Nature, must find his Heart raised and enlivened in thinking upon God. For these Truths cannot be believed without putting the Soul into a State of Prayer, Adoration, and Joy in God. The seeing thus far into Heaven, is seeing so many Motives to Praise and Thanksgiving.

It was this View of future Glory that made the Apostle break out in this Strain of Thanksgiving, *Blessed be the God and Father of our Lord Jesus Christ, who hath begotten us to a lively Hope by the Resurrection of Jesus Christ from the Dead, to an Inheritance undefiled and that fadeth not away.†* And would we Praise and Adore God with such Thanksgiving, as filled the Heart of this Apostle, we must raise it from a Contemplation of the same Truth ; that *incorruptible Inheritance* that is prepared for us.

Again, the same Apostle saith to the *Philippians, Our Conversation is in Heaven,* and as the Reason and Motive to this heavenly Conversation, he addeth, *Whence we look for the Saviour, the Lord Jesus Christ : Who shall change our vile Body, that it may be fashioned like unto his glorious Body.‡* So that the most powerful motive to Heavenly-mindedness, the plainest Reason for our Conversation in Heaven, is our Expectation of Christ's glorious Appearance, when he shall come to put an *End* to the Miseries of this Life, and clothe us with Robes of Immortality. These Truths much more effectually raise the Heart to God, than any particular Precepts to Prayer, they do not so much exhort, as carry the Soul to Devotion : He that feels these Truths, feels himself Devout, they leave a Light upon the Soul, which will kindle into holy Flames of Love and Delight in God.

The way therefore to live in true Devotion, is to live in the Contemplation of these Truths ; we must daily consider the End and Hope of our Calling, that our Minds may be formed and raised to such Tempers and Desires as are suitable to it, that all little Anxieties, worldly Passions, and vain Desires may be swallowed up in one great Desire of future Glory. When the Heart is in this State, then it is in a State of Devotion, tending to God in such a Manner as justly suits the Nature of our

---

* 1 Cor. xv.   † 1 Pet. i. 3.   ‡ Phil. iii. 20.

Religion. For whither should our Hearts tend, but where our Treasure is? This Devotion to God, is signified in Scripture, by living by *Faith and not by Sight*, when the invisible Things of the other Life, are the Reason, the Motive, and the Measure of all our Desires and Tempers. When Christians are thus settled in right Judgments of Things, and tending towards God in such Motions and Desires as are suitable to them, then are they devout Worshippers of God everywhere; this makes the common Actions of their Life, Acts of Religion, and turns every Place into a *Chapel*. And it is to this State of Devotion, that we are all called, not only by particular Precepts, but by the whole Nature and Tenor of our Religion.

Now as all States and Tempers of the Mind must be supported by Actions and Exercises suitable to them, so Devotion, which is an earnest Application of the Soul to God, as its only Happiness, must be supported and kept alive, by Actions and Exercises suitable to it, that is, by *Hours* and *Forms* of Prayer both public and private. The Devotion of the Heart disposes us to observe set Times of Prayer, and on the other Hand, set Times of Prayer as naturally increase and enliven the Devotion of the Heart. It is thus in all other Cases: Habits of the Mind dispose us to Actions suitable to them, and these Actions likewise strengthen and improve the Habits, from whence they proceeded.

It is the habitual Taste for *Music*, that carries People to *Concerts*, and again it is *Concerts* that increases the habitual Love of *Music*. So it is the right Disposition of the Heart towards God, that leads People to outward Acts of Prayer, and on the other Side, it is outward Acts of Prayer, that preserve and strengthen the right Disposition of the Heart towards God. As therefore we are to judge of the Significancy of our Prayers, by looking to the State and Temper of our Heart; so are we also to judge of the State of our Heart, by looking to the *Frequency, Constancy,* and *Importunity* of our Prayers. For as we are sure that our Prayers are insignificant, unless they proceed from a right Heart, so unless our Prayers be *frequent, constant,* and full of *Importunity,* we may be equally sure that our Heart is not right towards God.

Our Blessed Saviour has indeed condemned one sort of long Prayer. *But when ye pray, use not vain Repetitions as the Heathens do; for they think they shall be heard for their much speaking.** Now it is not *Length* or a *Continuance* of Prayer that is here forbid, but *vain Repetitions*, when instead of praying, the

---

* Matt. vi. 7.

same Words are only often repeated. *Secondly*, the *Heathens* are not here condemned for being *importunate* and *persevering* in their Prayer; but for a *wrong Judgment*, a false Devotion, in that they thought they were heard, because they *spoke much*, that is, often repeated the same Words. So that all that Christians are here forbid, is only this, they are not to think that the *Efficacy* of Prayer consists in vain and long Repetitions, but are to apply to God upon a better Principle, a more enlightened Devotion. Now though this is plainly all that is here condemned, yet some People imagine that a Continuance and Importunity of Prayer is here reproved, and thence conclude that Shortness is a necessary Qualification of Prayer.

But how willing must such People be to be deceived, before they can Reason in this manner. For the Words have plainly no Relation to *Length* or *Shortness* of Prayer, they no more condemn the one than the other, but speak altogether to *another* Matter. They only condemn an Opinion of *Heathens*, which supposed, that the Excellency and Power of Prayer consisted in a Multitude of Repetitions. Now to think, that a short Prayer is better, because it is *short*, is the same Error as to hold with the *Heathens*, that a Prayer is more powerful, the longer the same Words are repeated. It is the same Mistake in the Nature of Devotion.

But supposing the Meaning of these Words were something obscure (which it is not) yet surely it is plain enough, that our Saviour has *expressly* taught and recommended a *Continuance* and *Importunity* in Prayer. And how perversely do they read the Gospel, who can find his Authority against such kind of Devotion! For can he who was so often retiring to *Deserts*, to *Mountains*, to *Solitary* Places to pray, who spent *whole Nights* in Prayer, can he be supposed to have left a Reproof upon such as should follow his Example? But besides the Authority of his great Example, his Doctrine is on no Point more plain and certain, than where he teaches Frequency, Continuance, and Importunity in Prayer. *He spake a Parable unto them, to this End, that Men ought always to pray, and not to faint. Saying, there was in a City a Judge which feared not God, nor regarded Man. And there was a Widow in that City, and she came unto him, saying, Avenge me of my Adversary. And he would not for awhile: But afterwards he said within himself, Though I fear not God, nor regard Man, yet because this Widow troubleth me, I will avenge her. And shall not God avenge his own Elect, which cry Day and Night unto him?* The Apostle tells us, that this Parable was to teach Men to *pray always*, and *not to faint*, and it is plain to anyone that reads it, that it has no other intent, but to recom-

mend *Continuance* and *Importunity*, as the most prevailing Qualifications of Prayer. The Widow is relieved, not because she
asked Relief, but because she *continued* asking it, and God is said
to avenge his Elect, not because they cry to him now and then,
but because they *cry Day and Night.* Our Blessed Saviour
teacheth the same Doctrine in another Parable, of a Person
going to his Friend to borrow *three Loaves* of him at Midnight,
where it thus concludes, *I say unto you, though he would not rise
and give him, because he is his Friend, yet because of his Importunity, he will rise and give him as many as he needeth.* Here
again the sole Scope of this Passage is to show, the great Power
and Efficacy of Continuance and Importunity in Prayer.

Consider further in what manner Prayer is mentioned in
Scripture. St. *Paul* does not command us to pray, but to *pray
without ceasing.** The same Doctrine is thus taught in another
Place, *continue in Prayer.*† And again, *Praying always with all
Prayer and Supplication in the Spirit.*‡ It is said of *Anna, That
she served God in Fasting and Prayer Night and Day.* Now who
can imagine that *Shortness* is any Excellency of Prayer?

Clito says, he desires no more Time for rising, dressing, and
saying his Prayers, than a Quarter of an Hour. He tells this to
his Friends, not to show his want of Religion, but that he may
be thought to understand Devotion. You tell him that our
Saviour's Parables teach *Continuance* and *Importunity* in Prayer,
that the Apostles exhort to *pray without ceasing*, to pray *always*,
and that devout Persons are recorded in Scripture, as praying
Night and Day. Still *Clito* is for short Prayers. He at last finds
a Text of Scripture, and appeals to the Example of the *Angels*,
they only said, *Glory be to God on High, and on Earth Peace,
Goodwill towards Men.* *Clito* takes this to be an Argument for
short Prayer, because the Angels had done so soon. But *Clito*
must be told, that this is no Prayer. It is only a joyful Procla-
mation to Men. And surely the manner of *Angels* speaking to
Men, can be no Rule or Measure of the Devotion of Men speaking to God. The Angels had no more to tell the World, than
this Message of Joy, but does it therefore follow, that Sinners
are to be as short in their Addresses to God? The Scripture
tells us sometimes of *Voices* from Heaven, but it would be
strange, to make Things that were then spoken, the Measure of
our Prayers when we call upon God. If *Clito* must have an
Example from Heaven, he might have found one much more
proper than this, where it is said, *That they rest not Day and*

---

* 1 Thess. v. 17.   † Col. iv. 2.   ‡ Ephes. vi. 18.

*Night, saying, Holy, Holy, Holy, Lord God Almighty, which was and is, and is to come.**

Our Blessed Saviour saith, *But thou, when thou prayest enter into thy Closet, and when thou hast shut thy Door, pray unto thy Father, &c.*† Now here is indeed no mention of the Time that Prayer is to be continued, but yet this Preparation for Prayer, of *entering* into our Closet, and *shutting* the Door, seems to teach us that it is a Work of some Time, that we are not hastily to open our Door, but to allow ourselves time to continue and be importunate in our Prayers.

How long and how often all People ought to pray, is not to be stated by any one particular Measure. But this we may take as a general Rule, that relates to all Particulars, that every Christian is to pray so often and so long, as to show a Perseverance and Importunity in Prayer, as to show that he prays *without ceasing*, that he prays always, and that he *cries* to God *Night and Day*, for these are essential Qualifications of Prayer, and expressly required in Scripture. One would think it impossible for People to be sparing in their Devotions, who have read our Saviour's Parables, which teach us that the Blessings of Heaven, the Gifts and Graces of God's Holy Spirit are given to such as are importunate in their Prayers. I shall now only add a Word or two in Favour of frequent and *continued* Prayers.

First, *Frequent* and *continued* Prayers, are a likely Means to beget in us the *Spirit* of Prayer. A Man who is often in his Closet, on his Knees to God, though he may for some Time perform but a *Lip-labour*, will, if he perseveres, find the very Labour of his Lips altering the Temper of his Heart, and that he has learned to pray, by praying often.

This we find to be true in all Parts of Life, that we catch a Spirit and Temper from such Conversation and Ways of Life as we allow ourselves in. Use is called a second Nature, and Experience teaches us, that whatever we accustom ourselves to, it will by Degrees transform our Spirit and Temper into a Likeness to it.

Credula was for some Time a tender *Mother*, friendly and charitable to her Neighbours, and full of Good-will towards all People; she is now spiteful, malicious, envious, and delights in nothing but Scandal. How came *Credula* thus changed? Why she has been for several years spending her Time in *visiting*, she entered into *Scandal* and *evil Speaking* at first merely for the Sake of *Talk*, she has gone on talking, till she has talked her very Heart and Spirit into a Taste for nothing

---

* Rev. iv. 8.   † Math. vi. 6.

else; at first she only detracted from her Neighbours and Friends, because she was visiting, but now she visits for the Sake of Detraction. *Credula* is hardened and cruel in evil Speaking, for the same Reason, that *Butchers* are inhuman and cruel, because she has been so long used to murder the Reputation of her Neighbours. She has killed all her own Family over and over, and if she seeks new Acquaintance, it is to get fresh Matter for Scandal; now all this change in *Credula*, is purely owing to her *indulging* a talkative Temper.

Now everything that we use ourselves to, enters into our Nature in *this Manner*, and becomes a *part* of us before we are aware. It is common to observe, that some People tell a Story so long, till they have forgotten that they invented it. This is not as is supposed, through a bad Memory, but because the things which we make *constant* and *familiar,* will by Degrees steal the Approbation of the Heart. If therefore we would but be often on our Knees, putting up our Prayers to God, though for a while it was only *Form* and *outward* Compliance, yet our Hearts would by Degrees learn the *Language* of our Mouths. The Subject of our Prayers would become the Subject of our Hearts, we should pray ourselves into Devotion, and it would become a part of us, in the same manner that all other ways enter into our Nature. Our Reason and Judgment would at last consent to our lips, and by saying the same things often, we should come to *believe* and *feel* them in a proper Manner. For it is a very reasonable Thing, to Judge of the Effects of good Customs, by what we see to be Effects of bad ones. They therefore who are *hasty* in their Devotions, and think a little will do, are Strangers both to the Nature of *Devotion* and the Nature of *Man;* they do not know that they are to *learn* to pray, and that Prayer is to be learnt, as they learn all other things, by *Frequency, Constancy,* and *Perseverance.*

Secondly, There is another great Advantage in frequent and continued Prayers.

The Cares and Pleasures of Life, the Levity, Vanity, and Dulness of our Minds, make us all more or less unfit for our Devotions. We enter into our *Closets* thus unprepared for Prayer; now if our Petitions are very short, we shall end our Prayers before our Devotion is begun, before we have time to collect our Minds, or turn our Hearts to the Business we are upon.

Now continuance in Prayer, is as great relief against these Indispositions, not only as it gives the Heart leisure to fall from worldly Cares and Concerns, but as it Exercises the Mind upon such Subjects, as are likely to abate its Vanity and Distraction,

14

and raise it into a State of Seriousness and Attention. It is the Case of all People, to find themselves Inconstant in their Prayers, joining heartily with some Petitions, and wandering away from others; it is therefore but common Prudence to continue our Prayers, that our Minds which will wander from some Parts, may have others to join in. If we were Masters of our Attention, and could be as Fervent as we pleased, then indeed fewer Words might serve for our Devotion, but since our Minds are weak, inconstant, and ungovernable, we must endeavour to catch and win them to Devotion, by such Means as are suited to such a State of Weakness, Dulness, and Inconstancy. He that goes to his *Closet* in a *hurry*, only to repeat a *short Form* of Words, may pray *all his Life* without any Devotion, and perhaps he had been a devout Man long ago, if it had ever entered into his Head, that *Meditation* and *Continuance* in Prayer are necessary to excite Devotion. If a Man were to make it a *Law*, to himself, to *Meditate* a while before he began his Prayers, if he were to force his Mind to think, what Prayer is, what he prays for, and to whom he prays ; if he should again make it a Rule to stop in some Part of his Prayers, to ask his Heart, whether it really prays, or to let his Soul rise up in silence unto God ; prayers thus performed, thus assisted by Meditation and Continuance, would in all likelihood soon render the Mind truly Devout. It is not intended by this, to impose *any particular* Method upon all People ; it is only to show us, that there are *certain Means* of assisting our Devotion, some Rules, though *little* in themselves, yet of *great use* to render our Minds Attentive and Fervent in our applications to God. It is the Business therefore of every sincere Christian, to be as wise as he can in these Arts and Methods of Self-government. As we ourselves know most of the Falseness of our own Hearts, of the Temper of our Minds, and the Occasion of our Defects, so if we would but be so wise, as to think the Amendment of our Hearts, the best and greatest Work, that we can do, every one's Reason would help him to such useful Rules, as had a peculiar fitness to his own State. *Self-reflection* is the shortest and most certain Way of becoming truly Wise, and truly Pious.

There are *two Seasons* of our Hearts, which if we would but reflect upon, we might get much Knowledge of ourselves, and learn how to assist our Devotion. I mean the *time* when we are *most affected* with our Devotions, and the *time* when we are *most indisposed* to pray. Both these *Seasons* equally serve to instruct us in the Knowledge of ourselves, and how to govern the Motions of our Hearts.

Reflect with yourself, how it was with you, what *Circumstances* you were in, what had *happened* to you, what you had been *doing*, what *Thoughts* you had in your Head at such a Time, when you found yourself *so affected* with your Devotions. Now if you find out what State you were then in, when you were disposed to pray so Fervently, then you have found out a certain Way of raising your Devotion at another time. For do but put yourself in the same State, recall the same Thoughts, and do as you had then been doing, and you will find the same Causes will again produce the same Effects, and you will be again in the same Temper of Devotion. If you were then to put down in *Writing*, some short Remembrances of the *chief Things*, that ever raised your Heart to Fervency of Prayer, so that you might have Recourse to a full View of them, as often as your Mind wanted such Assistance, you would soon find a Benefit, that would well Reward your Labour. On the contrary, whenever you have found yourself *very much Indisposed* for Prayer, reflect with yourself, what State you were then in, what had *happened* unto you, what *Thoughts* you had in your Head, what *Passions* were then awakened, what you had been *doing*, or were *intending* to do; for when you have found out the State that you were then in, you have found out the real Hindrances of your Devotion, and are made certain what things you are to avoid, in order to keep yourself in a Temper of Devotion.

If you were here again to make short remembrances in *Writing*, of the chief Things which at such times rendered you indisposed for Prayer, and oblige yourself frequently to read them and reflect upon them, you would by this Means, set a *Mark* upon everything that did you any Hurt, and have a constant, faithful Information of what Ways of Life, you are most to avoid. If in Examining your State, you should find that sometimes *impertinent Visits, foolish Conversation*, or a Day idly Spent in *civil Compliances* with the Humours and Pleasures of other People, has rendered your Mind *dull* and *indisposed*, and less *affected* with Devotion, than at other times, then you will have found, that impertinent Visits, and Ceremonious Compliances in spending our time, are not *little, indifferent* Things, but are to be numbered amongst those Things which have a *great effect* upon our Minds, and such as are to be daily watched and guarded against, by all those who are so wise as to desire, to be daily alive unto God in the Spirit and Temper of Devotion.

I pass now to another Observation upon the Benefit of frequent Prayers.

Thirdly, *Frequent* and *continued* Prayer is the best Remedy against the Power of Sin. I do not mean as it procures the

14—2

Divine Grace and Assistance, but as it naturally *Convinces*, *Instructs*, and *Fortifies* the Mind against all Sin. For every endeavour to pray, is an endeavour to *feel* the Truth of our Prayers, to *convince* our Minds of the Reasonableness and Fitness of those Things, that are the Subject of our Prayers, so that he who prays most, is one that most labours to convince his Heart and Mind of the Guilt, Deformity, and Misery of Sin. Prayer therefore considered merely as an *Exercise* of the Heart upon such Subjects, is the most *certain way* to destroy the Power of Sin ; because so far as we pray, so far we *renew* our Convictions, *enlighten* our Minds and *fortify* our Hearts by fresh Resolutions. We are therefore to consider the Necessity and Benefit of Prayer, not only as it is that which God *hears*, but also as it is that, which by its natural Tendency *alters* and *corrects* our Opinions and Judgments, and forms our Hearts to such Ways of Thinking, as are suitable to the Matter of our Prayers.

Now this is an unanswerable Argument for *frequency* and *continuance* in Prayer, since if Prayer at all convinces the Mind, frequency and continuance in Prayer, must be the most certain way to establish the Mind in a steady well-grounded State of Conviction. They therefore who are for short Prayers, because they suppose, that God does not *need* much entreaty, ought also to show, that the Heart of Man does not need Assistance of *much Prayer*, that it is so regular and uniform in its Tendency to God, so full of right Judgments and good Motions, as not to *need* that Strength and Light, and Help, which arises from *much praying*. For unless this be the State of our Hearts, we shall want much Prayer to *move* and *awake* ourselves, though but little was necessary to *excite* the Goodness of God. If therefore Men would consider Prayer, not only as it is an *Invocation* of God, but also as it is an *Exercise of holy Thoughts*, as it is an endeavour to *feel* and be affected with the great Truths of Religion, they would soon see, that though God is so good, as not to *need* much calling upon, yet that Man is so weak as to need much Assistance, and to be under a constant Necessity of that Help, and Light, and Improvement which arises from praying much.

It is perhaps for this Reason, that God promises to give to those who are *importunate* and ask *without ceasing*, to encourage us to practise that Exercise, which is the most natural Cure of the Disorders of our Souls. If God does not give to us at our first asking, if he only give to those who are importunate, it is not because our Prayers make any *Change* in God, but because our Importunity has made a change in *ourselves*, it has *altered* our Hearts, and rendered us proper Objects of God's Gifts and Graces. When therefore we would know how much we ought to pray, we must consider how much our Hearts want to be altered, and remember that the great Work of Prayer, is to work upon ourselves ; it is not to *move* and affect God, but it is to *move* and affect our own Hearts and fill them with such *Tempers* as God delights to reward.

Prayer is never so good a Preservation against Sin, it never so corrects and amends the Heart, as when we extend it to all the *Particulars* of our State, enumerating all our Wants, Infirmities, and Disorders, not because God needs to be informed of them, but because by this Means we inform ourselves, and make our Hearts in the best Manner acquainted with our true Condition. When our Prayers are thus particular, descending to all the Circumstances of our condition, they become by this Means a faithful Glass to us, and so often as we pray, so often we see ourselves in a true Light.

This is the most likely Means to raise in us proper Affections, to make us feel the Force and Truth of such Things, as are the Subject of our Devotions. Don't be content therefore with confessing yourself to be a *Sinner*, or with praying against Sin in *general*, for this will but little affect your Mind, it will only show you to yourself in such a State as all Mankind are in ; but if you find yourself out, if you confess and lay open the Guilt of your own *particular Sins*, if you pray constantly against such particular Sins, as you find yourself most subject to, the *frequent Sight* of your own Sins, and your *constant deploring* of their Guilt, will give your Prayers Entrance into your Heart, and put you upon Measures how to amend your Life.

If you confess yourself only to be a *Sinner*, you only confess yourself to be a *Man*, but when you describe and confess your *own particular* Guilt, then you find Cause for your own *particular Sorrow*, then you give your Prayers all the Power they can have, to affect and wound your Hearts. In like manner, when you pray for God's Grace, don't be satisfied with a general Petition, but make your Prayers suitable to your Defects ; and continue to ask for such Gifts and Graces of the Holy Spirit, as you find yourself most Defective in, for this will not only give Life to your Petitions, and make your Heart go along with them, but will also be the surest Means to fit and prepare you for such Graces, as you pray for.

Lastly, This Particularity in our Prayers, is the greatest Trial of the *Truth* of our Hearts.

A Man perhaps thinks he prays for Humility, because he has the Word, *Humility*, in his Prayers. But if he were to branch out Humility into all its *particular Parts*, he would perhaps find himself not disposed to pray for them. If he were to represent to himself the several Particulars, which make a Man *poor in Spirit*, he would find his Heart not desirous of them. So that the only way to know the Truth of our Hearts, and whether we really pray for any Virtue, is to have all its Parts in our Prayers, and make our Petitions ask for it in all its Instances. If the *proud* Man were to pray daily, and frequently for Humility in all its Kinds, and to beg of God to remove him from all Occasions of *such Pride*, as is common to his *particular State*, and to disappoint him in all his Attempts, that were contrary to Humility, he would find, that such Prayers, would either conquer his Pride, or his Pride would put an End to his Prayers. For it would be impossible to live long in any Instances of Pride, if his daily and frequent Prayers, were Petitions against those particular Instances. Now everyone may make his private Devotions thus useful to him, if he has but Piety enough to intend it. For everyone may know his own State if he will; we indeed commonly say, that People are blind to themselves, and know the least of their true State. We pass this Judgment upon People, because we see them pretending to so many Virtues, which do not belong to them, and declaiming against Vices, to which they are the most subject. Therefore we say, that Men don't know themselves, but this is false Reasoning.

We see People often pretending to be *Rich*, now this is not, because they don't know their State, but because they would not have you to know it, and they presume it possible to impose upon you. Now the Case is just the same in all other Pretences. The false, the proud, the worldly Man that pretends to Fidelity, Humility, and Heavenly Affection, knows that he is neither Faithful, nor Humble, nor Heavenly-minded; he no more thinks he has these Virtues, than a Man thinks he has a great Estate, when he endeavours to be thought rich; he knows that he only affects the Reputation of these Virtues, and is only blind in this, that he imagines he imposes upon you, and passes for the Man he is not.

Every Man therefore has Knowledge enough of himself, to know how to make his Prayers particularly fitted to the Corruption and Disorders of his Heart, and when he is so desirous of Salvation, as to enter into such a Method of Prayer, he will find, that he has taken the best Means, to make his Prayers effectual Remedies against all his Sins. Let me now only add this one Word more, that he who has learned to *pray*, has learned the greatest Secret of a holy and happy Life. Which way soever else we let loose our Hearts, they will return unto us again *empty* and *weary.* Time will convince the *vainest* and *blindest* Minds, that Happiness is no more to be found in the Things of this World, than it is to be dug out of the Earth. But when the Motions of our Hearts, are Motions of Piety, tending to God in constant Acts of Devotion, Love and Desire, then have we found Rest unto our Souls, then is it, that we have conquered the Misery of our Nature, and neither Love nor Desire in vain ; then is it, that we have found out a Good suited to our Natures, that is equal to all our Wants, that is, a constant Source of Comfort and Refreshment, that will fill us with Peace and joyful Expectations here, and eternal Happiness hereafter. For he that lives in the Spirit and Temper of Devotion, whose Heart is always full of God, lives at the *Top* of human Happiness, and is the furthest removed from all the Vanities and Vexations, which disturb and weary the Minds of Men, who are devoted to the World.

Chapter XIII.

All Christians are required to imitate the Life and Example of Jesus Christ.

OUR Religion teaches us, that as we have *borne the Image of the Earthly, so we shall bear the Image of the Heavenly,* that after our Death we shall rise to a State of Life and Happiness, like to that Life and Happiness, which our Blessed Saviour enjoys at the Right Hand of God. Since therefore it is the great End of our Religion to make us Fellow-Heirs with Christ, and Partakers of the same Happiness, it is not to be wondered at, that our Religion should require us to be like Christ in this Life, to imitate his Example, that we may enter into that State of Happiness, which he enjoys in the Kingdom of Heaven.

For how can we think that we are going to the Blessed Jesus, that we are to be hereafter as he is, unless we conform to his Spirit in this Life, and make it our great Endeavour to be what he was, when he was here. Let it therefore here be observed, that the *Nature* of our Religion teaches us this Duty in a more convincing Manner, than any particular Precepts concerning it. For the most ordinary Understanding must feel the Force and Reasonableness of this Argument. You are born to depart out of this World, to ascend to that State of Bliss, to live in such

Enjoyment of God to all Eternity, as our Blessed Saviour now enjoys, you are therefore to live in the Spirit and Temper that he lived, and make yourselves first like him here, that you may be like him hereafter. So that we need not look for particular Texts of Scripture, which command us to imitate the Life of Christ, because we are taught this Duty by a Stronger and more convincing Authority; because as the End and Design of our Religion, is to make us one with Christ hereafter, Partakers of the same State of Life, so it plainly calls us to be one with him here, and to be Partakers of that same Spirit and Temper in which he lived on Earth. When it is said that we are to imitate the Life of Christ, it is not meant that we are called to the same manner of Life, or the same sort of Actions, for this cannot be, but it is certain that we are called to the same Spirit and Temper, which was the Spirit and Temper of our Blessed Saviour's Life and Actions. We are to be like him in Heart and Mind, to act by the same Rule, to look towards the same End, and to govern our Lives by the same Spirit. This is an Imitation of Jesus Christ, which is as necessary to Salvation, as it is necessary to believe in his Name. This is the sole End of all the Counsels, Commands and Doctrines of Christ, to make us like himself, to fill us with his *Spirit* and *Temper*, and make us live according to the Rule and Manner of his Life. As no Doctrines are true, but such as are according to the Doctrines of Christ, so it is equally certain, that no Life is regular or Christian, but such as is according to the Pattern and Example of the Life of Christ. For he lived as infallibly as he taught, and it is as irregular, to vary from his Example, as it is false, to dissent from his Doctrines. To live as he lived, is as certainly the one sole Way of living as we ought, as to believe as he taught, is the one sole Way of believing as we ought. I am, saith the Blessed Jesus, *The Way, the Truth, and the Life, no Man cometh unto the Father but by me.* Christians often hear these Words, and perhaps think that they have enough fulfilled them by believing in Jesus Christ. But they should consider, that when Jesus Christ saith he is the *Way*, his meaning is, that his way of Life is to be the way, in which all Christians are to live, and that it is by living after the manner of his Life, that any Man cometh unto the Father. So that the Doctrine of this Passage is this, that however we may call ourselves Christians, or Disciples of Christ, yet we cannot come unto God the Father, but by entering into that way of Life, which was the way of our Saviour's Life. And we must remember, that there is no other way besides this, nothing can possibly bring us to God, but that way of Life, which first makes us one with Christ, and teacheth us to walk as he walked. For we may as well expect to go to a Heaven where Christ is not, as to go to that where he is, without the Spirit and Temper which carried him thither. If Christians would but suffer themselves to reflect upon this Duty, their own Minds would soon convince them of the Reasonableness and Necessity of it. For who can find the least Shadow of a Reason, why he should not imitate the Life of Christ, or why Christians should think of any other Rule of Life? It would be as easy to show that Christ acted amiss, as that we need not act after his Example. And to think that these are Degrees of Holiness, which though very good in themselves, are yet not necessary for us to aspire after, is the same Absurdity as to think, that it was not necessary for our Saviour to have been so perfect himself as he was. For, give but the Reason why such Degrees of Holiness and Purity became our Saviour, and you will give as good a Reason for us to aspire after them. For as the Blessed Jesus took not on him the Nature of Angels, but the Nature of Man, as he was in all Points made like unto us, Sin only excepted, so we are sure, that there was no Spirit or Temper that was Excellent in him, that recommended him to God, but would be also Excellent in us, and recommend us to God, if we could arrive at it.

If it should be said, that Jesus was the *Saviour* of the World, that he was born to *redeem* Mankind, was the *Son of God*, and therefore in a Condition so different from ours, that his Life can be no Rule of our Life. To this it may be answered, That these Differences don't make the Life of Christ to be less the *Rule* and *Model* of all Christians. For, as I observed before, it is the *Spirit* and *Temper* of Christ, that all Christians are to imitate, and not his particular Actions, they are to do their *proper Work* in that Spirit and Temper, in which Christ did the Work on which he was sent. So that although Christians are not Redeemers of the World as he was, though they have not his extraordinary Powers, nor that great Work to finish which he had, yet they have their Work to do in the manner that he did his; they have their Part to act, which though it be a different Part, must not be performed with a different Spirit, but with such Obedience to God, such Regard to his Glory, for such Ends of Salvation, for such Good of others, and with all such Holy Dispositions, as our Blessed Saviour manifested in every Part of his Life. A *Servant* of the lowest Order is in a very different State from his Master, yet we may very justly exhort such a one, to follow the Example of a pious and charitable Master, not because he can perform the *same Instances* of Piety and Charity, but because he may show the *same Spirit* of Piety and Charity in the Actions, which are proper to his State. This may show us, that the different State of our Lord and Master leaves him still the *exact Rule* and *Pattern* of his lowest Servants, who though they cannot come up to the Greatness of his Actions, may yet act according to that Spirit from whence they proceeded ; and then are they true Followers of Christ, when they are following his Spirit and Temper, acting according to his Ends and Designs, and doing that in their several States, which Christ did in his.

The Blessed Jesus came into the World to save the World ; now we must enter into this same Design, and Make *Salvation* the greatest Business of our Lives ; though we cannot, like him, contribute towards it, yet we must contribute all that we can, and make the Salvation of ourselves and others, the one only great Care of our Lives.

The *poor Widow's Mites* were but a small Matter in themselves, yet as they were the utmost she could do, our Blessed Saviour set them above the larger Contributions of the Rich. This may encourage People in every State of Life to be contented with their *Capacity* of doing good, provided that they do but act up to it.   Let no one think that he is too low, too mean and private to follow his Lord and Master in the Salvation of Souls, let him but add his Mite, and if it be all that he hath, he shall be thought to have done much, and be reckoned amongst those who have best performed their Master's Will.   It is not meant by this, that all People are to be Preachers and Teachers of Religion, no more than all are to be *Apostles, or all Prophets, or all Workers of Miracles.*   Christians are like Members of one and the same Body, they are as different from one another as Hands and Eyes, and have as different Offices to perform, yet may their different Parts serve and promote the same common End.   As the *Eye cannot say to the Hand, I have no need of thee, nor again the Head to the Feet, I have no need of you,** so neither can the learned Teacher say he hath no need of the private unlearned Person.   For the Work of Salvation is carried on by all Hands, as well by him that is taught, as by him that teacheth. For an *unlearned* Person by being desirous of Instruction, and careful to comply with it, may by these very Dispositions promote Salvation in as true a Degree, as he who is able and willing to instruct.   This teachable Disposition may more effectually draw others to a like Temper of Mind, than another Man's Ability and Care of teaching.   And perhaps in many Instances, the Success of the Teacher is more owing to the Manners and Example of some Person that is taught, than to the Power and

---

* I Cor. xii. 21.

Strength of the Teacher. Therefore though, as the Apostle saith, all have *not the Gifts of Healing*, though all do not *speak with Tongues*, yet all have *some Part* that they may act in the Salvation of Mankind, and may follow their Lord and Master in the great Work, for which he came down from Heaven. We must not therefore think, that it is only the Business of *Clergymen* to carry on the Work of Salvation, but must remember, that we are engaged in the same Business, though not in the same Manner. Had the *poor Widow* thought herself excused from taking Care of the Treasury, had she thought that it belonged only to the *Rich* to contribute to it, we find that she had been mistaken, and had lost that great Commendation which our Saviour bestowed upon her. Now it may be that some Widows may be so very poor, as not to have so much as a *Mite* to give to the Treasury, who must therefore content themselves with the Charity of their Hearts; but this can never happen in the Business of Salvation, here no one can be so poor, so destitute, so mean and private, as not to have a *Mite* to contribute towards it. For no Circumstances of Life can hinder us from being *Examples* of Piety and Goodness, and making our Lives a *Lesson* of Instruction to all who are about us. And he that lives an exemplary Life, though his State be ever so *poor* and *mean*, is *largely* contributing to the Salvation of others, and proving himself the *best* Follower of his Lord and Master.

This therefore is the first great Instance in which we are to follow the Example and Spirit of our Blessed Saviour. He came to save the World, to raise Mankind to a Happiness in Heaven, we must therefore all consider ourselves as called to carry on this *great Work*, to concur with our Saviour in this glorious Design. For how can we think ourselves to be his *Followers*, if we do not follow him in that for which alone he came into the World? How can we be like the Saviour of the World, unless the *Salvation* of the World be our chief and constant Care? We cannot save the World as he saved it, but yet we can contribute our Mite towards it. *How knowest thou, O Wife,* saith the Apostle, *whether thou shalt save thy Husband? Or how knowest thou, O Man, whether thou shalt save thy Wife?* This shows very plainly, that *all Persons* may have a great Share in the Salvation of those who are near them, and that they are to consider themselves as expressly called to this great Work. For the Apostle uses it as the same Argument both to Husband and Wife, which supposes that it is a Business, in which one is as much concerned as the other. The *Woman* we know is not

---

* 1 Cor. vii. 16.

allowed to speak in the *Church*, yet is she here instructed with *some share* in the Salvation of the World, she is called to this great Work, and supposed equally capable of saving the Husband, as the Husband of saving the Wife. Now what is here said of Husband and Wife, we must extend to *every State* and Relation of this Life; *Brothers* and *Sisters, Relations, Friends,* and *Neighbours* must all consider themselves as called to the *Edification* and Salvation of one another. How knowest thou, *O Sister,* whether thou shalt save thy *Brother?* How knowest thou, O Man, whether thou shalt save thy *Neighbour,* is a Way of thinking that ought never to be out of our Minds. For this would make Brothers and Sisters bear with one another, if they considered that they are to do that for one another, which Christ has done for all the World. This Reflection would turn our Anger towards bad Relations into Care and Tenderness for their Souls, we should not be glad to get away from them, but give them more of our Company, and be more exact in our Behaviour towards them, always supposing it possible, that our *good Conversation* may some time or other affect them, and that God may make use of us as a Means of their Salvation.

Eutropius is very good and pious himself, but then his Fault is, that he seeks only the Conversation of pious and good People; he is careful and exact in his Behaviour towards his virtuous Friends and Acquaintance, always studying to oblige them, and never thinking he has done enough for them; but gets away from, and avoids those that are of another Temper. Now *Eutropius* should recollect, that this is acting like a *Physician* who would take care of the *Healthy,* and disregard those who are *Sick.* He should remember, that his irreligious Friends and Relations are the very Persons who are fallen to his Care, to be edified by him, and that he is as directly called to take care of their Salvation, as the Husband to take care of the unbelieving Wife. *Eutropius* therefore, if he would imitate his Lord and Master, must apply to the *lost Sheep of the House of Israel,* and endeavour by all the innocent Arts of pleasing and conversing with his Friends, to gain them to Repentance. We must not excuse ourselves from this Care, by saying that our Relations are obstinate, hardened, and careless of all our Behaviour towards them, but must support ourselves with the Apostle's Argument, how knowest thou, O Man, whether it will be always so, or whether thou mayest not at last save thy Relation?

The Apostle saith, *Destroy not him with thy Meat for whom Christ died.** We may therefore justly reason thus with our-

---

* Rom xiv. 15.

selves, that as it lies much in our Power to hinder the Salvation, so it must be in our Power in an equal Degree to edify and promote the Salvation of those whom Jesus Christ died to save. Destroy not therefore by thy Negligence, by thy Impatience, by thy Want of Care, that Relation for whom Christ died, nor think that thou hast done enough to save those who relate to thee, till there is no more that thou canst do for them. This is the State in which all Christians are to consider themselves, as appointed by God in their several Stations to carry on that great Work, for which Christ came into the World. *Clergymen* are not the only Men who have a *Cure* of Souls, but every Christian has some People about him, whose Salvation he is obliged to be careful of, with whom he is to live in all Godliness and Purity, that they may have the Benefit of his Example and Assistance in their Duty to God. So that all Christians, though ever so *low* and *mean*, and *private*, must consider themselves as *hired* by Christ to work in his *Vineyard;* for as no Circumstances of Life can hinder us from saving ourselves, so neither can they hinder us from promoting the Salvation of others. Now though we have according to our different Stations different Parts to act, yet if we are careful of that Part which is fallen to our Share, we may make ourselves equally Objects of God's Favours.

Thou, it may be, art not a *Prophet*, God has not honoured thee with this Post in his Service, yet needest thou not fall short of this Happiness; for our Saviour hath said, *That he that receiveth a Prophet in the Name of a Prophet, shall receive a Prophet's Reward.* Now this shows us that though all Men have not the same Part to act in the common Salvation, yet that none will be losers by that State they are in, if they be but true to the particular Duties of it. If they do all the Good they can in their *particular State*, they will be looked upon with such Acceptance as the *poor Widow* who gave all that she had. Hence we may learn the Greatness of their Folly, who neglecting the exact Performance of such Duties as fall within their Power, are pleasing themselves with the great Things they would do, were they but in another State.

Clemens, has his Head full of imaginary Piety. He is often proposing to himself what he would do if he had a great Estate; he would outdo all charitable Men who are gone before him : He would retire from the World, he would have no Equipage, he would allow himself only Necessaries, that Widows and Orphans, the Sick and Distressed, might find Relief out of his Estate. He tells you that all other Ways of Spending an Estate is Folly and Madness.

Now *Clemens* has at present a moderate Estate which he

spends upon himself in the same Vanities and Indulgences, as other People do : He might live upon one Third of his Fortune, and make the rest the Support of the Poor, but he does nothing of all this that is in his Power, but pleases himself with what he would do, if his Power were greater. Come to thy Senses, *Clemens*, do not talk what thou wouldst do, if thou wast an *Angel*, but consider what thou canst do as thou art a *Man*. Make the best Use of thy *present State*, do now as thou thinkest thou wouldst do with a great Estate, be *sparing*, *deny* thyself, *abstain* from all Vanities, that the Poor may be better maintained, and then thou art as Charitable as thou canst be in any Estate. Remember the poor *Widow's Mite*.

Fervidus, is a regular Man, and exact in the Duties of Religion, but then the Greatness of his Zeal to be doing Things that he cannot, makes him overlook those little Ways of doing Good, which are every Day in his Power. *Fervidus* is only sorry that he is not in Holy Orders, and that his Life is not spent in a Business the most desirable of all Things in the World. He is often thinking what Reformation he would make in the World, if he were a *Priest* or *Bishop ;* he would have devoted himself wholly to God and Religion, and have had no other Care, but how to save Souls. But do not believe yourself, *Fervidus*, for if you desired in earnest to be a Clergyman, that you might devote yourself entirely to the Salvation of others, why then are you not doing all that you can in the State that you are now in ? Would you take extraordinary Care of a *Parish* or a *Diocese*, why then are you not as extraordinary in the Care of your Family ? If you think the Care of other Peoples' Salvation, to be the happiest Business in the World, why do you neglect the Care of those who are fallen into your Hands ? Why do you show no Concern for the Souls of your Servants ? If they do their Business for which you hired them, you never trouble your Head about their Christianity. Nay, *Fervidus*, you are so far from labouring to make those who are about you truly Devout and Holy, that you almost put it out of their Power to be so. You hire a *Coachman* to carry you to Church, and to sit in the Street with your *Horses*, whilst you are attending upon Divine Service. You never ask him how he supplies the loss of Divine Service, or what means he takes to preserve himself in a State of Piety. You imagine that if you were a *Clergyman*, you would be ready to lay down your Life for your Flock, yet you cannot lay aside a *little State* to promote the Salvation of your Servants. It is not desired of you, *Fervidus*, to die a *Martyr* for your Brethren ; you are only required to go to *Church* on Foot, to spare some *State* and *Attendance*, to bear sometimes with a little *Rain* and *Dirt*, rather than keep those Souls which are as dear to God and Christ as your's is, from their *full Share* in the common Worship of Christians. Do but deny yourself such small matters as these, let us but see that you can take the least Trouble, to make all your Servants and Dependants true Servants of God, and then you shall be allowed to imagine, what Good you would have done, had you been devoted to the Altar.

Eugenia is a good young Woman, full of pious Dispositions; she is intending, if ever she has a Family, to be the *best Mistress* of it that ever was, her House shall be a *School* of Religion, and her Children and Servants shall be brought up in the strictest Practice of Piety; she will spend her time, and live in a very different Manner from the rest of the World. It may be so, *Eugenia*, the Piety of your Mind makes me think that you intend all this with Sincerity. But you are not yet at the Head of a Family, and perhaps never may be. But, *Eugenia*, you have now one Maid, and you do not know what Religion she is of; she dresses you for the Church, you ask her for what you want, and then leave her to have as little Christianity as she pleases. You turn her away, you hire another, she comes, and goes no more instructed or edified in Religion by living with you, than if she had lived with any Body else. And all this comes to pass, because your Mind is taken up with greater Things, and you reserve yourself to make a whole Family Religious, if ever you come to be Head of it. You need not stay, *Eugenia*, to be so extraordinary a Person; the Opportunity is now in your Hands, you may now spend your time, and live in as different a Manner from the rest of the World, as ever you can in any other State. Your *Maid* is your Family at present, she is under your Care, be now that religious Governess that you intend to be; teach her the *Catechism*, hear her read, exhort her to pray, take her with you to Church, persuade her to love the Divine Service, as you love it, edify her with your Conversation, fill her with your own Notions of Piety, and spare no Pains to make her as Holy and Devout as yourself. When you do thus much Good in your present State, then are you that extraordinary Person that you intend to be, and till you thus live up to your present State, there is but little Hopes that the altering of your State, will alter your Way of Life.

I might easily produce more Instances of this Kind, where People are vainly pleasing themselves with an *imaginary* Perfection to be arrived at some time or other, when they are in different Circumstances, and neglecting that real Good which is proper to their State, and always in their Power. But these are, I hope, sufficient to show my Reader how to examine his own Life, and find out himself, if I have not done it for him.

There is no Falseness of our Hearts, that leads us into greater Errors, than imagining that we shall some time or other be better than we are, or need be now ; for *Perfection* has no Dependence upon *external* Circumstances, it wants no *Times* or *Opportunities*, but it is then in its highest State, when we are making the *best Use* of that Condition in which we are placed. The *poor Widow* did not stay till she was *rich*, before she contributed to the Treasury, she readily brought her Mite, and, little as it was, it got her the Reward and Commendation of great Charity. We must therefore all of us imitate the Wisdom of the poor Widow, and exercise every Virtue in the same Manner, that she exercised her Charity. We must stay for no Time or Opportunities, wait for no *Change* of Life, or *fancied Abilities*, but remember that every time is a time for Piety and Perfection. Everything but Piety has its Hindrances, but Piety, the more it is hindered, the higher it is raised. Let us therefore not vainly say, that if we had lived in our Saviour's Days, we would have followed him, or that if we could work Miracles, we would devote ourselves to his Glory. For to follow Christ as far as we can in our present State, and to do all that we are able for his Glory, is as acceptable to him, as if we were working Miracles in his Name.

The Greatness that we are to aim at, is not the Greatness of our Saviour's *particular Actions*, but it is the Greatness of his Spirit and Temper, that we are to act by in all Parts of our Life. Now every State of Life, whether *public* or *private*, whether *bond* or *free*, whether *high* or *low*, is capable of being conducted and governed by the same *Spirit* and *Temper*, and consequently every State of Life may carry us to the same Degree of Likeness to Christ. So that though we can in *no respect* come up to the Actions, yet we must in every respect act by the Spirit and Temper of Christ. *Learn of me*, saith our Blessed Lord, *for I am meek and lowly in Heart.* He doth not say, be ye in the State and Condition that I am in, for that were impossible, yet though ever so different in State and Condition, he calls upon us to be like him in Meekness and Lowliness of Heart and Spirit, and makes it necessary for us to go through our particular State with that Spirit and Temper, which was the Spirit and Temper of his whole Life. So far therefore as we can learn the Heart and Spirit of our Saviour, so far as we can discover the Wisdom, Purity, and Heavenliness of his Designs, so far we have learned of what Spirit and Temper we ought to be of, and must no more think ourselves at liberty to act by any other Spirit, than we are at liberty to chose another Saviour. In all our Actions and Ways of Life we must appeal to this Rule, we must reckon ourselves no further living like Christians, than as we live like Christ, and be assured, that so far as we depart from the Spirit of Christ, so far we depart from that State to which he has called us. For the Blessed Jesus has called us to live as he did, to walk in the same Spirit, that he walked, that we may be in the same Happiness, with him when this Life is at an end. And indeed who can think that anything but the *same Life,* can lead to the *same State?*

When our Blessed Saviour was upon the Cross, he thus prayed for his Enemies, *Father, forgive them, for they know not what they do.** Now all Christians readily acknowledge that this Temper of Christ, is to be the *exact Rule* of our Temper on the like Occasion, that we are not to fall short of it, but must be perfectly like Christ in this Charity towards our Murderers. But then perhaps they do not enough consider, that for the very same Reason, every other Temper of Christ, is as much the *exact Rule* of all Christians, as his Temper towards his Murderers. For are we to be thus disposed towards our Persecutors and Murderers, because Christ was so disposed towards his? And is it not as good an Argument that we are to be so, and so disposed towards the World and all worldly Enjoyments, because Christ was so disposed towards them? He was as right in one case as the other, and no more erred in his Temper towards *worldly Things,* than in his Temper towards his *Enemies.* Should we not fail to be good Christians, if we fell short of that forgiving Spirit, which the Blessed Jesus showed upon the Cross? And shall we not equally fail to be good Christians, if we fall short of that humble and meek Spirit which he showed in all his Life? Can any one tell why the Temper of Christ towards his Enemies, should be more the exact Measure of our Temper, than any other Spirit that he showed upon any other Occasion? Think, *Reader,* if thou canst find a Reason, why thou mayest not as well forgive thy Enemies less than Christ forgave his, as to love the World more than he loved it? If thou canst tell why it is not as dangerous to be wanting in the Humility, Meekness, and other Tempers of Christ, as to be wanting in his Charity, towards his Enemies. We must therefore either own, that we may be good Christians, without the *forgiving Spirit,* which Christ then exercised, or we must own that we are not good Christians, whenever we depart from the Spirit of Christ in any *other Instances.* For the Spirit of Christ consisted as much in Meekness,

---

* Luke xxiii. 34.

Humility, Devotion, and Renunciation of the World, as in the *forgiving* his Enemies: They therefore who are contrary to Christ in any of these Tempers, are no more like to Christ, than they who are contrary to him in this forgiving Spirit. If you were to see a Christian dying without this Temper towards those that destroyed him, you would be frightened at it; you would think that Man in a dreadful State, that died without that Temper in which Christ died. But then, remember, that he judges as rightly, who thinks it equally dreadful to live in any other Spirit, that is not the Spirit of Christ. If thou art not living in that *Meekness* and *Lowliness* of Heart, in that *Disregard* of the World, that *Love of God*, that *Self-denial* and *Devotion* in which our Saviour lived, thou art as unlike to him, as he that *dies* without that *Temper*, in which he died.

The short of the Matter is this, the Spirit and Temper of Christ, is the *strict Measure* of the Spirit and Temper of all Christians. It is not in this or that particular Temper of Christ, that we are to follow his Example, but we are to aspire after his whole Spirit, to be in all things as he was, and think it as dangerous to depart from his Spirit and Temper in one Instance, as in another. For besides that there is the same Authority in all that our Saviour did, which obliges us to conform to his whole Example: Can any one tell us why we should have more value for this World, than our Saviour had? What is there in our *State* and *Circumstances*, that can make it proper for us to have more affection for the Things of this Life, than our Saviour had? Is the World any more our *Happiness* than it was his Happiness? Are Riches, and Honours, and Pleasures, any more our *proper Good*, than they were his? Are we any more born for this Life, than our Saviour was? Are we in less danger of being *Corrupted* by its Enjoyments, than he was? Are we more at leisure to take up *our rest*, and spend our time in worldly Satisfactions than he was? Have we a work upon our Hands that we can *more easily* finish, than he could finish his? That requires of us less *Mortification* and *Self-denial*, less *Devotion* and *Watching*, than our Saviour's required of him? Now as nothing of this can be said, so nothing can be said in our Excuse, if we follow not our Saviour's Temper in this Respect. As this World is as little our Happiness, and more our Danger, than it was his, as we have a Work to finish that requires *all our Strength*, that is as *contrary* to the World, as our Saviour's was, it is plain, there was no Reason or Necessity of his Disregard of the World, but what is the same Reason and Necessity for us to disregard it in the same Manner.

Again, take another Instance of our Blessed Saviour's Spirit,

I came down from Heaven, saith he, *not to do my own Will, but the Will of him that sent me.**

And again, *My Meat and Drink is to do the Will of him that sent me.* Now can any Christian show, why he may think otherwise of himself, than our Saviour here thought? Or that he need be *less devoted* to the Glory of God than he was? What is there in our *Nature* and *Condition* to make any Difference of this Kind? Do we not stand in the same Relation to God that our Saviour did? Have we not the same Nature that he had? Are we too great to be made Happy in the same Way that he was? Or can anything else be the Happiness of our Nature, but that which was the Happiness of his? Was he a *sufferer,* a *loser,* did he leave the true Happiness of *human Life,* by devoting himself to the Will of God? Or can this be our Case, though it was not his? Can we be *losers,* by looking to God *alone,* and *devoting* ourselves to his Glory? Was it not the Greatness and Happiness of our Saviour that he lived to God alone? And is there any other Happiness or Greatness for us, but by making that the End and Aim of our Life, which he made the End and Aim of his Life? For we may as well seek out for another God, as for another Happiness, or another Way to it, than that in which Christ is gone before us. He did not mistake the Nature of *Man,* or the Nature of the *World,* he did not overlook any *real Felicity,* or pass by any *solid Good,* he only made the best Use of human Life, and made it the Cause of all the Happiness and Glory that can arise from it. To find a Reason therefore, why we should live otherwise than he lived, why we should less seek the Glory of God than he sought it, is to find a Reason why we should less promote our own Greatness and Glory. For our State and Condition in this Life lays us under *all the Obligations,* that our Saviour was under to live as he did, his Life is as much our *right Way,* as it was his, and his Spirit and Temper is as *necessary* for our Condition, as it was for his. For this World and all the Things of the World signify as *little* to us, as they did to him; we are no more in our *true State,* till we are got out of this World, than he was; and we have no other way to arrive at true Felicity and Greatness, but by so *devoting* ourselves to God, as our Blessed Saviour did. We must therefore make it the great Business and Aim of our Lives, to be like Christ, and this not in a *loose* or *general* Way, but with great *Nicety* and *Exactness,* always looking to his *Spirit,* to his *Ends* and *Designs,* to his *Tempers,* to his Ways and Conversation in the World, as the *exact Model* and *Rule* of our Life.

---

* John vi. 38.

15—2

Again, *Learn of me*, saith our Blessed Saviour, *for I am Meek and Lowly of Heart*, Now this Passage is to be considered, not as a Piece of good Advice, that would be of use to us, but as a *positive* Command requiring a *necessary* Duty. And if we are commanded to learn of Christ Meekness and Lowliness, then we are commanded in the same positive Manner, to learn *his* Meekness and Lowliness. For if we might take up with a Meekness and Lowliness of Heart, that was *not his*, then it would not be necessary to learn them of him. Since therefore we are commanded to learn them of him, it is plain, that it is his Meekness and Lowliness that we are commanded to learn ; that is, we are to be Meek and Lowly, not in any *loose* or *general* Sense of the Words, not according to the *Opinions* and *Practices* of Men, but in such *Truth* and *Reality* as Christ was Meek and Lowly.

It ought also to be observed, that there must be something very *Extraordinary* in these Dispositions of the Heart, from the manner in which we are taught them. It is only in this Place, that our Saviour says expressly, *Learn of me ;* and when he says, *Learn of me*, he does not say, for I am just and equitable, or kind or holy, but *I am meek and lowly of Heart;* as if he would teach us, that these are the Tempers which most of all *distinguish* his Spirit, and which he most of all requires his Followers to learn of him. For consider, does Christ when he describes himself, choose to do it by *these Tempers ?* When he calls upon us to learn of him, does he only mention *these Tempers ?* And is not this a sufficient Proof that these are Tempers, which the Followers of Christ, are most of all obliged to learn, and that we are then most *unlike* to Christ, when we are wanting in them ? Now as our great Lord and Master has made these Characters, the *distinguishing* Characters of his Spirit, it is plain, that they are to be the *distinguishing* Characters of our Spirit, for we are only so far his, as we are like him. Consider also, was he *more lowly* than he need have been ? Did he practise any Degrees of Humility that were *unnecessary ?* This can no more be said, than he can be charged with Folly. But can there be any Instances of Lowliness which became him, that are not necessary for us ? Does our State and Condition excuse us from any kind of Humility, that were necessary for him ? Are we higher in our Nature, more raised in our Condition, or more in Favour of God than he was ? Are there *Dignities, Honours,* and *Ornaments* of Life which we may delight in, though he might not ? We must own these Absurdities, or else acknowledge, that we are to breathe the same *lowly Spirit*, act with the *same Meekness*, and practise the *same humble* Behaviour that he did. So that the Matter comes plainly to this Conclusion, either that Christ was more humble and lowly than his Nature and Condition required, or we are under the same Necessity of as great Humility, till we can prove that we are in a higher state than he was.

Now as it is plainly the Meekness and Lowliness of Christ, that we are to Practise, why should we think, that we have attained unto it, unless we show forth these Tempers in *such Instances*, as our Saviour showed them? For, can we suppose, that we are Meek and Lowly as he was, if we live in *such Ways* of Life, and seek after *such Enjoyments* as his Meekness and Lowliness would not allow him to follow? Did he mistake the *proper Instances* of Lowliness? If not, it must be our great Mistake not to follow his Steps. Did his Lowliness of Heart make him disregard the Distinction of this Life, avoid the Honours, Pleasures, and Vanities of Greatness? And can we think that we are living by the same lowly Spirit, whilst we are seeking after all the Dignities and Ornaments both of our Persons and Conditions? What may we not think, if we can think after this Manner? For let us speak home to this Point, either our Saviour was *wise, judicious*, and governed by a *Divine Spirit* in these Tempers, or he was not; to say that he was not, is horrid *Blasphemy*, and to say that he was, is saying, that we are neither *wise*, nor *judicious*, nor governed by a *Divine Spirit*, unless we show the *same Tempers*. Perhaps you will say, that though you are to be *lowly in Heart* like Christ, yet you need not disregard the Ornaments, Dignities, and Honours of Life, and that you can be as truly meek and lowly in the *Figure and Show* of Life, as in any other State.

Answer me, therefore, this one Question. Was our Saviour's Lowliness, which showed itself in an utter disregard of all *Pomp* and *Figure* of Life, a *false Lowliness* that mistook its *proper Objects*, and showed itself in Things *not* necessary? Did he abstain from Dignities and Splendour, and deny himself Enjoyments which he might with the *same Lowliness* of Heart have taken Pleasure in? Answer but this Question plainly, and then you will plainly determine this Point; if you justify our Saviour, as being *truly* and *wisely* Humble, you condemn yourself, if you think of any *other* Humility, than *such* as he practised. Consider further, that if you were to hear a Person reasoning after this Manner in any other Instance, if he should pretend to be of an *inward Temper* contrary to the *outward Course* of his Life, you would think him very absurd. If a Man that lived in an outward Course of *Duels* and *Quarrels*, should say, that in his Heart he forgave all Injuries, allowed of no Resentments. If another whose common Life was full of *Bitterness*, and *Wrath*, and *Evil-Speaking*, should pretend that in his Heart he loved

his Neighbour as himself, we should reckon them amongst those
that were more than a little touched in their Heads. Now to
pretend to any Temper contrary to our *outward Actions*, is the
same Absurdity in one Case as in another. And for a Man to
say, that he is lowly in Heart, whilst he is seeking the *Ornaments, Dignities,* and *Show* of Life, is the same Absurdity, as for
a Man to say, that he is of a *meek* and forgiving Spirit, whilst he
is seeking and revenging *Quarrels.* For to disregard and avoid
the Pomp and Figure, and vain Ornaments of worldly Greatness,
is as essential to Lowliness of Mind, as the avoiding of *Duels*
and *Quarrels* is essential to Meekness and Charity. As therefore there is but *one way* of being charitable as our Saviour was,
and that by such outward Actions towards our Enemies as he
showed, so is there but *one way* of being lowly in Heart as he
was, and that by living in such a Disregard of all vain and
worldly Distinctions, as he lived. Let us not therefore deceive
ourselves ; let us not fancy that we are truly Humble, though
living in all the *Pride* and *Splendour* of Life ; let us not imagine
that we have any Power to render ourselves Humble and Lowly
any other way, than by an humble and lowly Course of Life.
Christ is our *Pattern* and *Example,* he was content to be *one
Person,* he did not pretend to *Impossibilities,* to reconcile the
Pride of Life with the *Lowliness* of Religion, but renounced the
one, that he might be a true Example of the other. He had
a Power of working Miracles, but to *reconcile* an humble and
lowly Heart with the vain *Ornaments* of our Persons, the
Dignities of *State* and *Equipage,* was a *Miracle* he did not pretend to. It is only for us great Masters in the science of Virtue,
to have this mighty Power ; we can be humble, it seems, at *less
Expense* than our Saviour was, without supporting ourselves in it
by a way of Life suitable to it. We can have *Lowliness* in our
Hearts, with *Paint* and *Patches* upon our Faces, we can deck and
adorn our Persons in the Spirit of Humility, make all the Show
that we can in the *Pride* and *Figure* of the World, with Christian
Lowliness in some *little Corner* of our Hearts.

But suppose now that all this was possible, and that we could
preserve an humble and lowly Temper in a way of Life contrary
to it. Is it any advantage to a Man to be one Thing in his *Heart,*
and another Thing in his *Way of Life?* Is it any excuse, to say
that a Man is kind and tender in his Heart, though his Life hath
a Course of contrary Actions? Is it not a greater Reproach to
him, that he lives a churlish Life with Tenderness in his Heart?
Is he not that Servant that shall be beaten with many stripes
for sinning against his Heart and Conscience? Now it is the
same Thing in the Case before us. Are you *humble* and *lowly*

in your Heart, is it not therefore a greater Sin in you, not to practise Humility and Lowliness in *your Life?* If you live contrary to Conscience, are you not in a State of greater Guilt? Are not lowly Actions, an humble Course of Life, as much the proper Exercise of Humility, as a charitable Life and Actions, is the proper Exercise of Charity?

If therefore a Man may be excused for not living a charitable Life, because of a supposed Charity in his Heart, then may you think it excusable to forbear a Lowliness of Life and Actions, because of a pretended Humility in your Mind. Consider further, is any Thing so agreeable to a proud Person, as to *shine* and make a *Figure* in the Pride of Life? Is such a Person content with being high in *Heart* and *Mind?* Is he not uneasy till he can add a way of Life *suitable* to it? Till his *Person,* his *State,* and *Figure* in Life appear in a Degree of Pride suitable to the Pride of his Heart? Nay, can any Thing be a greater Pain to a proud Man, than to be forced to live in an humble lowly State of Life? Now if this be true of Pride, must not the contrary be as true of Humility? Must not Humility in an equal Degree dispose us to ways that are contrary to the Pride of Life, and *suitable* and *proper* to Humility? Must it not be the same Absurdity, to suppose a Man content with *Humility of Heart,* without adding a Life *suitable* to it, as to suppose a Man content with a *secret Pride* of his Heart, without seeking such a *State* of Life as is according to it? Nay, is it not the same Absurdity, to suppose an humble Man seeking all the *State* of a Life of Pride, as to suppose a proud Man desiring only *Meanness* and *Obscurity,* and unable to relish any Appearance of Pride? These Absurdities are equally manifest and plain in one Case as in the other. So that what way soever we examine this Matter, it appears, that a Humility of Mind, that is not a Humility of *Person,* of *Life* and *Action,* is but a *mere Pretence,* and as contrary to common Sense, as it is contrary to the *Doctrine* and *Example* of our Saviour.

I shall now leave this Subject to the Reader's own Meditation, with this one further Observation.

We see the Height of our calling, that we are called to follow the Example of our Lord and Master, and to go through this World with his Spirit and Temper. Now nothing is so likely a Means to fill us with his Spirit and Temper, as to be frequent in reading the *Gospels,* which contain the History of his Life and Conversation in the World. We are apt to think, that we have sufficiently read a Book, when we have so read it, as to know what it contains, this reading may be sufficient as to many Books, but as to the *Gospels,* we are not to think that we have ever read them enough, because we have often read and heard what they contain. But we must read them, as we do our *Prayers*, not to know what they contain, but to fill our Hearts with the Spirit of them. There is as much Difference betwixt reading, and reading, as there is betwixt praying, and praying. And as no one prays well, but he who is daily and constant in Prayer, so no one can read the Scriptures to sufficient Advantage, but he who is daily and constant in the reading of them. By thus conversing with our Blessed Lord, looking into his Actions and manner of Life, hearing his Divine Sayings, his Heavenly Instructions, his Accounts of the Terrors of the Damned, his Descriptions of the Glory of the Righteous, we should find our Hearts formed and disposed to *Hunger and Thirst after Righteousness*. Happy they, who saw the Son of God upon Earth converting Sinners, and calling *fallen Spirits* to return to God! And next happy are we, who have his Discourses, Doctrines, Actions, and Miracles which then converted *Jews* and Heathens into *Saints and Martyrs*, still preserved to fill us with the same Heavenly Light, and lead us to the same State of Glory.

Chapter XIV.

An Exhortation to Christian Perfection.

WHOEVER hath read the foregoing Chapters with Attention, is, I hope, sufficiently instructed in the Knowledge of *Christian Perfection*. He hath seen that it requireth us to *devote* ourselves *wholly* unto God, to make the Ends and Designs of Religion, the Ends and Designs of all our Actions. That it calleth us to be *born again of God*, to live by the Light of his Holy Spirit, to *renounce the World* and all *worldly Tempers*, to practise a constant, *universal Self-denial*, to make daily War with the Corruption and Disorder of our Nature, to prepare ourselves for *Divine Grace* by a Purity and Holiness of Conversation, to avoid all Pleasures and Cares which *grieve the Holy Spirit*, and separate him from us, to live in a *daily constant State* of Prayer and Devotion, and as the Crown of all to imitate the *Life and Spirit* of the Holy Jesus.

It now only remains, that I exhort the Reader to labour after this Christian Perfection. Were I to exhort anyone to the Study of *Poetry* or *Eloquence*, to labour to be *Rich* and *Great*, or to spend his Time in *Mathematics* or other Learning, I could only produce such Reasons as are fit to delude the Vanity of Men, who are ready to be taken with any Appearance of Excellence. For if the same Person were to ask me, what it signifies to be a *Poet* or *Eloquent,* what Advantage it would be to him, to be a great *Mathematician,* or a great *Statesman,* I must be forced to answer, that these Things would signify just as much to him, as they now signify to those Poets, Orators, Mathematicians, and Statesmen, whose Bodies have been a long while lost amongst common Dust. For if a Man will but be so thoughtful and inquisitive, as to put the Question to every human Enjoyment, and ask what real Good it would bring along with it, he would soon find, that every Success amongst the Things of this Life, leaves us just in the same State of Want and Emptiness in which it found us. If a Man asks why he should labour to be the first *Mathematician, Orator,* or *Statesman,* the Answer is easily given, because of the *Fame* and *Honour* of such a Distinction, but if he were to ask again, why he should thirst after Fame and Honour, or what Good they would do him, he must stay long enough for an Answer. For when we are at the *Top* of all human Attainments, we are still at the *Bottom* of all human Misery, and have made no further Advancement towards true Happiness, than those, whom we see in the Want of all these Excellences. Whether a Man die before he has written *Poems,* compiled *Histories,* or raised an *Estate,* signifies no more than whether he died an hundred, or a thousand Years ago.

On the contrary, when anyone is exhorted to labour after Christian Perfection, if he then asks what Good it will do him, the Answer is ready, that it would do him a Good, which Eternity alone can measure, that it will deliver him from a State of Vanity and Misery, that it will raise him from the poor Enjoyments of an animal Life, that it will give him a glorious Body, carry him in spite of Death and the Grave to live with God, be Glorious among Angels and Heavenly Beings, and be full of an infinite Happiness to all Eternity. If therefore we could but make Men so reasonable, as to make the shortest Inquiry into the Nature of Things, we should have no Occasion to exhort them to strive after Christian Perfection. *Two Questions,* we see, put an End to all the vain Projects and Designs of human Life, they are all so empty and useless to our Happiness, that they cannot stand the Trial of a *second* Question. And on the other Hand, 'tis but asking whether Christian Perfection tends, to make us have no other Care. One single Thought upon the eternal Happiness that it leads to, is sufficient to make all People *Saints.*

This shows us how inexcusable all Christians are, who are devoted to the Things of this Life, it is not because they want *fine Parts*, or are unable to make *deep Reflections*, but it is because they reject the first Principles of *common Sense*, they won't so much as ask what those Things are, which they are labouring after. Did they but use thus much Reason, we need not desire them to be wiser, in order to seek only eternal Happiness. As a Shadow at the first Trial of the Hand, appears to have no Substance, so all Human Enjoyments sink away into nothing at the first Approach of a *serious* Thought. We must not therefore complain of the Weakness and Ignorance of our Nature, or the deceitful Appearances of worldly Enjoyments, because the lowest Degree of Reason, if listened to, is sufficient to discover the Cheat. If you will, you may *blindly* do what the rest of the World are doing, you may follow the *Cry*, and run yourself out of *Breath*, for you know not what. But if you will but show so much Sense, as to ask why you should take such a Chase, you will need no deeper a Reflection than this, to make you leave the Broad-way, and let the Wise and Learned, the Rich and Great be mad by themselves. Thus much common Sense will turn your Eyes towards God, will separate you from all the Appearances of worldly Felicity, and fill you with one only Ambition after eternal Happiness.

When *Pyrrhus* King of *Epirus*, told *Cineas* what great Conquests he intended to make, and how many Nations he would subdue, *Cineas* asked him what he would do, when all this was done? He answered, we will then live at Ease and enjoy ourselves and our Friends. *Cineas* replied to this Purpose, Why then, Sir, do we not *now* live at Ease and enjoy ourselves? If Ease and Quiet, be the utmost of our Views and Designs why do we run away from it at present? What Occasion for all these Battles and Expeditions all over the World?

The *Moral* of this Story is very extensive, and carries a Lesson of Instruction to much the greatest part of the Christian World.

When a Christian is eager after the Distinctions of this Life, proposing some mighty Heights to which he will raise himself, either in *Riches, Learning*, or *Power*, if one was to ask him what he will do when he has obtained them, I suppose his Answer would be, that he would then retire, and devote himself to *Holiness and Piety*. May we not here justly say with *Cineas*, if Piety and Holiness is the *chief End* of Man, if these are your last Proposals, the upshot of all your Labours, why do you not enter upon Happiness at present? Why all this wandering out of your Way? Why must you go so far about? For to devote yourself to the World, though it is your last Proposal to retire from it to Holiness and Piety, is like *Pyrrhus's* seeking of *Battles*, when he proposed to live in Ease and Pleasure with his Friends. I believe there are very few Christians, who have it not in their Heads at least, to be some Time or other Holy and Virtuous, and readily own, that he is the happy Man that dies truly Humble, Holy, and Heavenly-minded. Now this Opinion which all People are possessed of, makes the Projects and Designs of Life, more Mad and Frantic than the Battles of *Pyrrhus.* For one may not only say to such People, why do you neglect the *present* Happiness of these Virtues, but one must further add, why are you engaged in ways of Life, that are quite contrary to them? You want to be *Rich* and *Great,* is it that Riches and Greatness may make you more *Meek* and *Humble,* and *Heavenly-minded?* Do you aspire after the distinctions of Honour, that you may more truly feel the *Misery* and *Meanness* of your Nature, and be made more lowly in your own Eyes? Do you plunge yourself into worldly Cares, let your Passions fix upon Variety of Objects, that you may love God with all your Heart, and raise your Affections to Things above? You acknowledge Humility to be essential to Salvation, yet make it the chief Care of your Life to run away from it, to raise yourself in the *Show* and *Figure* of the World? Is not this fighting of *Pyrrhus's* Battles? Nay, is it not a much more egregious Folly? For your own, that you cannot be saved without true Humility, a real Lowliness of Temper, and yet are doing all that you can to keep it out of your Heart. What is there in the Conduct of the maddest Hero, that can equal this Folly?

Suppose, that *strict Sobriety* was the sole End of Man, the necessary Condition of Happiness, what would you think of those People, who knowing and believing this to be true, should yet spend their Time in getting Quantities of all Sorts of the *strongest Liquors?* What would you think if you saw them constantly enlarging their *Cellars,* filling every Room with *Drams,* and contending who should have the *largest Quantities* of the strongest Liquors? Now this is the Folly and Madness of the Lives of Christians, they are as Wise and Reasonable, as they are who are always providing strong Liquors in order to be *strictly Sober.* For all the Enjoyments of human Life, which Christians so aspire after, whether of *Riches, Greatness, Honours,* and *Pleasures,* are as much the Dangers and Temptations of a Christian, as strong and pleasant Liquors, are the Dangers and Temptations of a Man that is to drink only Water. Now if you were to ask such a Man, why he is continually increasing his Stock of Liquors, when he is to abstain from them all, and only to drink Water, he can give you as good a Reason, as those Christians, who spare no Pains to acquire Riches, Greatness, and Pleasures, at the same time that their Salvation depends upon their Renouncing them all, upon their Heavenly-mindedness, great Humility, and constant Self-denial.

But it may be, you are not devoted to these Things, you have a greater Soul, than to be taken with *Riches, Equipage,* or the *Pageantry* of State. You are deeply Engaged in *Learning* and *Sciences.*

You are, it may be, squaring the *Circle,* or settling the Distances of the *Stars,* or busy in the Study of *exotic Plants.*

You, it may be, are comparing the ancient Languages, have made deep Discoveries in the *Change of Letters,* and perhaps know how to write an *Inscription* in as obscure Characters, as if you had lived above two Thousand Years ago. Or, perhaps, you are meditating upon the *Heathen Theology,* collecting the History of their *Gods* and *Godesses;* or you are scanning some ancient *Greek* or *Roman* Poet, and making an exact Collection of their *scattered* Remains, *Scraps* of Sentences, and *broken* Words.

You are not exposing your Life in the Field like a mad *Alexander* or *Cæsar,* but you are again and again fighting over all their Battles in your *Study,* you are collecting the Names of their *Generals,* the Number of their *Troops,* the Manner of their Arms, and can give the World a more exact Account of the Times, Places, and Circumstances of their Battles than has yet been seen.

You will perhaps ask whether this be not a very commendable Inquiry? An excellent Use of our Time and Parts? Whether People may not be very reasonably Exhorted to these Kind of Studies? It may be answered, that all Inquiries (however Learned they are reckoned) which do not improve the Mind in some useful Knowledge, that do not make us Wise in *religious Wisdom,* are to be reckoned amongst our greatest Vanities and Follies. All Speculations that will not stand this Trial, are to be looked upon as the Wanderings and Impertinences of a *disordered Understanding.*

It is strange Want of Thought to imagine, that an Inquiry is ever the better, because it is taken up in *Greek* and *Latin.* Why is it not as Wise and Reasonable for a *Scholar* to dwell in the *Kitchen* and converse with *Cooks,* as to go into his Study, to meditate upon the *Roman* Art of *Cookery,* and learn their Variety of *Sauces.*

A *grave Doctor* in Divinity would perhaps think his time very ill Employed, that he was acting below his Character, if he were to be an *Amanuensis* to some *modern Poet.* Why then does he think it suitable with the Weight of his Calling, to have been a *Drudge* to some *ancient Poet*, counting his Syllables for several Years, only to help the World to read, what some *irreligious, wanton,* or *Epicurean* Poet has written.

It is certainly a much more reasonable Employment to be making *Clothes,* than to spend one's Time in reading or writing Volumes upon the *Grecian* or *Roman* Garments.

If you can show me a Learning that makes Man truly *sensible* of his Duty, that fills the Mind with *true Light,* that reforms the *Heart,* that disposes it right towards God, that makes us more *reasonable* in all our Actions, that inspires us with *Fortitude, Humility, Devotion,* and Contempt of the *World,* that gives us right Notions of the *Greatness* of Religion, the *Sanctity* of Morality, the *Littleness* of every Thing but God, the *Vanity* of our Passions, and the *Misery* and Corruption of our Nature, I will own myself an Advocate for such Learning. But to think that time is well employed, because it is spent in such Speculations as the Vulgar cannot reach, or because they are fetched from *Antiquity,* or found in *Greek* or *Latin,* is a Folly that may be called as great as any in human Life.

They who think that these Inquiries are consistent with a Heart *entirely devoted* to God, have not enough considered human Nature ; they would do well to consult our Saviour's Rebuke of *Martha.* She did not seem to have wandered far from her proper Business, she was not busy in the History of *Housewifery,* or inquiring into the *Original of the Distaff,* she was only taken up with her present Affairs, and *cumbered about much serving,* but our Blessed Saviour said unto her, *Martha, Martha, thou art careful and troubled about many Things. But one thing is needful.*

Now if *Scholars* and *Divines* can show, that they only apply to such Studies as are serviceable to the *one thing needful,* if they are busy in a Philosophy and Learning that has a necessary Connection with the Devotion of the Heart to God, such Learning becomes the Followers of Christ. But if they trifle in *Greek* and *Latin,* and only assist other People to follow them in the same Impertinence, such Learning may be reckoned amongst the Corruptions of the Age. For all the Arguments against *Pride, Covetousness,* and *Vanity,* are as good Arguments against *such Learning,* it being the same Irreligion to be devoted to any false Learning, as to be devoted to any other *false Good.*

A Satisfaction in any vain Ornaments of the Body, whether of *Clothes* or *Paint,* is no greater a Mistake, than a Satisfaction in the *vain Accomplishments* of the Mind.

A Man that is eager and laborious in the Search and Study of that which does him *no good*, is the same poor, little Soul, as the *Miser*, that is happy in his *Bags*, that are laid by in Dust. A ridiculous Application of our *Money, Time*, and *Understanding*, is the same Fault, whether it be found amongst the Finery of *Fops*, the Hoards of *Misers*, or the Trinkets of *Virtuosos*. It is the same false Turn of Mind, the same Mistake of the Use of Things, the same Ignorance of the State of Man, and the same Offence against Religion.

When we see a Man brooding over *Bags* of Wealth, and labouring to die *Rich*, we do not only accuse him of a poor Littleness of Mind, but we charge him with great Guilt, we do not allow such a one to be in a State of Religion. Let us therefore suppose that this covetous Man was on a sudden changed into another Temper, that he was grown *Polite* and *Curious*, that he was fond and eager after the most useless Things, if they were but *ancient* or *scarce;* let us suppose that he is now as greedy of *original Paintings*, as he was before of *Money*, that he will give more for a *Dog's-Head*, or a *Snuff* of a Candle by a good *Hand*, than ever he gave in Charity all his Life, is he a wiser Man, or a better Christian than he was before? Has he more overcome the World, or is he more devoted to God, than when his Soul was locked up with his Money? Alas! his Heart is in the same false Satisfaction, he is in the same State of Ignorance, is as far from the true Good, as much separated from Good, as he whose Soul is cleaving to the Dust; he lives in the same Vanity, and must die in the Misery, as he that lives and dies in *Foppery or Covetousness*.

Here therefore I place my first Argument for *Christian Perfection*, I exhort thee to labour after it, because there is no choice of anything else for thee to labour after, there is nothing else that the Reason of Man can exhort thee to. The whole World has nothing to offer thee in its stead, choose what other way thou wilt, thou hast chosen nothing but Vanity and Misery; for all the different Ways of the World, are only different Ways of deluding thyself, this only excels that, as one Vanity can excel another. If thou wilt make thyself more Happy than those who pursue their own Destruction, if thou wilt show thyself wiser than *Fops*, more reasonable than *sordid Misers*, thou must pursue that Happiness, and study that Wisdom which leads to God, for every other Pursuit, every other Way of Life, however *polite* or *plausible* in the Opinions of the World, has a Folly and Stupidity in it, that is equal to the Folly and Stupidity of *Fops* and *Misers*.

For a while shut thine Eyes, and think of the *silliest Creature* in human Life, imagine to thyself something, that thou thinkest the most *poor*, and *vain* in the Way of the World. Now thou art thyself that poor and vain Creature, unless thou art devoted to God, and labouring after Christian Perfection: Unless this be thy Difference from the World, thou canst not think of any Creature more silly than thyself. For it is not any *Post*, or *Condition*, or *Figure* in Life, that makes one Man wiser or better than another, if thou art a proud *Scholar*, a worldly *Priest*, an indevout *Philosopher*, a crafty *Politician*, an ambitious *Statesman*, thy Imagination cannot invent a Way of Life, that has more of Vanity or Folly than thine own.

Every one has Wisdom enough to see, what Variety of Fools and Madmen there are in the World.

Now perhaps we cannot do better, than to find out the true Reason of the Folly and Madness of any Sort of Life. Ask thyself therefore wherein consists the Folly of any Sort of Life, which is most condemned in thy Judgment.

Is a drunken *Fox-hunter* leading a foolish Life? wherein consists the Folly of it? Is it because he is not getting Money upon the *Exchange*? Or because he is not wrangling at the *Bar*? Or not waiting at *Court*? No, the Folly of it consists in this, that he is not living like a *reasonable Christian*, that he is not acting like a Being that is *born again* of God, that has a Salvation to work out with *fear and trembling*, that he is throwing away his Time amongst *Dogs*, and Noise, and Intemperance, which he should devote to Watching and Prayer, and the Improvement of his Soul in all holy Tempers. Now if this is the Folly (as it most certainly is) of an intemperate *Fox-hunter*, it shows us an equal Folly in every other Way of Life, where the same great Ends of Living are neglected. Though we are shining at the *Bar*, making a Figure at *Court*, great at the *Exchange*, or famous in the *Schools* of Philosophy, we are yet the same despicable Creatures, as the intemperate *Fox-hunter*, if these States of Life keep us as far from the improvements of Holiness, and heavenly Affections. There is nothing greater in any Way of Life than *Fox-hunting*, it is all the same Folly, unless Religion be the Beginning and Ending, the Rule and Measure of it all. For it is as *noble* a Wisdom, and shows as *great a Soul*, to die less Holy and Heavenly for the sake of *Hunting* and *Noise*, as for the sake of anything that the World can give us.

If we will judge and condemn things, by our Tempers and Fancies, we may think some Ways of Life mighty wise, and others mighty foolish, we may think it Glorious to be pursuing Methods of *Fame* and *Wealth*, and foolish to be killing *Foxes*, but if we will let Reason and Religion show us the Folly and Wisdom of Things, we shall easily see, that all Ways of Life are *equally*

Little and Foolish, but those that perfect and exalt our Souls in Holiness.

No one therefore can complain of Want of Understanding in the Conduct of his Life, for a small Share of Sense is sufficient to condemn *some Degrees of* Vanity, which we see in the World; everyone is able and ready to do it. And if we are but able to condemn the vainest Sort of Life upon *true Reasons*, the same Reasons will serve to show, that all Sorts of Life are equally vain, but the *one Life* of Religion. Thou hast therefore, as I observed before, no choice of anything to labour after instead of Christian Perfection : If thou canst be content to be the *poorest, vainest, miserablest* Thing upon Earth, thou mayst neglect Christian Perfection. But if thou seest anything in human Life that thou *abhorrest* and *despisest*, if there be any Person that lives so, as thou shouldst *fear* to live, thou must turn thy Heart to God, thou must labour after *Christian Perfection*, for there is nothing in Nature but this, that can set thee above the *vainest, poorest,* and most *miserable* of human Creatures. Thou art everything that thou canst abhor and despise, everything that thou canst fear, thou art full of every Folly that thy Mind can imagine, unless thou art all devoted to God.

Secondly, Another Argument for *Christian Perfection* shall be taken from the necessity of it.

I have all along shown, that Christian Perfection consists in the right Performance of our *necessary Duties*, that it implies such holy Tempers, as constitute that common Piety, which is necessary to Salvation, and consequently it is such a Piety as is equally necessary to be attained by all People. But besides this, we are to consider, that God only knows what *Abatements* of Holiness he will accept; and therefore we can have no Security of our Salvation, but by doing our utmost to deserve it.

There are different Degrees of Holiness, which it may please God to Reward, but we cannot State these different Degrees ourselves ; but must all labour to be as eminent as we can, and then our different Improvements must be left to God. We have nothing to trust to, but the Sincerity of our Endeavours, and our Endeavours may well be thought to want Sincerity, unless they are Endeavours after the utmost Perfection. As soon as we stop at any Degrees of Goodness, we put an End to our Goodness, which is only valuable by having all the Degrees, that we can add to it. Our highest Improvement, is a State of great Imperfection, but will be accepted by God, because it is our highest Improvement. But any other State of Life, where we are not doing all that we can, to purify and perfect our Souls, is a State that can give us no Comfort or Satisfaction, because so far as we are wanting in any Ways of Piety that are in our Power, so far as we are defective in any holy Tempers, of which we are capable, so far we make our very Salvation uncertain. For no one can have any Assurance that he pleases God, or puts himself within the Terms of Christian Salvation, but he who serves God with his whole Heart, and with the utmost of his Strength. For though the Christian Religion be a Covenant of Mercy, for the Pardon and Salvation of *frail* and *imperfect* Creatures, yet we cannot say that we are within the Conditions of that Mercy, till we do all that we can in our frail and imperfect State. So that though we are not called to such a Perfection, as implies a *sinless State*, though our Imperfections will not prevent the Divine Mercy, yet it cannot be proved, that God has any Terms of Favour for those, who do not labour to be as Perfect as they can be.

Different Attainments in Piety will carry different Persons to Heaven, yet none of us can have any Satisfaction, that we are going thither, but by arriving at all that Change of Nature, which is in our Power. It is as necessary therefore to labour after Perfection, as to labour after our Salvation, because we can have no Satisfaction that a failure in one, will not deprive us of the other. When therefore you are exhorted to Christian Perfection, you must remember, that you are only exhorted to secure your Salvation, you must remember also, that you have no other Rule to judge of your Perfection, but by the Sincerity and *Fulness* of your Endeavours to arrive at it.

We may judge of the Measure and Extent of *Christian Holiness*, from the one Instance of *Charity*. This Virtue is thus described, *Charity seeketh not her own, beareth all Things, believeth all Things, hopeth all Things, endureth all Things.* Now this Charity though it be in Perfection, is yet by the Apostle made so absolutely Necessary to Salvation, that a failure in it, is not to be supplied by any other, the most shining Virtues. *Though I have all faith, so that I could remove Mountains, though I bestow all my Goods to feed the Poor, though I give my Body to be burned, and have not Charity, it profiteth me nothing.* The Apostle expressly teaches us, that this Perfection in Christian Charity, is so necessary to Salvation, that even *Martyrdom* itself is not sufficient to Atone for the want of it. Need we now any other Argument to convince us, that to labour after our Perfection, is only to labour after our Salvation? For what is here said of Charity, must in all Reason be understood of every other Virtue, it must be practised in the same Fulness and Sincerity of Heart as this Charity. It may also justly be affirmed, that this Charity is so holy a Temper, and requires so many other Virtues as the Foun-

16

dation of it, that it can only be exercised by a Heart, that is far advanced in Holiness, that is entirely devoted to God. Our whole Nature must be changed, we must have put off the *old Man*, we must be *born again* of God, we must have *overcome the World*, we must live *by Faith*, be full of the Spirit of Christ, in order to Exercise this Charity.

When therefore you would know, whether it be necessary to labour after Christian Perfection, and live wholly unto God, read over *St. Paul's* Description of *Charity*: If you can think of any *Negligence* of Life, any *Defects* of Humility, any *Abatements* of Devotion, any *Fondness* of the World, any Desires of *Riches* and *Greatness*, that is consistent with the *Tempers* there described, then you may be content with them; but if these Tempers of an exalted Charity cannot subsist, but in a Soul that is devoted to God, and resigned to the World, that is humble and mortified, that is full of the Spirit of Christ, and the Cares of Eternity, then you have a plain Reason of the Necessity of Labouring after all the Perfection, that you are capable of; for the Apostle expressly saith, that without these Tempers, the very Tongues of *Angels*, are but as *sounding Brass or a tinkling Cymbal*. Do not therefore imagine, that it only belongs to People of a *particular Piety and Turn of Mind*, to labour after their Perfection, and that you may go to Heaven with much less Care; there is only one *strait Gate* and one *narrow Way that leadeth unto Life*, and there is no Admission, but for those who *strive* to enter into it. If you are not *striving*, you neglect the express condition which our Lord requires, and it is flat Nonsense to think that you *strive*, if you do not use all your Strength. The Apostle represents a Christian's striving for eternal Life in this Manner, *Know ye not that they which run in a Race, run all, but one receiveth the Prize? So run that ye may obtain.* So that, according to the Apostle, he only is in the *Road* to Salvation, who is so contending for it, as he that is running in a *Race*. *Further*, you can have no Satisfaction that you are sincere in any one Virtue, unless you are endeavouring to be Perfect in all the Instances of it. If you allow yourself in any Defects of Charity, you have no Reason to think yourself sincere in any Acts of Charity. If you indulge yourself in any Instances of Pride, you render all your Acts of Humility justly suspected, because there can be no *true Reason* for Charity, but what is as good a Reason for *all Instances* of Charity; nor any religious Motive for Humility, but what is as strong a Motive for all Degrees of Humility. So that he who allows himself in any known Defects of Charity, Humility, or any other Virtue, cannot be supposed to practise any Instances of that Virtue upon true Reasons of Religion. For if it was a right Fear of God, a true Desire of being like Christ, a hearty Love of my Fellow-Creatures that made me give *Alms*, the same Dispositions would make me *love and forgive* all my Enemies, and deny myself all kinds of *Revenge*, and *Spite*, and *Evil-speaking*.

So that if I allow myself in known Instances of Uncharitableness, I have as much Reason to suppose myself void of true Charity, as if I allowed myself in a Refusal of *such Alms* as I am able to give. Because every Instance of Uncharitableness, is the same Sin against all the Reasons of Charity, as the allowed Refusal of *Alms*. For the Refusal of *Alms* is only a great Sin, because it shows that we have not a right Fear of God, that we have not a hearty Desire of being like Christ, that we want a *true Love* of our Fellow Creature. Now as every allowed Instance of Uncharitableness shows a Want of all these Tempers, so it shows, that every such Instance is the same Sin, and sets us as far from God, as the Refusal of *Alms*.

To forbear from *Spite and Evil-speaking*, is a proper Instance of Christian Charity, but yet it is such a Charity as will not profit those, who are not charitable in *Alms*, because by refusing *Alms*, they sin against as many Reasons of Charity, as he that lives in *Spite and Evil-speaking*. And on the other Hand, he that allows himself in *Spite and Evil-speaking*, sins against all the same Reasons of Charity, as he that lives in the Refusal of *Alms*. This is a Doctrine that cannot be too much reflected upon by all those who would practise a Piety, that is pleasing to God.

Too many Christians look at *some Instances* of Virtue which they practise, as a sufficient Atonement for their known Defects in some other Parts of the same Virtue. Not considering, that this is as absurd, as to think to make some apparent Acts of *Justice*, compound for other allowed Instances of *Fraud*.

A *Lady* is perhaps satisfied with her Humility, because she can look at some apparent Instances of it ; she sometimes visits *Hospitals and Alms-houses*, and is very familiar and condescending to the Poor : Now these are very good Things, but then it may be, that these very Things are looked upon as sufficient Proofs of Humility ; she *Patches and Paints*, and delights in all the Show and Ornaments of *personal Pride*, and is very easy with herself, because she visits the *Hospitals*. Now she should consider, that she places her Humility in that which is but a Part, and also the smallest and most deceitful Part of it. For the hardest, the greatest, and most essential Part of Humility, is to have low Opinions of ourselves, to love our *own Meanness*, and to renounce all such Things, as gratify the Pride and Vanity of our Nature. Humility also is much better discovered by our Behaviour towards our *Equals and Superiors*, than towards those who are so much below us. It does no hurt to a *proud* Heart, to stoop to some low Offices to the meanest People. Nay, there is something in it that may gratify *Pride,* for perhaps our own Greatness is never seen to more Advantage, than when we stoop to those who are so far below us. The lower the People are to whom we stoop, the better they show the Height of our own State. So that there is nothing difficult in these Condescensions, they are no *Contradictions* to Pride.

The truest Trial of Humility, is our Behaviour towards our *Equals,* and those that are our Superiors or Inferiors but in a *small Degree.* It is no Sign of Humility, for a private Gentleman to pay a profound Reverence, and show great Submission to a *King*, nor is it any sign of Humility for the same Person to condescend to great Familiarity with a *poor Almsman.* For he may act upon the same Principle in both Cases.

It does not hurt him to show *great* Submission to a *King*, because he has no Thoughts of being *equal* to a *King*, and for the same Reason it does not hurt him to condescend to poor People, because he never imagines, that they will think themselves *equal* to him. So that it is the great Inequality of Condition, that makes it as easy for People to condescend to those who are a great Way below them, as to be submissive, and yielding to those who are vastly above them.

From this it appears, that our most splendid Acts of Virtue, which we think to be sufficient to atone for our other known Defects, may themselves be so Vain and Defective as to have no worth in them. This also shows us the absolute Necessity of labouring after *all Instances* of Perfection in every Virtue, because if we pick and choose what Parts of any Virtue we will perform, we sin against all the same Reasons, as if we neglected all Parts of it. If we choose to *give* instead of *forgiving,* we choose something else instead of *Charity.*

Thirdly, Another Motive to induce you to aspire after *Christian Perfection,* may be taken from the double Advantage of it in this Life, and that which is to come.

The Apostle thus exhorts the *Corinthians,* wherefore *my beloved Brethren, be ye steadfast, immovable, always abounding in the Work of the Lord, forasmuch as ye know, that our Labour will not be in vain in the Lord.* This is an Exhortation founded upon solid Reason; for what can be so Wise and Reasonable, as to be

---

* 1 Cor. xv.

always abounding in *that Work*, which will never be *in vain?* Whilst we are pleased with ourselves, or pleased with the World, we are pleased with Vanity, and our most prosperous Labours of this Kind are, as the *Preacher* saith, *but Vanity of Vanities, all is Vanity.* But whilst we are labouring after Christian Perfection, we are labouring for Eternity, and building to ourselves higher Stations in the Joys of Heaven. *As one Star differeth from another Star in Glory, so also is the Resurrection of the Dead:* We shall surely rise to different Degrees of Glory, of Joy and Happiness in God, according to our different Advancements in Purity, Holiness, and good Works.

No Degrees of Mortification and Self-denial, no private Prayers, no secret Mournings, no Instances of Charity, no Labours of Love will ever be forgotten, but all treasured up to our everlasting Comfort and Refreshment. For though the Rewards of the other Life, are free Gifts of God, yet since he has assured us, that every Man shall be rewarded according to his Works, it is certain that our Rewards will be as different as our Works have been.

Now stand still here a while, and ask yourself, whether you really believe this to be true, that the more Perfect we make ourselves here, the more Happy we shall be hereafter. If you do not believe this to be strictly true, you know nothing of God or Religion. And if you do believe it to be true, is it possible to be *awake*, and not aspiring after Christian Perfection? What can you think of, what can the World show you, that can make you any amends for the Loss of *any Degree* of Virtue? Can any way of Life make it reasonable for you to die *less perfect*, than you might have done?

If you would now devote yourself to Perfection, perhaps you must part with some Friends, you must displease some Relations, you must lay aside some Designs, you must refrain from some Pleasures, you must alter your Life, nay, perhaps you must do more than this, you must expose yourself to the Hatred of your Friends, to the Jest and Ridicule of *Wits*, and to the Scorn and Derision of worldly Men; but had you not better do and suffer all this, than to die *less perfect*, less prepared for Mansions of eternal Glory? But, indeed, the suffering all this, is suffering nothing. For why should it signify anything to you, what *Fools* and *Madmen* think of you? And surely it can be no Wrong or rash Judgment, to think those both Fools and Mad, who condemn what God approves, and like that which God condemns. But if you think this too much to be done, to obtain Eternal Glory, think, on the other hand, what can be gained instead of it.

Fancy yourself living in all the Ease and Pleasure that the World can give you, esteemed by your Friends, undisturbed by your Enemies, and gratifying all your *natural Tempers*. If you could *stand still* in such a State, you may say, that you had got *something ;* but alas ! every Day that is *added* to such a Life, is the same thing as a Day taken from it, and shows you that so much Happiness is gone from you ; for be as Happy as you will, you must see it all sinking away from you, you must feel yourself *decline*, you must see that your Time *shortens apace*, you must hear of *sudden Deaths*, you must fear *Sickness*, you must both dread and desire *old Age*, you must fall into the Hands of Death, you must either die in the painful, bitter Sorrows of a deep Repentance, or in sad, gloomy Despair, wishing for *Mountains to fall upon you, and Seas to cover you.* And is this a *Happiness* to be chosen ? Is this all that you can gain, by neglecting God, by following your own Desires, and not labouring after Christian Perfection ? Is it worth your while to separate yourself from God, to lose your Share in the Realms of Light, to be *thus Happy*, or I may better say, to be thus Miserable even in this Life ? You may be so blind and foolish as not to think of these Things, but it is impossible to think of them, without labouring after Christian Perfection. It may be, you are too young, too happy, or too busy to be affected with these Reflections, but let me tell you, that *all* will be over before you are aware, your *Day* will be spent, and leave you to such a *Night*, as that which surprised the *foolish Virgins. And at Midnight there was a great Cry made, behold the Bridegroom cometh ; go ye out to meet him.**

The *last Hour* will soon be with you, when you will have nothing to look for, but your *Reward* in another Life, when you will stand with nothing but *Eternity* before you, and must begin to be *something*, that will be your State for ever. I can no more *reach* Heaven with my *Hands*, than I can describe the Sentiments, that you will then have, you will then feel Motions of Heart that you never felt before, all your Thoughts and Reflections will pierce your Soul in a Manner, that you never before experienced, and you will feel the Immortality of your Nature, by the Depth and piercing Vigour of your Thoughts. You will then know what it is to die, you will then know, that you never knew it before, that you never thought worthily of it, but that dying Thoughts are as *new* and *amazing*, as that State which follows them.

Let me therefore exhort you, to come prepared to this Time

---

* Matt. xxv. 6.

of Trial, to look out for Comfort, whilst the Day is before you, to treasure up such a *Fund* of good and pious Works, as may make you able to bear that State, which cannot be borne without them. Could I any way make you apprehend, how dying Men feel the Want of a pious Life, how they lament Time lost, Health and Strength squandered away in Folly, how they look at Eternity, and what they think of the Rewards of another Life, you would soon find yourself one of those, who desire to live in the highest State of Piety and Perfection, that by this Means you may grow old in Peace, and die in full Hopes of eternal Glory.

Consider again, that besides the Rewards of the other Life, the labouring after Christian Perfection, or devoting yourself wholly to God, has a great Reward even in this Life, as it makes Religion *doubly* pleasant to you. Whilst you are divided betwixt God and the World, you have neither the Pleasures of Religion, nor the Pleasures of the World, but are always in the Uneasiness of a divided State of Heart. You have only so much Religion as serves to disquiet you, to check your Enjoyments, to show you a *Hand-writing upon the Wall*, to interrupt your Pleasures, to reproach you with your Follies, and to appear as a *Death's-head* at all your Feasts, but not Religion enough, to give you a Taste and Feeling of its proper Pleasures and Satisfactions. You dare not wholly neglect Religion, but then you take no more than is just sufficient to keep you from being a Terror to yourself, and you are as loth to be *very good*, as you are fearful to be *very bad*. So that you are just as Happy, as the *Slave* that dares not run away from his Master, and yet always serves him against his Will. So that instead of having a Religion that is your *Comfort* in all Troubles, your Religion is itself a *Trouble*, under which you want to be Comforted; and those Days and Times hang heaviest upon your Hands, which leave you only to the Offices and Duties of Religion. *Sunday* would be very dull and tiresome, but that it is but one Day in *seven*, and is made a Day of *dressing* and *visiting*, as well as of Divine Service: You don't care to keep away from the Public Worship, but are always glad when it is over. This is the State of a *Half-piety*; thus they live who add Religion to a worldly Life; all their Religion is mere *Yoke* and *Burden*, and is only made tolerable by having but little of their Time.

Urbanus, goes to Church, but he hardly knows whether he goes out of a Sense of Duty, or to meet his Friends. He wonders at those People who are *Profane*, and what Pleasure they can find in Irreligion; but then he is in as great wonder at those who would make every Day, a Day of Divine Worship, he feels no more of the Pleasures of Piety, than of the Pleasures of Profaneness. As Religion has everything from him, but his *Heart*, so he has everything from Religion, but its *Comforts*. *Urbanus* likes Religion, because it seems an *easy* Way of pleasing God, a *decent* thing, that takes up but little of our Time, and is a proper *Mixture* in Life. But if he were reduced to take *Comfort* in it, he would be as much at a loss, as those who have lived without God in the World. When *Urbanus* thinks of Joy, and Pleasure, and Happiness, he does not think at all of Religion. He has gone through a hundred Misfortunes, fallen into a Variety of Hardships, but never thought of making Religion his *Comfort* in any of them, he makes himself Quiet and Happy in another Manner. He is content with his Christianity, not because he is *pious*, but because he is not *profane*. He continues in the same Course of Religion, not because of any real Good he ever found in it, but because it does him no hurt.

To such poor Purposes as these do Numbers of People profess Christianity. Let me therefore exhort you to a *solid Piety*, to devote yourself wholly unto God, that entering deep into Religion, you may enter deep into its Comforts, that serving God with all your Heart, you may have the Peace and Pleasure of a Heart that is at Unity with itself. When your Conscience once bears you witness, that you are *steadfast, immovable, and always abounding in the Work of the Lord,* you will find that your Reward is already begun, and that you could not be less Devout, less Holy, less Charitable, or less Humble, without lessening the most substantial Pleasure, that ever you felt in your Life. So that to be content with any lower Attainments in Piety, is to rob ourselves of a present Happiness, which nothing else can give us.

You would perhaps devote yourself to Perfection, but for this or that *little Difficulty*, that lies in your Way, you are not in so convenient a State for the full Practice of Piety as you could wish. But consider, that this is Nonsense, because Perfection consists in conquering Difficulties. You could not be Perfect, as the present State of Trial requires, had you not those Difficulties and Inconveniences to struggle with. These things therefore which you would have removed, are laid in your Way, that you may make them so many Steps to Perfection and Glory.

As you could not Exercise your Charity, unless you met with Objects, so neither could you show, that you had *overcome* the World, unless you had many worldly Engagements to overcome. If all your *Friends* and *Acquaintance*, were Devout, Humble, Heavenly-minded, and wholly intent upon the one End of Life, it would be less Perfection in you to be like them. But if you are *Humble* amongst those that delight in Pride, *Heavenly-*

minded, amongst the Worldly, *Sober* amongst the Intemperate, *Devout* amongst the Irreligious, and labouring after *Perfection* amongst those, that despise and ridicule your Labours, then are you truly devoted unto God. Consider therefore, that you can have no Difficulty, but such as the World lays in your Way, and that Perfection is never to be had, but by parting with the World. It consists in nothing else. To stay therefore to be Perfect, till it suits with your Condition in the World, is like staying to be Charitable, till there were no Objects of Charity. It is as if a man should intend to be Courageous some time or other, when there is nothing left to try his Courage.

Again, You perhaps turn your Eyes upon the World, you see all Orders of People full of other Cares and Pleasures, you see the Generality of *Clergy* and *Laity,* Learned and Unlearned, your Friends and Acquaintance mostly living according to the Spirit that reigneth in the World, you are perhaps content with such a *Piety,* as you think contents great *Scholars,* and *famous* Men, and it may be, you cannot think that God will reject such Numbers of Christians. Now all this is amusing yourself with Nothing, it is only losing yourself in vain Imaginations, it is making that a *Rule,* which is no Rule, and cheating yourself into a false Satisfaction. As you are not censoriously to damn other People, so neither are you to think your own Salvation secure, because you are like the generality of the World.

The *foolish Virgins* that had provided no Oil for their Lamps, and so were shut out of the Marriage-Feast, were only thus far foolish, that they trusted to the *Assistance* of those that were *Wise.* But you are more *foolish* than they, for you trust to be saved by the *Folly* of others, you imagine yourself safe in the *Negligence, Vanity,* and *Irregularity* of the World. You take confidence in the *broad Way,* because it is *broad,* you are content with yourself, because you seem to be along with *the many,* though God himself has told you, that *narrow* is the Way, that leadeth unto Life, and *few* there be that find it.

Lastly, one Word more and I have done, think with yourself, what a Happiness it is, that you have it in your Power to secure a Share in the Glories of Heaven, and make yourself one of those blessed Beings that are to live with God for ever. Reflect upon the Glories of bright Angels, that shine about the Throne of Heaven, think upon that Fulness of Joy, which is the State of Christ at the Right Hand of God, and remember, that it is this same State of Glory and Joy that lies open for you. You are less, it may be, in worldly Distinctions than many others, but as to your Relation to God, you have no Superior upon Earth. Let your Condition be what it will, let your Life be ever so mean, you may make the End of it, the Beginning of eternal Glory. Be often therefore in these Reflections, that they may fill you with a wise Ambition of all that Glory, which God in Christ hath called you to. For it is impossible to understand and feel anything of this, without feeling your Heart affected with strong Desires after it. The Hopes and Expectations of so much Greatness and Glory, must needs awake you into earnest Desires and Longings after it. There are many Things in human Life, which it would be in vain for you to aspire after, but the Happiness of the next, which is the Sum of all Happiness, is secure and safe to you against all Accidents. Here no Chances or Misfortunes can prevent your Success, neither the Treachery of Friends, nor the Malice of Enemies can disappoint you, it is only your own false Heart that can Rob you of this Happiness. Be but your own true Friend, and then you have nothing to fear from your Enemies. Do you but sincerely labour in the Lord, and then neither Height nor Depth, neither Life nor Death, neither Men nor Devils, can make your Labour in vain.

FINIS.